DAVID DUKE

Evolution of a Klansman

Michael Zatarain

PELICAN PUBLISHING COMPANY
Gretna 1990

Library of Congress Cataloging-in-Publication Data

Zatarain, Michael.
    David Duke, evolution of a Klansman / by Michael Zatarain.
        p. cm.
    Includes index.
    ISBN 0-88289-817-5
    1. Duke, David Ernest. 2 Politicians – Louisiana – Biography.
3. Ku Klux Klan (1915-   ) – Biography. 4. Louisiana – Politics and
government – 1951-   . 5. White supremacy movements – Louisiana –
History – 20th century. 6. Louisiana – Race relations. I. Title
F376.3.D84Z38   1990
976.3'063'092 – dc20
[B]   90-7339
                                                                       CIP

*Quoted material from the NAAWP News, copyright © 1982, reprinted
with permission.*

Manufactured in the United States of America
Published by Pelican Publishing Company, Inc.
1101 Monroe Street, Gretna, Louisiana 70053

To My Father
CHARLES CLEMENTS ZATARAIN, JR.

Contents

Preface

I FIRST HEARD OF DAVID DUKE in 1969 when I was still in high school. My brother, who was attending Louisiana State University, told me about an outrageous student who drew huge crowds by standing on a soapbox debating political issues. This in itself would not have been unusual because the Vietnam War and the civil rights movement were burning issues on college campuses across the United States.

What made this situation unique was the student my brother spoke of was a racist who consistently attacked blacks and Jews. He denounced communism and the decline of the white middle class with passion. Already a member of the Ku Klux Klan, David Duke involved himself with neo-Nazis and finally formed his own college racist group to further the causes he championed. Most students dismissed Duke as a just another campus radical, but many were still intrigued by his fervor and charisma.

Shortly after arriving at LSU, Duke had become one of the best-known students on campus. Everyone had to choose sides in the Duke debate. Twenty years later, in 1989, the same people who once gawked at the lone figure stood in voting lines and once again were forced to take sides. David Duke was elected as the newest Republican member of the Louisiana legislature.

I followed David Duke's career from afar with curiosity, knowing he would continue to surface with his racist message.

There was something about his delivery and commitment to even the most unpopular positions that made people stop and listen. All through his years with the Knights of the Ku Klux Klan, Duke continued to rewrite what the image of the radical right was supposed to be. As he found new forums for his beliefs, he preached his new brand of white power to increasingly larger audiences.

In 1988, Duke ran for president of the United States in the Democratic primary and later as the candidate of the far-right Populist party. No one, including David Duke, thought he had any chance of victory, but he nevertheless campaigned as though the race were winnable. As expected, he was trounced, but he drew a great deal of attention from the news media wherever he spoke. The positions he took were not in the mainstream of conventional American politics, but he still managed to be included in the process by keeping his platform before the public.

His ability to bring out human emotion is equalled in politics only by the Reverend Jesse Jackson. No one changes the television channel when David Duke's name is mentioned. No newspaper article about Duke goes unread. He has become a political rock star of sorts, despite a racist and anti-Semitic past. With the message of George Wallace, the communicative ability of Ronald Reagan, and the movie-star attraction of Tom Selleck, David Duke is not simply going to fade into the sunset.

Researching information on the public life of David Duke was as easy as going to my local library. Newspapers and magazines from across the world were filled with articles from as far back as 1969. When someone has been linked with the Nazi party and has been grand wizard of the Ku Klux Klan and president of the National Association for the Advancement of White People, there is no shortage of material.

What I did find incredible was the lack of information on David Duke, the person. There are volumes of articles printed about the student activist, Klan leader, and racist politician. But there is very little about Duke the way he is, was, or is going to be in the future. Only through hundreds of hours of interviews with relatives, former students, Klan members, and politicians, as well as with Duke himself, was it possible to write a biography of one of the most complex, radical political figures in America today.

The David Duke I interviewed over a period of more than a year was in direct contrast to the ignorant bigot normally associated with the Ku Klux Klan and racism. Smooth, well-dressed, and totally dedicated, he is obviously intelligent, but he is so wrapped up in racism that he cannot see the forest for the trees.

I abhor the racist and anti-Semitic philosophies Duke espouses. But I have acquired a fuller understanding of why he has devoted his life to negative politics. I do not purport to be an expert on politics, nor do I claim to be a psychologist. Any conclusions I may have made regarding Duke in this book were derived entirely from what I believe are facts.

There is no simple answer to Duke's bizarre behavior because his racism and anti-Semitism have taken a lifetime of specific events to develop. He is as much the product of his environment as of genetics.

After I finished this book, I found that I did not detest David Duke as a person, but rather pitied him. The cross of hatred is a heavier burden than I would ever wish to carry.

It is not my intention to glorify or vilify Duke. I will leave that to others. I do hope, however, that I can enlighten the reader so that through careful examination of the facts an informed judgment may be made about David Duke.

MICHAEL ZATARAIN
New Orleans, Louisiana

Acknowledgments

I want to express my appreciation to the scores of individuals who offered assistance in the preparation of this book, even those many who insisted on anonymity.

I also want to offer special thanks to Peter Miller, my literary agent, for his faith in and commitment to this project, and to Tatum and Michael for their patience and understanding while I was researching, interviewing, and writing.

And, finally, to my wife, Lynn, I express gratitude for her steadfast support and counsel.

DAVID DUKE
Evolution of a Klansman

David Duke campaigns for president of the United States, 1988. (Photo by Nancy Moss)

CHAPTER ONE

Victory—The Beginning

CAMERAMEN AND NEWS REPORTERS from across the nation crowded into the Lions Club Hall in the New Orleans suburb of Metairie to witness the election night voting results of former Ku Klux Klan grand wizard David Duke's campaign. From volunteer campaign workers standing in the jammed Lions Club parking lot to the president of the United States sitting by his Oval Office telephone, people anxiously awaited the outcome of a minor state election that had captured the attention of the world.

The mood of the room was heightened by the very thought that the man who leads the racist right could actually be elected to office. Some in attendance were outwardly angry at the monumental attacks directed toward Duke by civic leaders, the political establishment, and the news media preceding election day. They hoped a victory by their candidate would vindicate their belief that they were right in supporting his racist positions. Others, who were with Duke during his Klan days, were simply joyous at the thought that their longtime leader had a realistic chance of winning political acceptance.

Polls taken just before the election showed the race was a dead heat. Long considered too extreme to win an election, Duke shocked politicos by challenging the establishment until

15

the bitter end. Votes were being tabulated, but the race remained too close to call.

Suddenly, Duke strode into the hall and headed for the stage. The crowd grew silent with anticipation. Overcoming his past affiliation with racist groups, Duke stood at the podium and announced to the all-white audience that he had indeed been elected to office. To the disgust of those who opposed his racist views, and to the thunderous applause and cheers of the people who had become his ardent supporters, David Duke was finally part of the establishment. The frustrated crowd blamed blacks and liberals for what they believed was the deterioration of their way of life and saw Duke as their only salvation. Chants of "Duke! Duke! Duke!" filled the packed hall. The victorious candidate finally was able to quiet his supporters so he could deliver the speech he had repeated in his mind since he was fourteen years old:

> "There is a deep and abiding thankfulness that is up inside of me. No man ever had more loyal friends. The hopes you have placed in me, the faith, I shall never forget. But you made it us, and not just me. No candidate has ever been attacked more than what we sustained. The [New Orleans] *Times-Picayune* ran eight editorial columns against us and dozens of negative news articles. Television news, from the local to the national level, ran new allegations against us almost every day. Practically every elected official, from the governor on down, attacked us. The PACs spent tens of thousands of dollars against us. In the end, even Ronald Reagan and George Bush campaigned against us.
>
> "But we overcame, and we prevailed against almost impossible odds because our cause is a just one, because God gave us strength to endure and the people of this district [the] ability to really hear the sincerity in our hearts.
>
> "I am thankful that I am an American. For only in America could a candidate facing such establishment op-

position succeed. Only in America could this story have been written.

"I can't begin to tell you how much I love you all. This isn't a victory for me, it was a victory for those who believe in true equal rights for all, not the racial discrimination of affirmative action and minority set asides.

"It was a victory for those who choose to work hard rather than abuse welfare.

"It was a victory for the poor people who want the drug dealers and abusers out of their housing projects and away from their children.

"It was a victory for the hard-pressed taxpayer and homeowner.

"It was a victory for those that are determined to save the precious environment of Louisiana from those special interests that would foul our air and our waterways, destroy our precious ecology and our people's precious health for thirty pieces of silver.

"It was a victory for the victim rather than the brutal criminal.

"It was a victory for the young people of Louisiana who demand the right to attend their own neighborhood schools, to be safe and sound there, and to be educated to the extent of their ability.

"Yet, most of all it was a victory from the political control of the mass media, the special interest PACs, and the political power-brokers who have ruled us for too long. The long sleeping tiger of the American majority is awakening. Listen to it roar. You can hear it in the rich delta country and the pine-scented foothills of Louisiana, in the smokey Piedmont of the Carolinas, the concrete canyons of New York City, the mists of the Great Lakes, the crisp air of the Rockies, and in the sunshine of California. But nowhere can you hear it louder than from the good people of Metairie. In this historic election they have spoken in a way that has been heard around the world. God bless and godspeed you all."

It had all begun in November 1988, after Duke had spent the previous two years crisscrossing America as a candidate for president of the United States in the Democratic primaries and later as the candidate of the far-right-wing Populist party. He had returned to his home in suburban New Orleans after being defeated, as expected, for the nation's highest office. The number of votes Duke had gathered was minuscule compared to those of the Republican candidate, Vice-President George Bush, and the Democratic nominee, Massachusetts Gov. Michael Dukakis. He knew he had no chance to win, but Duke nevertheless campaigned day and night throughout the country trying to spread the message that his racist policies were good for America. What he did accomplish during the presidential campaign, however, was to keep his pro-white ideas and name before the public. Afterward, he had come home to rest and continue as president of the National Association for the Advancement of White People when a series of events began that forever changed the life of David Duke and perhaps American politics.

A special election had been called to fill the unexpired term of state Rep. Charles ("Chuck") Cusimano II, who had recently been elected to the 24th Judicial District Court. What should have been a quiet local House race turned into a campaign with a lion's roar.

For the previous six years, Louisiana had been suffering through the worst economic recession since the Great Depression. Long a poor state, Louisiana had an economy that was heavily dependent upon revenues from the oil and gas industry. While the rest of the United States flourished under the Reagan administration, oil-producing states such as Texas, Oklahoma, and Louisiana were decimated economically. Things seemed to be getting worse as unemployment statewide reached 11.3 percent and people were ready to try almost anything to change the outlook.

Change came in October of 1987, when Congressman Charles ("Buddy") Roemer defeated three-term Gov. Edwin W. Edwards. Elected on a strong reform platform, Roemer called for sweeping changes in the way government operated in Louisiana. The state was so financially desperate when he took office he was forced to call three special legislative sessions intended to raise taxes.

The governor planned a special session in October 1988 to rewrite certain tax codes in the state constitution. The plan was widely supported by big business, but was opposed by many, especially small businessmen, rural legislators, and powerful local tax assessors.

One main component in the rewrite was the reduction of the homestead exemption, which excludes the first $75,000 of a home's value from any local parish (county) property tax. There is no state ad valorem tax, so most houses are assessed nothing in the way of local taxes. Governor Roemer's proposed fiscal reform package fell ten votes short of the necessary two-thirds majority in the House of Representatives. The governor angrily proclaimed he would call another special session soon.

In the meantime, two legislators had resigned from the House, leaving their seats vacant. One was held by Rep. Kathleen Blanco (D—Lafayette), who had been elected to the state Public Service Commission. The other was Representative Cusimano of Metairie, the new district judge. Blanco had supported Roemer and voted for the tax reform package, while Cusimano had voted against it. It was crucial for the governor to hold these elections before his next special session because he needed seventy votes for passage. The two vacated seats could make the difference. What resulted was a bizarre chain of events that helped propel David Duke to world attention.

The 81st legislative district of Louisiana was tailor-made for David Duke. It is located in Jefferson Parish, bordering the city of New Orleans, and most importantly for Duke, 99.6

percent white. There are 12,100 registered Democrats, 7,500 Republicans, and 1,800 Independents. The area is more than 65 percent Roman Catholic and boasts the highest educational level in the state. Residents include some of the wealthiest people in Louisiana, and the majority of residents are middle income.

They have one thing in common: they almost all own their homes and live there as a result of white flight from New Orleans. These issues would help determine the outcome of the election.

Although Governor Roemer is a Democrat, he is considered a conservative, and at the time he enjoyed good rapport with the Republican delegation in the legislature. The 81st district has been called the Orange County of Louisiana—in other words, a safe seat for Republicans. It was decided that longtime Republican activist and home builder John Treen would be the chosen candidate of the GOP. He is a brother of former Republican Gov. David C. Treen, who for many years lived in the district and enjoyed immense popularity. A meeting took place between the Treen people and Roemer, with the resulting agreement that a John Treen victory would be a yea vote for the governor's tax package.

As expected, others were looking at the seat Cusimano had held since 1980. One was David Vitter, a young Harvard graduate and Rhodes scholar, who could cause trouble for the sixty-four-year-old Treen. Vitter had moved into the district only months before, but was well known and was attracting press attention as a possible candidate for the District 81 seat. His problem was that in Louisiana one must be a resident of a district for at least a year to qualify for a seat in the legislature.

Treen forces got wind of Vitter's residency shortfall, and the governor quickly called the election for January 21, 1989. That ended any chance of Vitter's entering the race. With

Vitter out of the way, the campaign could progress as planned for Treen and Roemer.

The qualifying date for the House seat was December 2, and those throwing their hats in the ring were Treen, former school board member Delton Charles, real estate broker D. J. ("Bud") Olister, businessman Roger Villere, lawyer Ron Court-ade, engineering consultant Bobby Savoie, and most surprising of all, former Ku Klux Klan leader David Duke. All were Republicans, with the exception of Savoie and Olister, who were Democrats. Only three days earlier, Duke had changed his lifelong affiliation from Democrat to Republican, much to the future consternation of Republican National Committee Chairman Lee Atwater.

His party switch was prompted by a meeting held at Duke's Metairie office to discuss what avenue he should take next if he were ever going to be a serious political candidate. Duke decided he could never get anywhere in politics as long as he remained in the Democratic party.

"I had been a Democrat all my life," he explained, "but the Democrats have become the party of Jesse Jackson and not the party envisioned by Thomas Jefferson."

After conferring with political friends, Duke decided to join the Republican party. Although he was outside the mainstream of most Republican politics, he was closer in ideology and racial thinking to the GOP than to the Democrats.

The next step was to find an election Duke could win.

"We had to find a winnable race if David was ever going to get his message across," recalled Howie Farrell, Duke's long-time friend and campaign manager. Farrell is a man of forty with a big mustache and a fervent belief in Duke. "The presidential race was too big," he said seriously. "There was going to be a parish council seat opening up the next year, but that was too local. When Cusimano's seat opened up, it looked good. We looked at the makeup of the district, the numbers of NAAWP members, and thought this might be the right race for David."

To be successful in Jefferson Parish politics, a candidate usually must be supported by one or more elected officials. It is very much like a Southern version of Cook County, Illinois, where political bosses attempt to control power by electing "their people." Treen's campaign managers would be his brother, former Gov. Dave Treen, and Jefferson Parish President Mike Yenni.

Delton Charles was endorsed by Jefferson Parish tax assessor Lawrence E. Chehardy, one of the most powerful politicians in Louisiana. Chehardy had gained fame as chief supporter of the homestead exemption and was a leading foe of Governor Roemer's tax plan. Olister was the candidate of the local sheriff, Harry Lee. The sheriff (who is of Oriental descent and wears cowboy suits) made national headlines in 1986 by instituting an executive order for his deputies to stop and question any blacks found roaming white neighborhoods in "his parish."

The remaining candidates did not have any established endorsements, especially David Duke. The deals had been cut and the players were in place for an election that looked like John Treen and Delton Charles in a showdown.

Neither the candidates nor the news media took David Duke seriously. Everyone knew him from his radical days at Louisiana State University and his years as grand wizard of the Ku Klux Klan.

"We just didn't take him as a threat," said Treen coordinator state Rep. James Donelon (R—Metairie). "We just assumed it would be us and Delton Charles."

Both Treen and Charles hired professional pollsters and set up phone banks within weeks of qualifying. The polls showed Treen well ahead, with Charles a distant second. Everyone still thought it was a two-man race, and the election remained quiet. Other candidates were showing single-digit numbers in the polls with the exception of Duke, who was almost a non-candidate.

Louisiana has an open voting law under which candidates from all parties run in the same primary. It permits Democrats, Republicans, and Independents to challenge each other simultaneously. Because of this, it is not uncommon for local parish political parties to endorse candidates, even if more than one party member is running for the same seat. On December 5, the Republicans called a meeting to decide whom to endorse. It was assumed that the battle would be between Treen and Charles, but all Republicans were invited, including the newest member, David Duke, who received a personal invitation from local chairwoman Sandy Emerson.

Republican party leaders were surprised by Duke's unexpected decision to run for the House seat and began publicly distancing themselves from the former Klansman. Their statements to the news media made it seem as though the official party sentiment was one of censure, but Farrell remembers the story differently.

"We all met at the Republican headquarters on Veterans Highway in Kenner for a pre-nominating meeting," he insists. "Everyone there acted as though they were pleased to have David and me on the Republican side, including John Treen. Sandy Emerson told us that it was the best thing that ever happened to the Republican party."

The last thing Republican officials wanted was infighting among party members, and they tried to get the candidates in attendance to unite behind the winner of the committee's balloting.

"They asked each candidate present if he would support the winner of the night's nomination, and we told them David was in the race to be elected by the voters of the 81st district," said Farrell.

Villere had already spent thousands of dollars and was too deeply involved to get out, and Courtade wanted to get political exposure, so no one had a reason to bow out in favor of Treen or Charles.

There was a deep division over whether to endorse Treen or Charles, and no decision was made that evening. The nominating committee consisted of elected Jefferson Parish Republicans, state executive committee members, elected state central committee members, the chairperson, and a number of members chosen by the chairperson.

The most memorable aspect of the night was that of all the candidates who spoke, David Duke was by far the most articulate. His polished delivery and grasp of the issues were in stark contrast to the other candidates who were banking on past affiliations with committee members to give them enough votes to win the nomination. Rather than simply being written off by the committee as just a former Klansman, Duke finally was being taken seriously.

At the closed-door meeting, state Republican party Chairman Bill Nungesser told Duke, "David, you gave the best speech of the evening."

Only Delton Charles took Duke as a threat, even though he greeted the former Ku Klux Klansman warmly that night as a fellow Republican. He believed Duke should not be allowed a free ride away from his racist past, but felt Duke's supporters would be needed in the runoff against Treen and thus did nothing to alienate his opponent. Ultimately, Duke's racist past was brought up continually during the election, but it merely made the voters aware of his views, with which many of them agreed.

It also made him a major force because he had become the center of media attention.

When the endorsement votes were counted, Treen led, with Charles second and Duke a surprising third. "We couldn't believe we got the support we did," said Farrell. Without a majority of votes another meeting would have to be called to choose the party's candidate.

A special meeting of the Republican committee was hastily called three days later to get Treen the endorsement. Delton Charles was out of town, and his campaign staffers were not able to muster enough committee members favorable to Charles, so the meeting proceeded with a majority of Treen members present. The strategy worked, and John Treen was named the official candidate of the party, but not without inflicting serious wounds that later would come back to haunt him. Charles resented what he felt was an unfair coup d'etat by the old guard of the Republican party and did little to help Treen in the runoff election.

The Alliance for Good Government sponsored a forum the next evening. For the first time, the general public and the news media had the chance to see David Duke as a candidate working within the system.

"It was amazing to see the difference in style," remarked a Treen official. "Duke was really head and shoulders above the rest of the candidates in getting his platform across to the Alliance. But we still figured the public looked at him as some Klan kook and he would hurt the other guys running."

Treen got the Alliance's endorsement but Duke got a tremendous boost from the media, especially television. Most people watching the news saw a new David Duke, not a radical wearing a white Klan robe but a polished speaker dressed in a conservative business suit who took positions with which many of them agreed.

"People came up to me in waves after the forum and shook my hand," remembered Duke. "I knew something different was about to happen. They thought my ideals [*sic*] would only attract a minority of voters. I just kept saying what I have always said and people began to listen."

Duke's message, or "ideals," as he prefers to say, about government suppression of whites was being listened to seriously by a group that previously had been turned off by his Ku Klux Klan background. Since his early days at LSU, Duke's positions had not changed, only his method of delivery and the public's acceptance of him were different.

After the qualifying period ended, there were rumors that Duke might not have lived in the district for the mandatory year. Since none of the candidates felt Duke was a threat, the matter was dropped for the moment. Although Duke had changed his voting address two weeks earlier, the law requires that a residency challenge be made within ten days after qualifying. No formal charge was filed, and it was too late to exclude Duke from the race. The very same law that John Treen and Governor Roemer had used against David Vitter was not invoked with Duke. The chance to end David Duke's rise to power was overlooked by candidates who may have concluded that the racist candidate would siphon votes from other opponents.

Two weeks before the primary, Delton Charles began to worry because "Duke for Representative" signs were cropping up in yards throughout the district. Although polls still showed the former Klan leader a nonentity, something just did not seem right. Charles drew up a campaign mailer that compared his record to both Treen's and Duke's. The flyer was designed to make certain that the reader was aware of Duke's past affiliation with the Ku Klux Klan and right-wing groups.

Some campaign advisers saw this attack as too risky a move and the idea was dropped. The *Times-Picayune*, television news programs, and radio talk shows were already filled with stories concerning Duke's racist past. Charles' aides still believed their candidate would run first, and by dropping the idea of the mailing they would eliminate any possibility of alienating Duke supporters in the runoff.

During the first two months of 1989, New Orleans was experiencing a record-setting murder every day. It was almost entirely black-on-black crime resulting from drug wars within the city's poverty-filled public housing projects. However distant the murders were from the 81st district, daily headlines in the New Orleans *Times-Picayune* helped to galvanize racial fears. As the death-a-day spree continued, Duke made the most of it by accenting the lack of protection for whites and the working poor. Also, he publicly endorsed Sheriff Lee's action to curb black penetration of white neighborhoods.

Most politicians are afraid to speak out on the specific issues of poverty and crime because they fear they might be labeled racist, something that has never bothered Duke. He was actually able to use his Klan past to advantage in the election. People who might never before have considered voting for Duke were now listening to him denigrate affirmative action and minority set-aside programs, as well as promote his plans to reduce the illegitimate birthrate by rewarding welfare mothers who practice birth control.

As chance would have it, on January 16, just five days before the primary election, a parade honoring Dr. Martin Luther King, Jr.'s, birthday was held on Canal Street in New Orleans. A near-riot broke out, and television news reports depicted young black youths kicking and punching any whites they could find. Police finally moved in and restored order, but not until the evening news programs were filled with pictures of horrified whites fleeing for their lives from hordes of terrorizing blacks.

One television station showed a white woman huddled in a store that had been chained closed. A fear that has been instilled in many Southern whites since the days of slavery was now being rekindled for all to see. According to William Hess of the New Orleans Anti-Defamation League, Duke may have had a hand in the fracas.

"I wouldn't put it past David Duke to pay some black kids to start a riot," he declared.

To make matters even more complicated, the Mardi Gras season had begun in earnest. Some whites were afraid to go to New Orleans, and many remained in suburban Metairie to watch the carnival parades there. At every parade Duke could be seen handing out campaign literature portraying himself as the only candidate offering solutions to whites' fears. He was now being greeted with warmth and enthusiasm almost everywhere he went. Duke would shake hands with parade-goers and tell them what a shame it was that they could not enjoy carnival as they had in the past. He blamed wasteful welfare programs for the lack of police protection in New Orleans.

"If the hardworking people of this state wouldn't spend so much tax money on wasteful welfare and drug users," he argued, "then there would be more than enough money to make the streets safe."

Campaign adviser and former Jefferson Parish Councilman Larry Heaslip said, "We knew we would be in the runoff. The support we were getting was great. I've never seen anybody get the kind of devoted followers David has."

Unlike most states, Louisiana holds elections on Saturdays. Polls taken a few days before the election still showed the race to be between Treen and Charles.

According to Charles' pollster, Dr. Ed Renwick, "One problem you had in polling this race was that you had such an enormous amount of undecided voters and people who wouldn't answer. Frankly, a lot of people flat out lied about who they were going to vote for." He added, "It wasn't easy for someone to tell a stranger over the phone that he or she was voting for the former grand wizard of the Ku Klux Klan."

Election night brought a surprise to everyone except Duke and his few advisers. After all thirty-four precincts had reported, the results were:

Duke	3,995	33%
Treen	2,277	19%
Charles	2,011	17%
Olister	1,150	10%

Villere	1,142	9%
Courtade	791	7%
Savoie	697	6%

Duke's victory celebration was held at the Lions Club Hall on Metairie Road.

"The place was electric," said a grinning Heaslip. "The moment David walked through the door, the place went wild."

A smiling Duke was greeted by a sparse but enthusiastic group of supporters. During the first primary, Duke was still considered by many to be an extremist ex-Klan member and at best a long shot to make the runoff. As a result, barely one hundred people came out to join him for the election night returns. Dressed in sport coat and tie, Duke stood on the podium to say what everyone wanted to hear.

"We came in first!" shouted an exuberant Duke. The room broke out with chants of "Duke! Duke! Duke!" Never really taken seriously by anyone before, David Duke had used the political system and finally had come out on top.

David Duke pickets a speech by anti-war activist William Kunstler at Tulane University, 1970. (Photo by Michael P. Smith)

CHAPTER TWO

Over the Hill

THE MOOD AT TREEN HEADQUARTERS was subdued. The candidate had made the runoff, but trailed badly. And now he had to run a race against a former Klansman.

"We had figured all along to be in the runoff with Delton Charles," said Treen coordinator James Donelon. "Our whole approach would have to be changed to deal with Duke. I told John [Treen] that the quiet little House race was over, and the next four weeks would be like nothing we had ever seen. I just didn't know how right I was."

Immediately, press coverage turned from a local state campaign story to a worldwide media spectacle. No longer would local issues be the focus of the campaign. Duke's racist past and his new designation as a contender would now dominate the race.

Voter turnout was 54 percent, an unusually high figure in Louisiana for a special legislative race. The thinking among political insiders was that Duke had peaked at 33 percent, because voters who supported Duke's racist ideas would have come out en masse to support their hero. Pundits also theorized that the remaining votes gathered by the five defeated candidates would be Treen's by default. Ron Courtade, Roger Villere, and Bobby Savoie endorsed Treen and worked in the runoff to defeat Duke. But the other two candidates either gave a passive written endorsement or remained neutral.

Delton Charles had not forgotten how the Treen forces had used their considerable influence within the party to hastily call the Republican committee together at the eleventh hour to capture the party's endorsement while Charles was out of town. The very thing that helped Treen win the party nomination would cost him in the runoff.

In any normal election, a candidate in a runoff with a former Ku Klux Klan leader could be assured unlimited support, but John Treen defied the obvious. Throughout his life, Treen has been described as a maverick. He joined the Republican party in 1947 at a time when there were fewer than 3,000 Republicans in the state. He ran unsuccessfully for the state Senate in 1972 and for the Jefferson Parish Council in 1975. A former chairman of the Jefferson Parish Republican party, Treen had served for many years on the state central committee. In 1984 and 1988, he also was a delegate to the Republican National Convention. So how could someone with a lifetime of party dedication have trouble winning support from fellow Republicans? The answer lies with John Treen himself.

In 1987, Parish President Joseph Yenni died, and Republicans endorsed Councilman Willie Hof to fill the unexpired seat. Treen, however, supported Yenni's son, Mike, a Democrat. Yenni won the election, and many Republicans resolved they would not forget Treen for abandoning the party.

"He's just not the kind of guy you want to be friends with," said one local Republican official of Treen. "He can tell you good morning and piss you off."

Just days after the election, Larry Heaslip phoned Sheriff Harry Lee to seek his support for Duke. He reminded Lee that the former Klan leader had always supported the sheriff in the past. Lee responded, "You know what this election gets down to, Larry? A choice between a bigot and an ass. . . ."

There are many, however, who find John Treen to be a loyal man of principle. "He didn't need to run for this seat," insisted one legislator, "but he saw that he could do some good in Baton Rouge and stepped to the line for his state and the Republican party."

Stepping to the line to defeat the former grand wizard of the Ku Klux Klan would become a popular thing to do. The Catholic church even got involved. Archbishop Philip Hannan wrote in the February 5 issue of the archdiocesan newspaper, the *Clarion Herald*: "The election will determine the convictions of the voters of the district about the basic dignity of persons, recognition of human rights of every person and the equality of races made by Divine Providence."

Archbishop Hannan instructed that these sentiments be read at every mass in the New Orleans area, including District 81. Because Lenten season is the most holy time for Catholics, the letter was expected to have a great impact. It did, but not in the way the Treen forces had hoped.

At a number of masses, members rose from their pews and challenged the letter, which they felt was inappropriate in church. Some actually left the services. Hundreds of Catholics who supported Duke protested the church's political involvement, while those opposed to his racist views defended it.

Because of church doctrine, the archbishop could not publicly endorse Treen, but little was left to the imagination of Catholics on where he stood in the race. Duke, who had attended Catholic mass in Laos during the Vietnam War and openly recruited Catholics for the Ku Klux Klan, was stung by the rebuke. He asked for and was granted an audience with the archbishop. After the meeting, Archbishop Hannan announced it was up to the voters to decide whether Duke had repudiated his racist past. In a letter to the *Times-Picayune,* the archbishop said, "At no time have I stated, either verbally or in writing, that I support either of these candidates."

The Reverend James C. Carter, president of Loyola University, sent 783 letters to Loyola alumni living in the 81st district criticizing the National Association for the Advancement of White People. He never directly used Duke's name, however. He wrote that the NAAWP was anti-black, anti-Catholic, and anti-Semitic. Although the letter never endorsed Treen directly, it urged voters to become better informed about candidates who agreed with church doctrine. Duke and many of his supporters were incensed by the letter.

Duke's campaign manager Howie Farrell, a practicing Catholic, said on a radio talk show, "There is not one shred of evidence suggesting that David Duke has ever been anti-Catholic. On the contrary, he has repeatedly praised the conservatism and moral stance of the church." Farrell challenged Carter to produce a single anti-Catholic utterance or writing by Duke. There was no reply.

While Treen was busy seeking endorsements, Duke was busy walking door to door, standing on street corners, and visiting every restaurant where he might find potential voters. He was relentless in his search for every available vote. As a result, more and more dark-blue Duke signs began popping up throughout the district. He said later, "I kept getting positive feedback from the people I met. I've been at this long enough to know that my ideals were being accepted."

Positions taken by the two candidates were virtually identical in the runoff. Treen had long been an advocate of conservative causes popular with Republicans. Although not considered racists, Treen and his brother David were leaders in the States Rights party in the 1950s. That was believed by many to have been a major reason David Treen was denied a federal judgeship by a U.S. Senate committee in 1989. The States Rights party espoused segregation and was opposed to changes in certain laws, particularly those designed to allow blacks to vote more freely. When the Treen campaign concentrated on

Duke's racist past, the former Klansman depicted himself as the victim of political hypocrisy.

Most politicians try to avoid controversy, but Duke thrived on it. He took positions no other candidate would admit to supporting, even though the same candidate may have agreed with him privately. He may have been the first candidate to make opposition to affirmative action programs and "reducing the illegitimate welfare birthrate" the cornerstones of a serious political campaign. However, he did not neglect the more traditional Republican issues of opposition to higher taxes and support for law and order. He also advocated a more stringent environmental protection policy, a philosophy more closely identified with liberal Democrats.

In a detailed campaign flyer, he professed exactly what people in District 81 wanted to hear:

1) CUT THE FAT, NOT THE HOMESTEAD EXEMPTION

I am absolutely committed to preserving and protecting the Homestead Exemption. Hardworking, productive, middle class people are already taxed too much! In a sea of exorbitant taxes, tremendous waste and flagrant corruption, the exemption is just about the only break the middle-class and the elderly have left. I will defend it.

2) I AM OPPOSED TO ANY NEW TAX INCREASES

Sales taxes, gasoline taxes, and some business taxes are already among the highest in the nation.

3) GET TOUGH ON CRIME

We need real teeth in repeat offender laws, tougher penalties for drug pushers, more concern for the victim than the criminal, and ways to select more competent jurors.

4) ELIMINATE UNFAIR AND WASTEFUL MINORITY SET-ASIDES

Minority set-asides in state and municipal contracting cost the taxpayers millions in higher costs and poorer quality work, and it is grossly unfair to the more qualified, lower bidder.

5) EQUAL RIGHTS FOR ALL. END UNJUST AFFIRMATIVE ACTION

The truth is that today, better qualified white people face racial discrimination in hiring, promotions, scholarships, college admissions, union admittance, and in the awarding of contracts. I believe that the best qualified regardless of race should be favored. Government or Corporate programs of affirmative action should be prohibited.

6) WORKFARE NOT WELFARE

Able-bodied welfare recipients should be required to do some kind of work to get benefits.

7) REDUCE THE ILLEGITIMATE WELFARE BIRTHRATE

Poverty and crime are breeding, and we the taxpayers pay for it. Productive people who cannot afford children of their own should not have to pay for massive welfare illegitimacy. The cycle of poverty and all its accompanying ills can be broken only by slowing the birthrate.

8) PROTECT OUR WETLANDS, WATERS, AND NATURAL RESOURCES

Coastal erosion and toxic waste buildup hurt the quality of life and our fishing industry.

9) VOUCHER SYSTEM IN EDUCATION

In many areas of the state, such as Orleans and parts of Jefferson, parents cannot let their children use the school system that they have paid for through their taxes. Violence and academic mediocrity are prevalent. We need a voucher system to lessen the burden on parents who would like to choose parochial or private schooling for

their children. Tracking in public schools is needed for
students to achieve their potential.

10) PROTECT THE RIGHT TO KEEP AND BEAR
    ARMS

I am unalterably opposed to gun control.

11) LET THE PEOPLE DECIDE

I am in favor of popular referendum on issues such as
a proposed lottery.

Duke hammered at this message each day. But the election
was now receiving international media attention because of
who the candidate was, and so positions on the issues were
hardly noticed. David Duke and his Klan past were in
headlines across the nation, and any philosophical differences
between the candidates were suddenly irrelevant to the
election.

Duke has always caused concern among the Jewish community because of the outspoken anti-Semitism of his youth,
which continues to plague him to this day. Local rabbis were
particularly critical of Duke throughout the first primary, and
their criticism escalated in the runoff. When Mordechi Levy,
head of the small, radical, New York-based Jewish Defense
Organization, involved himself in the election, Duke became
an underdog.

"Mordechi Levy is an extremist who does not represent all
Jews," declared Bill Hess, who by this time was active in fund-
raising efforts for Treen. "There is no unified Jewish community in New Orleans, and there was nothing we could do to
prevent Levy or anyone else from speaking out against Duke."

Levy vowed to stop a Duke victory even if it meant violence.
In late January he announced, "We will do everything we can
to destroy the David Duke campaign. If anyone brings about
bloodshed, it's the foolish people who voted for someone who
wants to put me in a gas chamber."

The fear that Duke instills in many Jewish people cannot be overstated, and Levy saw the former Klansman as a real threat to Jews. Levy later told reporters, "To me, David Duke is a small-time Hitler who is trying to be a big-time Hitler."

Duke called Levy a terrorist and suggested he should stay in New York to "clean up his own city. I'm appalled that he has the nerve to come down here and tell us how to vote."

Duke made the most of the JDO involvement by skillfully playing to the news media. He appeared on the evening news, asking voters to look at him and see if there was anything anti-Semitic about what they saw. Newspapers and television gave Duke prime time to answer Levy's charges and he took full advantage of the opportunity. It was as though Duke controlled the flow of the daily news.

The Treen campaign was aghast at the prospect of a radical New York Jewish leader coming to suburban New Orleans and telling people how they "have to vote."

Treen media consultant and political strategist James St. Raymond, a state representative (R — New Orleans), said, "It was just another boost for Duke. He has been saying all these things about how he has changed from his Klan days and has some people believing him. Now here comes Mordechi Levy who makes Duke look like a saint."

Levy arrived in New Orleans to find that city law required that parade permit applications be filed at least fifteen days in advance of a march. Because he therefore was unable to hold a public demonstration, Levy spent most of his time handing out anti-Duke leaflets at Tulane University. That gave the news media another opportunity to make Duke into something larger than life.

A sparsely attended stop-Duke rally finally was held in the ballroom of the New Orleans Sheraton Hotel, but it did little to dissuade anyone from voting for the former Klansman. In the end the JDO left local Jewish leaders on the defensive, John Treen in the middle, and David Duke in the headlines.

One of Duke's methods of drawing attention to his philosophies is to accuse the minority groups that oppose him of being the true racists. A report on Mordechi Levy on local ABC-TV affiliate WVUE only helped validate in the minds of voters Duke's contention that Levy was an extremist. For a 5 P.M. newscast, WVUE had arranged a satellite hookup between New Orleans and New York in which Levy bashed Duke. When the live interview concluded, Levy mistakenly thought the camera was turned off and referred to the people of the 81st district as "asshole-idiot white devils." The station later aired the remark on the 10 P.M. news show. Metairie residents were infuriated by Levy's outrageous comment.

By this time, Duke was receiving unprecedented news coverage from across the world. He was the top story on every television station in Louisiana, not to mention NBC, ABC, CBS, and CNN network news programs. *Newsweek* and *Time* magazines carried articles about the campaign. The ex-Klan leader, of course, could never have bought such an avalanche of advertising. The media made Duke a political superstar and he took every advantage it offered him. He has few equals in his mastery of the news media. Like a white Jesse Jackson, Duke has the ability to run a campaign on a tight budget merely by being a media star.

Fund raising is an important element in any political race, and this election would be no exception. Money—in five- and ten-dollar amounts—poured into the Duke campaign from all over the country.

Although he raised only a small fraction of his total war chest locally, Duke nevertheless was able to keep within striking distance of Treen. When Treen and the media brought up the fact that most of Duke's finances came from out of state, Duke responded that most of Treen's money had come from "PACs of national and international corporations, which ultimately came from outside the state and have strings attached. I am the only real independent candidate in this race."

Some of the help Duke received was unwelcome. While he was trying to distance himself from his years of association with the Ku Klux Klan, his past kept following him. The *Times-Picayune* carried a story that the Northwest Knights of the Ku Klux Klan, located in Spokane, Washington, had a telephone hotline urging its callers to contribute to Duke's campaign. The message claimed a Duke victory would bring about change sought by the racist movement. The recording ended with the slogan, "White Victory."

Duke vehemently denied any connection with the Klan solicitations. "I don't know these people. I have not asked for their help, and I don't want their help," he said. "We can run our own campaign without them."

It was impossible for Duke to disassociate himself totally from his Ku Klux Klan past. In the euphoria of the runoff, his two young daughters visited from Florida to help their father in the campaign. The girls' mother, long since divorced from Duke, had remarried Don Black, who happens to be one of Duke's most loyal political confidants as well as a former Ku Klux Klan wizard himself. The entire Black family campaigned with Duke throughout the runoff election, although no one in the media picked up the Klan association.

Also adding to Duke's trouble were his past ties with members and former members of right-wing extremist groups. Ralph P. Forbes, allegedly a Nazi party officer in the 1960s, had worked on Duke's 1988 presidential race in the Populist party. Although Duke tried to distance himself from his past affiliations, Forbes delighted in giving his opinions to the press. This only heightened speculation that the new David Duke was actually no more than a Klansman in a suit and a tie.

Treen's media people, headed by Rep. James St. Raymond, knew something drastic and hard-hitting was necessary to turn the tide. Television advertisements showing John Treen, the grandfather, or John Treen, the businessman, were not generating enough enthusiasm among the voters to create the strong turnout needed for victory. Treen's advisors decided to film a commercial directly linking Duke to Nazis.

"We knew this spot would be all or nothing," St. Raymond later recalled. "Any other candidate would have been blown out of the water being seen in a Nazi uniform."

The ad began with a huge swastika fading to a 1970 picture of a boyish David Duke dressed in a Nazi uniform. The scene was from an actual protest by Duke at Tulane University against the appearance of anti-war activist William Kunstler. Duke held a sign that read: "Gas the Chicago 7." The Chicago 7 were anti-war protestors who had been charged with inciting riots that disrupted the 1968 Democratic National Convention in Chicago. In the ad, a background voice announced that David Duke was trying to infiltrate the Louisiana legislature. Viewers were reminded that the swastika is a symbol of hate, and were urged not to forget the men and women who died in World War II. There was a picture of John Treen at age nineteen wearing a U.S. Army uniform next to a picture of Duke sporting a swastika armband.

"When John Treen was nineteen," the background voice intoned, "he was defending his country against the Nazis." The commercial ended with a contemporary photograph of Treen and the simple message, "Vote John Treen . . . someone you can be proud of."

Duke retorted, "I shouldn't have picketed Kunstler in that fashion . . . not that we should forget that Kunstler worked for a Viet Cong victory." He also countered that he had a patriotic record during the Vietnam War by "serving my country in Laos."

Although the picture made a powerful impact at first, it lost its shock value as the campaign wore on. All the while, Duke claimed it was "a youthful mistake." It seemed that no matter what the former grand wizard had done, many voters saw him as a well-groomed politician, not a seasoned radical. He soon became known as "the Teflon Racist."

At the same time Duke was defending his past, according to St. Raymond, the Treen organization was in disarray. After the dismal showing the night of the first primary, a meeting of Treen advisers was called for the next afternoon. Those present knew something had to be done or the election and the reputation of the Republican party could be jeopardized. A decision was made to call the Republican National Committee for help. So important was this formerly unimportant House race that National Committee Chairman Lee Atwater became personally involved.

The RNC helped with beefed-up phone banks, polling, and some fund raising. Treen was so busy lining up endorsements that little time was spent raising money.

"A deal had been made with Governor Roemer to raise $20,000 for Treen in the runoff against Duke," contends a Treen insider. "But the governor never raised the first dime. Not a dime. He had a chance to do something about Duke, but he did absolutely nothing." Even so, Treen out-spent Duke by almost $50,000.

As the final week of the campaign approached, both camps were in a frenzy. Duke still walked the streets, talking to anyone who would listen to his plea "for white rights." He appeared on television and radio stations every day while Treen looked for more endorsements. The endorsements came and with them came some surprises.

Treen had locked up the support of virtually every elected official in Jefferson Parish and New Orleans. Not endorsing Treen had become tantamount to supporting Duke, which in turn labeled one a racist. Louisiana's U.S. senators and congressmen, both Republican and Democrat, gave their support to Treen. Things had gotten so out of hand that Chairman Atwater assured the *Wall Street Journal* he would do anything to defeat Duke.

"Anything" came in unprecedented endorsements from President George Bush and former President Ronald Reagan.

Residents living in District 81 were treated to a letter from President Bush urging them to vote for John Treen. Although Duke's name was never mentioned, the message was clear. Reagan went so far as to do a radio spot asking voters to cast their ballots for "my friend John Treen."

The headlines generated by the presidential endorsements focused even more attention on Duke. He appeared on the evening news looking dumfounded as to why George Bush and Ronald Reagan would want to get involved in a local House race.

"I felt like the whole world was after me," Duke joked. "The only one who didn't endorse my opponent was the Ayatolla Khomeini."

By the last week of the campaign, it was clear that no candidate for local office in America had ever undergone such thorough scrutiny by the media as had David Duke. Allegations were leveled against him every day in the news, which forced him to respond. At least a half-dozen mailings were sent to District 81 voters blasting the former Klansman for his racist background, linking him with every imaginable evil.

It seemed television news programs began every broadcast with photographs of Duke wearing a Klan robe or picketing in a Nazi uniform. Flyers accusing Duke of anti-Catholicism and unChristian-like behavior were placed on cars in church parking lots. Treen campaigners expected the grueling attacks to take their toll and draw an angry—and hopefully fatal—response from the ex-Klansman. They waited, but such a response never came. Whenever he was asked about the accusations, Duke calmly diverted the conversation to his campaign for "equal rights for whites."

Unknown to most observers, the attacks did take their toll, and Duke felt the pressure. He called the accusations "unfair," but still refused to show any public emotion about the personal hurt he was feeling.

"Sometimes at night," he remembers, "after a particularly vicious attack and the campaigning was done, I would take a long, steamy shower and let the pain slowly fall away with the tears."

Howie Farrell remembers the election as particularly mean-spirited, recalling, "I was amazed at the resilience of the man. I only saw him terribly depressed two or three times. But the next morning, he was full of enthusiasm and ready for the fight."

The end of the campaign was a blur to Duke. "I really don't remember sleeping much," he says. "It was campaign, do television interviews, and more campaigning. It seemed like it never stopped."

In the last days of the election, Duke's campaign was in full gear. It was as though he could do nothing wrong. Even the impressive list of endorsements brought together by his opponent seemed to aid Duke. There was a feeling of overkill by the RNC. It had gotten to the point where voting for John Treen was almost the same as giving away your freedom of choice. Americans love an underdog, and the Treen camp, the RNC, and the news media made David Duke a champion to many. "You could feel the backlash among the voters," said one Treen insider.

Just when Treen thought Duke had gotten all the breaks he could get, the U.S. Supreme Court handed down a ruling in a Richmond, Virginia, case, declaring many forms of set-aside programs unconstitutionally discriminatory. It was just what Duke had been saying all along and would prove to be the icing on the cake.

Duke relished saying, "If my position on minority set-aside programs makes me a racist, then a majority of the members of the Supreme Court of the United States are racist."

On Thursday before the Saturday election, Duke purchased a half-hour of local television time to get his views to the people. There sat David Duke, dressed in a blue suit with the

American flag behind him. A young lady asked rehearsed questions, and Duke then articulated what many at home wanted to hear. He attacked affirmative action and welfare programs, as well as forced integration, crime, and taxes.

"The truth is," he said, "that no other politician has the guts to stand up for honest, hardworking people and protect their rights." Near the end he looked in the camera and noted that one of his daughters had asked him, "Daddy, why do those people say such bad things about you? You're not like that at all." It was very effective.

Just before the election, New Orleans television station WWL, a CBS affiliate, broadcast an editorial denouncing Duke and urging voters to cast their ballots for John Treen. Duke immediately called station executive and editorialist Phil Johnson demanding equal time. Johnson said no. Duke then contacted the Federal Communications Commission in Washington, insisting that his civil rights were being violated by WWL's refusal to follow the equal-time doctrine. The FCC agreed with Duke and on Friday night, election eve, WWL allowed Duke free time to tell his side of the story. Once again the media had handed Duke the role of David fighting Goliath.

On election day the streets and medians of Metairie were filled with signs for both Duke and Treen. Duke positioned himself and his supporters at the corner of Veterans Highway and Bonnabel Boulevard, the busiest intersection in the area. Cars honked horns and people waved as they passed. Drivers and passengers rolled down their windows and shouted "Go Duke!" or "Go Treen!" There was a bevy of campaign workers wearing tee shirts and holding blue-and-white Duke signs in an effort to convince any voter who had not yet made up his mind. Wherever Duke went, television teams from across the world followed him. It became more of a presidential-style campaign than a local House race. Few sat on the sidelines and watched. Either because of fear the former grand wizard's election would cause untold international embarrassment to

Louisiana, or because of admiration for someone perceived as standing up for rights of oppressed whites, the election had moved the voting public in Louisiana as never before.

ABC News correspondent Mike von Freund expressed amazement at the response Duke was receiving and commented that Duke could win an election for the U.S. Senate were it not for his Klan background. After watching the euphoria for another five minutes, he said, "No, I think you could win anyway!"

Treen waited restlessly at his home as an army of campaign volunteers phoned, walked door to door, and stood on street corners, begging people not only to vote for John Treen but to save America by defeating David Duke. Treen disliked campaigning and almost never went door to door seeking votes.

According to Elizabeth A. Rickey, a member of the Republican State Central Committee and a Treen supporter, "Campaigning is just not something John likes to do. I went with him one day in his home precinct and he was miserable the entire time."

Workers from the RNC were busy polling and trying to get a handle on the Treen campaign. They knew the election was a virtual dead heat and thought a large turnout would ensure a Treen victory. Duke felt a large turnout would work to *his* advantage, and so every possible voter was regarded as a prize.

Lee Atwater remained in daily communication with various officials of the Treen camp. The pollsters could not accurately predict the outcome because of the large number of undecided voters—or who would not publically state a preference. Lawrence Chehardy remembers speaking with Atwater a few days before the election. "I told him that Duke was on a roll and things didn't look good."

When the polls closed at 8 P.M., Duke and Farrell stood alone and said a prayer before going to the First Parish Court to watch election results being tallied. Duke paced back and forth as they awaited the count. The first to report was a blue-collar precinct and Duke won by a large margin. He would need all the middle-class Democratic voters he could get to make up for Treen's commanding strength with the Republican establishment. As expected, the upper-income voting boxes were decidedly Treen's, and the tabulation seesawed back and forth.

"It was so close," Duke said, "I knew it could swing either way. But something inside told me I was going to win."

With only one precinct missing, he stood 299 votes ahead of Treen. He waited without saying a word until the last vote was tabulated. It was official. Duke had 8,459 votes, or 51 percent, to Treen's 8,232 votes, or 49 percent. It was a victory margin of 227 votes.

"We did it!" Duke shouted, then ran from the room without another word. He telephoned his father and mother to give them the news.

"I was never prouder in my life than when I told my Dad the news," said Duke.

Every son wants his father to be proud of his accomplishments, and Duke had spent a lifetime trying in his own way to be successful in the eyes of the father he idolizes.

The final victory party once again was held at the Lions Club Hall on Metairie Road. This time, the room was overflowing, and the parking lot was filled with supporters. Sheriff Harry Lee had arrived prior to the closing of the polls in hopes of congratulating Duke before television cameras could catch him meeting with the controversial candidate—or so observers concluded. Lee had been perceived as a Duke supporter throughout the runoff because of his inaction on behalf of Treen and because deputies and political allies were allowed to work for Duke.

Rumors that Duke had won filled the room, but no one would confirm anything before Duke spoke. The room grew silent as he stood in front of the microphone and said quietly, "I spoke with the clerk of court." He paused, savoring the moment, then with a broad grin shouted, "And we won!" The audience went berserk. Chants of "Duke! Duke! Duke!" filled the hall. "Duke for Governor" signs were lifted above the crowd, and the glaring lights from dozens of television cameras made the moment almost surrealistic.

The excitement brought on by international attention only increased the euphoria. People long frustrated by what they regarded as unfair treatment by the federal government through affirmative action and set-aside programs, and by what they perceived blacks had wrongly taken from them, finally saw victory. Supporters in the crowd came not only from Metairie, but from as far away as New York and California. Unlike the first primary victory, the runoff election appealed to many people who were previously turned off by Duke's Klan legacy.

Treen waited at the Howard Johnson Hotel on Causeway Boulevard. When the final vote came in, he was devastated. He wept when the news was given to him. He refused to concede and lashed out verbally at his opponent. On seeing Treen's display, one Republican shook his head, motioned toward Treen, and remarked, "This is exactly why Treen lost. He's a royal jerk." Treen had personally taken on the responsibility for saving Louisiana from David Duke, but it was more than John Treen, two United States presidents, and the Republican National Committee could accomplish.

So important was this race, according to James Donelon, that he reported the results that night personally to the president. "I could tell I was on a speaker box at the White House. I gave them the bad news, and I heard the unmistakable voice of George Bush thanking us for a gallant effort."

Media attention and a tremendous job by both the Duke and Treen forces produced a voter turnout of 78 percent. For a presidential election, such a figure would be outstanding, but in a special House election it was historic.

According to Dr. Ed Renwick, "When you get a vote of this magnitude, you virtually have a 100 percent turnout. Taking into account people moving, dying, or out of town, you can't expect much more."

The crowd inside the Lions Club Hall was so large that after Duke spoke to them, he fought his way out into the parking lot where he stood on the back of a sheriff's car to thank the overflow crowd who could not fit into the hall. With his hands held above his head in a display of victory, he could only smile until the cheers died down. Without an overcoat, he spoke in the bitter cold above the repeated chants of "Duke! Duke! Duke!"

In an impassioned speech, the exhausted candidate thanked his supporters and said:

> "I had to come out here to be with you, too, out in the cold, for this is what this campaign has been all about, the fact that the founding elements of this country, many of the men and women whose ancestors built America, are now out in the cold of affirmative action. Many are out in the cold by not being able to send their children to schools their very own taxes pay for.
>
> "We are braving the cold tonight because we have a vision for America; a vision of being able to walk on our streets safely, being able to use our schools, and [having] true equal rights for all in America, not special privilege for a few. We share a vision of truly helping the poor by reforming the liberal welfare system that has actually increased poverty, drugs, and crime.
>
> "We demand an America based on merit. We are dedicated to our children striving toward excellence.
>
> "You, my brave and stalwart ones, you will not be cold too long. Next time we meet, we'll exchange our greetings in the great warm House that Huey [Long] built, the House of Representatives in Baton Rouge."

Duke remembers being elated, but exhausted, that night. "I was too tired to really remember much of anything," he said. "I just wanted to get home and get a full night's sleep."

The following morning, Duke held a news conference to formally meet the press as a representative-elect. As had been the case the previous night, the room was filled with news people from around the world. Duke read a prepared statement in which he said his opponents had claimed, like Chicken Little, that the sky would fall if he were elected.

"Ladies and gentlemen," he said, "David Duke has been elected and the sky hasn't fallen." He tried to temper the mood by extending an olive branch to blacks and Jews, saying he would represent all people of the 81st district. Finally, he lost his composure when reporters persisted in asking him about his past affiliations with the Ku Klux Klan. He tersely responded that he was no longer going to talk about "things that happened ten years ago." It was not going to be easy to remove twenty years of public doubt about his racist past.

The same day, Rep. Odon L. Bacque, Jr., an Independent from Lafayette, announced he would challenge Duke's seating in the legislature. The special session was going to begin in three days and the newly elected House members would be sworn in as the first item on the agenda.

Bacque, who represents Cajun Catholics, reasoned that if Duke had not lived in the district for the one-year period, members of the House had an obligation not to seat him. Once again, Duke's past would follow him. The law that was not tested in the primary election would finally be examined in the legislature.

"I was just trying to follow the law," insists Bacque. "I don't agree with David Duke, but that's not why I opposed his being seated. What kind of signal would we send out to the rest of the country if we didn't at least look at the evidence that other people said was there?"

Some agreed with Bacque, while most took the approach that if the people of the 81st district wanted David Duke as their representative, then that was their choice. No duly elected legislator in the history of Louisiana has ever been denied a seat by the House. A state that has lived through Huey Long and Edwin Edwards knows what a powerful governor can do. The thought of a governor's persuading fifty-three members to expel opposing legislators encouraged more than one representative vote in favor of the former Klansman.

On February 22, the legislature convened at ten o'clock in the morning. Security at the capitol was extremely tight. State troopers were positioned at all entrances to the House of Representatives chamber and everyone passing through was searched. Television cameras jammed the press area, and some reporters were forced to set up their equipment in the capitol rotunda. The balcony was filled with Duke supporters from across the country who came to Baton Rouge to witness the historic occasion of the first Ku Klux Klan grand wizard to be sworn in as an elected official.

The first newly elected member to be sworn in was Jerry Luke LeBlanc, a Democrat from Lafayette. He stood with his family and quietly took the oath of office. The chamber politely applauded and then moved to the next matter on the agenda. When House Speaker Jimmy N. Dimos (D—Monroe) brought up Duke's installation, Bacque raised his hand in opposition. He requested that a vote be taken on a proposal to investigate allegations that Duke had not lived in District 81 for the mandatory one-year period.

He outlined his reasons why Duke's residency should be thoroughly investigated by the Committee on House and Governmental Affairs.

"It would be a travesty," he said, "to seat anyone where a question existed as to whether or not he was truly a legal resident of the district."

As Bacque spoke, Duke's supporters jamming the upper gallery began to yell, prompting Speaker Dimos to threaten to clear the chamber. Duke stood alone behind the speaker's chair waiting to learn if he would be sworn in that day or have to wait for a protracted committee hearing.

"I could hardly breathe," remembered Duke. "I didn't know if I could go through another battle."

Rising in opposition to Bacque's motion was former House Speaker John A. Alario, Jr. (D—Westwego), who represents another area of Jefferson Parish. Alario has long been associated with organized labor and minority rights, and he painstakingly addressed the silent legislative body. Every member knew Alario opposed what Duke had championed throughout his racist career. But he said the voters of the 81st district had chosen the person they wanted to represent them and that their wishes should be respected by the House. Immediately after Alario's remarks, the vote was taken, and by a margin of sixty-nine to thirty-three Bacque's motion to deny the seating of Duke was defeated. Some members of the Black Caucus tried to bring up another vote, but the effort failed.

As the world watched via live television broadcasts, Duke was sworn in as the newest member of the Louisiana House of Representatives. For almost anyone else who in the previous twenty years had been grand wizard of the Ku Klux Klan and president of the National Association for the Advancement of White People, this symbol of political acceptance would have been a fitting end to a remarkable career. But for David Duke, it was just the beginning.

CHAPTER THREE

An American Family

PERSISTENCE IN ATTAINING GOALS, however lofty they may be, is a trait David Duke has possessed all his life. Even during the darkest hours of his bizarre and controversial career, he has never wavered from his basic belief that white people are the real minority on earth and that they need someone to protect their interests and heritage.

In speeches and writings, Duke has continually echoed the theme that white Christian people "should live as our fathers did." In his mind, the United States was better off before the administration of Franklin Roosevelt and the progressive New Deal. He longs for a country based on Rugged Individualism. Convinced that minority elements have perverted society, he believes "a nation's greatness lies within its people, not in a welfare state influenced by the liberal-controlled press." He visualizes an America dominated by hard work, Christianity, and the values he associates with the white race.

Such is the philosophy of a family whose American roots allegedly can be traced back to John Walker and the arrival of the *Mayflower*. The early nineteenth century was a time of great expansion in the United States as the country spread westward, answering the call of Manifest Destiny. Immigrants from Europe, filled with hopes of a better life in the land across the Atlantic Ocean, streamed into the new nation to seek opportunities they could not find at home.

One of these "new Americans" was John Duke, the great-great-grandfather of America's most vocal white rights advocate. All that is known about him is he was born in Edinburgh, Scotland, in 1799, raised as a Methodist, and arrived in the new world in 1820. He first settled in Woodville, Ohio, where he became a farmer. Within a few years he was married and later had seven children before moving to Missouri near New Sedalia, where he continued farming until his death in 1851.

It is known that two of his sons, William and Matthew, fought in the Civil War on the side of the Union. William Duke was captured by Confederates at the Battle of Gettysburg and was sent south by ship to a prisoner of war camp. He never arrived because the boat carrying him was sunk by federal artillery. Family legend has it that Private Duke was rescued from drowning by a Rebel soldier, who helped him escape the Confederate Army and return to Missouri. After the war, William and the Rebel soldier remained close, lifelong friends. The Confederate's new friend would be the progenitor of the future leader of the Ku Klux Klan.

Matthew Duke next moved from his home in Missouri to the new state of Kansas, settling on a farm not far from the city of Lawrence. Records indicate that he continued the family tradition of farming and was active in Republican politics until his death in 1926. Four children were born to the Dukes, two girls named Cordie and Gossie, a boy named Ernest, and a fourth child who died at birth. Matthew Duke was a firm believer that education was the only way to escape the drudgery of farm life, and each of his three children would be highly motivated to better themselves.

The third child, Ernest, was born on July 30, 1877. He was an industrious youngster who knew from an early age that he was not going to spend his life on a farm. He was able to put aside money by working at odd jobs and in 1895 entered the University of Kansas, majoring in history.

Ernest Duke attended college for only three years and did not graduate. The education he received, however, allowed him to find employment outside of farming with the U.S. Post Office. He moved to Kansas City, Missouri, where he eventually rose to the position of chief postal clerk.

While at college, Ernest Duke had met and married Florence Hedger of Allen County, Kansas. She was an exceptionally bright woman who in 1904, long before women's liberation became a slogan, received a bachelor of science degree from the University of Kansas. She later joined the faculty, becoming one of the first women chemistry professors at the university. Her sister, Carolyn Hedger, was also interested in science and later became one of the first female surgeons in the United States, practicing medicine in Chicago for many years.

Florence Duke firmly believed that the more education one could receive, the better off one's life would be. The family were strict Methodists, and Christian beliefs were instilled along with the importance of mathematics, science, and history. Although never directly involved in politics, the Dukes maintained their loyalty to the Republican party even during the difficult period of the Great Depression. Religion, science, and politics were passions that would be passed on to Florence's son and become important factors in the unusual development of her grandson, David.

Florence Duke gave birth to a son in 1907 and named him William C. after his Civil War uncle. On March 18, 1912, Florence bore a second son, in Blue Rapids, Kansas, christening him David Hedger Duke. As soon as the children were old enough, Florence returned to teaching chemistry. She very much wanted to raise her sons to be scientists and leaders, and the children were told from an early age that as long as they stayed in school and made good grades, their parents would help support them.

The Methodist church, work, and school were the only things David Hedger remembers being involved in while growing up.

"We were never rich by any means," he emphasized, "but we were never without." The family was fortunate, as Matthew Duke remained employed throughout the Depression in his position at the post office, and Mrs. Duke retained her job at the University of Kansas.

David Hedger Duke was born with his mother's drive to learn and his father's desire to better himself. He was a high-energy child who today might be diagnosed as suffering from hyperactivity. When his uncle became ill, his father was forced to take on the additional burden of supporting a second family, which left little money for his own children. To help out, David Hedger worked at various times at the Central Drug Store and the Independence Stove Foundry throughout high school.

Sleep was considered a nuisance by David Hedger, who has never required more than three or four hours of rest a day. It is a trait he has passed on to his son, the former grand wizard. Although industrious, he pushed even harder, knowing that "if I failed at school, I failed with the family."

Florence Duke's dream of seeing her sons grow up to be scientists and doctors was cut short when she died of cancer in 1926. Ernest was left with the difficult task of rearing two children alone and holding down a job, in addition to supporting his brother's family. He was a man who needed the companionship of a wife, and being a single parent was not a role he enjoyed. Later, he met and married an Irish immigrant named Margaret Fergerson, who had two young children of her own. They became the best of friends and the marriage lasted fifty years, although Ernest's only true love was Florence.

David Hedger continued working and graduated from Rosedale High School in 1929. He attended Kansas City Junior College through 1932, working summers as a surveyor for the

Southern Bell Telephone Company. This work with the telephone company helped him decide to become an engineer.

In 1932, he met Maxine Crick, whom he would later marry. She was born on December 20, 1913, in Independence, Missouri, and grew up as a member of the Independent Church of Latter-day Saints. Her father was Thomas Crick, the wealthy owner of the Independence Manufacturing Company, which specialized in making stoves and heavy-iron products. Their Independence neighbors included Bess and Harry Truman.

The Cricks had three daughters, with Maxine being the middle and most-pampered one. Her parents made sure that all three girls received good educations and provided for their every whim. They wore the finest clothes and traveled extensively, living the good life of the Roaring Twenties.

Maxine was a bright girl who excelled in writing and poetry, as is reflected in her notebooks of the period. When not ill with scarlet fever or some other sickness, she excelled in athletics, especially golf.

In 1934 Maxine enrolled at the University of Kansas and on May 15, 1937, married a fellow student, David Hedger Duke, in a large ceremony in Independence. David H. Duke was a dashing young man with dreams of conquering the world, but he had little money and no family position. So Maxine was forced to adjust to being a middle-class housewife.

While at the University of Kansas, David Hedger took his father's advice and "did the smartest thing I ever did in my life." He joined the ROTC program and immediately fell in love with the military. It brought extra income for college, but more importantly, helped give him direction in life. He was used to discipline and hard work, and the military seemed a way to move up the ladder of success quickly.

Shortly after graduation from college, David Hedger landed a job with Shell Oil Company. For the next few years the Dukes followed the new oil boom in Oklahoma, Kansas, and North Texas. Soon they were living in Wichita, Kansas, where at age twenty-seven David was promoted to chief engineer. At the end of 1939 Duke relocated to Centralia, Illinois, to explore new oil fields in the southern part of the state. Things looked promising for the oil business, but the United States was gearing up for the growing prospect of war in Europe, and David Hedger was called to active duty by the army on December 6, 1940.

Lieutenant Duke was assigned to Air Defense and was stationed at Fort Crockett and later at Fort Bliss in Texas. He became part of the 63rd Coast Artillery, known as the "AA." Later, he would often proudly recall that he was a part of the giant summer maneuvers in Louisiana, where he served as an aide to Gen. Dwight Eisenhower.

"One night, I was ordered to drive from Lake Charles, Louisiana, to Monroe, in the northern part of the state, to deliver a top secret memo to Gen. George S. Patton," Duke said. "When I reached him, I was taken aback by what a larger-than-life figure he was. The memo was the order to end maneuvers and head to Europe."

On Sunday, December 7, 1941, Lieutenant Duke boarded a train bound for the West Coast. His final destination was to be the Philippines. The same day, however, the Imperial Japanese Navy attacked Pearl Harbor, launching America's involvement in World War II. Because of the outbreak of war, Duke made it only as far as San Francisco and subsequently was stationed with the AA in Seattle, Washington. Because he remained in the United States, he insisted that his wife Maxine come to live with him, and they spent much of the war in Seattle. The young officer, now a captain, yearned for advancement, and in 1943 was sent to the Command General College at Fort Leavenworth, Kansas.

The Dukes wanted to start a family, but Maxine's first pregnancies had ended in miscarriages. In 1944, with the world war raging, Maxine became pregnant for the third time. As in the first two pregnancies, she was careful about exercise, diet, and abstention from any alcoholic beverages. On March 12, 1945, while still in Seattle, Maxine gave birth by Caesarean section to a girl named Dorothy. Like all Dukes before her, she could be expected to be reared in a conservative Methodist family. Maxine had been brought up in the Church of Latter-day Saints but converted to Methodism after she married.

Captain Duke was soon promoted to the rank of major and was reassigned to the Philippines. He was there only long enough to be outfitted with winter clothes in anticipation of the planned invasion of Japan. The atomic bombing of Hiroshima and Nagasaki, however, quickly ended the war, and Major Duke returned to the states.

"I would have remained in the army after the war, but there were too many officers and not enough jobs to go around," he remembers. "I wanted to excel in the world, not get locked into a static position."

Major Duke returned to his job with Shell Oil, but maintained his commission in the Army Reserves. Because his job kept him on the move, he would take his active reserve duty each year at Fort Bliss in El Paso, Texas. He soon immersed himself in the government's new anti-aircraft missile program. This was a new area of defense, and Maj. David H. Duke wanted to be a leader in missile research. He studied everything he could get his hands on and soon was recognized as one of the leading experts on the subject.

The next years were devoted to his job with Shell and to his fascination with missile defense. As was typical in the oil business in the mid-1950s, the Dukes moved from city to city, following the boom. Maxine once again became pregnant, and on July 1, 1950, a son, David Ernest Duke, was born at St. John's Hospital in Tulsa, Oklahoma. The delivery was complicated, and an emergency Caesarean section was necessary to save the baby. He was known by the family as "the prayer baby" because Maxine had come so close to losing him. The child's grandmother predicted the baby would one day become a preacher. Major Duke would personally see to it that his daughter and son would be raised as he had been, with strict, conservative, Christian values.

Maj. David Hedger Duke, father of the former Klansman. (Photo courtesy of Dotti Duke)

CHAPTER FOUR

His Father's Son

By 1954, MAJOR DUKE not only had been able to maintain his status as an expert in the field of anti-aircraft missiles, but had moved up the corporate ladder with Royal Dutch Shell. He was offered a position at the company's headquarters at The Hague in the Netherlands. Although moving to another country can be an emotional event, this particular move proved a good one for the Duke family. The children were still very young, and time spent with their parents over the next few years would help shape them as the individuals they are today.

Major Duke had more time to spend with his family while they were living in Europe. Both Dorothy, or Dotti, as she was now called, and David attended Dutch schools and learned to speak the language. Major Duke knew the importance of education and was determined that his children would excel in whatever endeavors they chose later in life. They were expected to do their studies before they were allowed to play.

Time normally spent in the oil fields could now be devoted to the family, and Major Duke would see that the children spent an hour a day reading. One can only imagine a four-year-old and an eight-year-old sitting at a desk reading for an hour. But like their father, Dotti and David accepted, even at an early age, the Duke philosophy: "Failure at school means failure at home." This obsession to excel would dominate the relationship with their father throughout their childhood.

But all the time spent in The Hague was not dedicated to work. The family traveled almost every weekend, and found time to visit England and Italy. These family outings would become a special part of the Duke family life for many years, until Major Duke went to Vietnam in 1966.

Both Dotti and David remember the time spent in Europe as pleasant. Although Dotti was only eight and David four, each has fond memories of The Hague and the people they met. Most importantly, they remember the family life. "It was a good time," Dotti recalled." We traveled and did things like a family."

Throughout the Dukes' stay in the Netherlands, Major Duke maintained his commission in the U.S. Army. He worked with anti-aircraft missiles in Europe for NATO. The Cold War had put a strain on East-West relations, and Major Duke's commitment to the national defense of the United States increased. He was one of many post-World War II veterans who believed that democracy and the freedom it brings should be enjoyed throughout the world. The more he traveled, the more convinced he became that his extremely conservative views were right, and he passed them on to his children, especially his son.

Maxine, who had always been a social drinker, began drinking more heavily while the family was living in The Hague, according to Dotti. The long periods when Major Duke was working in other countries were difficult for Maxine, and alcohol became a way of dealing with the problem. She had been raised in wealthy surroundings by parents who saw to her every wish, says Dotti, and Major Duke was not in a position to keep up financially with the Cricks. Maxine was thirty-two when Dotti was born and thirty-seven when David arrived. She had, as Dotti put it, "a hard time adjusting to motherhood." For a woman who has been described as brilliant,

William Duke, Union soldier during the Civil War and great-uncle of David Ernest Duke. (Photo courtesy of Dotti Duke)

David Duke and sister Dotti, 1955. (Photo courtesy of Dotti Duke)

David Duke in school picture, 1958. (Photo courtesy of Dotti Duke)

Maxine Crick Duke, mother of David. (Photo courtesy of Dotti Duke)

being a housewife and mother seemed to leave her, in Dotti's words, "without purpose."

With Major Duke absent most of the time, the Dukes were able to make few friends, and Maxine needed more than staying at home with two small children. Her husband's main interests were his work at Shell, a military career, and seeing to it that Dotti and David were raised as perfect children. To a man with a military mind, excessive drinking was a weakness that would not exist if a person wanted to do something about it, and a rift inevitably developed between the couple. They dealt with their marriage problems in different ways—with Major Duke immersing himself in work and Maxine drinking too much. Later, he did see to it that Maxine got help for her illness, but by that time it was too late to resolve the problem.

Shell decided Major Duke could better serve the company back in the United States, so the family packed up and moved briefly to Lake Charles, Louisiana, and in 1955 to New Orleans, where they remained for the next fourteen years. They purchased a modest, two-story house at 4768 St. Ferdinand Street in an all-white neighborhood in the middle-class area of the city known as Gentilly Woods.

The Dukes joined the Elysian Fields Methodist Church, where Major Duke taught Sunday school to high school students. It was at this time that the Dukes began attending other churches. Major Duke remained devoutly Christian, but found it difficult to follow certain liberal church doctrine in the progressive 1950s and 1960s.

"He was looking for a church that could fit his philosophy," said Dotti. At a time when integration and other post-war liberal ideologies were becoming increasingly prominent in America, Major Duke remained steadfastly conservative.

According to Dotti, "He was very conservative. Much more conservative than Ronald Reagan."

Dotti and David Duke in Christmas card
photograph from the Netherlands, 1955.
(Photo courtesy of Dotti Duke)

Dotti and David Duke in Halloween costume, 1955. David is
dressed as a mammy. (Photo courtesy of Dotti Duke)

If a minister gave a sermon that was at odds with Major Duke's way of thinking, he and the children would look for another church. "I was more concerned," he said, "about the quality of the minister than the denomination."

Dotti and David were enrolled at William C. C. Claiborne Elementary School at 4617 Mirabeau Avenue, not far from their home. It was a small, traditional elementary school, just the kind young children need when they move to a new town. Although it was a public school, New Orleans was still segregated in the mid-1950s and the school, like the neighborhood, was all white. Major Duke would prepare the children's breakfast each morning and Dotti and David would walk to school.

The first time someone outside the Duke family made a lasting influence on David was at Claiborne Elementary. His second-grade teacher was Mrs. Zena Strole, who, as he remembers, "was an older lady who devoted a great deal of time to me. She made me want to be academically excellent."

Again David learned that if he tried hard at school, he could gain some of the attention and love all children need. Already, the fear that "failure at school means failure at home" was instilled in the young child. The attention Mrs. Strole gave Duke was important because David still retained a Dutch accent, which caused him difficulty with the English language. Her work with him improved his skills.

Major Duke was now Colonel Duke, and he was spending more and more time with the government and his passion for anti-aircraft missiles. Maxine stayed at home and did the best she could to care for the children while Colonel Duke divided his time between Shell Oil Company and the U.S. Army. She tried to be a wife of the 1950s, and as Dotti remembers, her mother "wanted to be a good mom."

The Dukes had a black housekeeper named Pinkie, who as Dotti describes her, "was not a maid, but more of a nanny. She looked after David and me, fixed our meals and, on my

Dad's insistence, ate every meal with us at our table. He [Colonel Duke] was conservative but treated black people with love and respect. She really was a part of our family and we all loved her. When she passed away, my mom and David were the only white people at her funeral."

Disaster struck the family on July 1, 1956, when Maxine's younger sister Mildred was killed. She and her husband were aboard a Trans World Airlines flight that crashed over the Grand Canyon. It was a tragedy that compounded Maxine's already fragile condition. She reacted to her sister's death by withdrawing from her family much of the time.

By 1957, Mrs. Duke's illness had grown progressively worse. She would drink alone at home, says Dotti. She never went to bars or nightclubs, although she drank a great deal during the day. Her problem had gotten so bad that Dotti did not want other children to visit the Duke residence.

David, who was only seven, usually remained outside playing with friends every day until dark. He then would come home and read alone or watch television, so he was not cognizant of his mother's problems. She was not a typical housewife who enjoyed housework, but often would take her son with her when she ran errands or went shopping. She still devoted much of her time to playing golf and taught David the game. It was easy for her to relate to a young boy as a teacher on a golf course, and she took great pride in her son's athletic ability.

The family still traveled whenever the opportunity arose. Sometimes it would just be a day trip to the Mississippi Gulf Coast. Dotti fondly recalls a boat trip to Ship Island off the coast of Gulfport, Mississippi. "The whole family went. David even brought his dog, Friskey." The Dukes had two fox terriers and, at David's insistence, both of them were named Friskey.

Colonel Duke and a friend formed a construction company in the late 1950s, and they built a total of "five or six spec houses." David recalls going with his father to the job sites. He would help by carrying tools or doing whatever a seven-year-old could do. He viewed his father in a different role as construction supervisor. He noticed Colonel Duke commanded respect on the job site, just as he did in the military.

"My dad instilled a strong work ethic in me," Duke said. "He told me that if I wanted something bad enough and worked hard enough, I could do anything I wanted to do."

David remembers one particular time he and his father went out together on Mardi Gras. He was seven years old and the two of them went to Felix's Oyster Bar in the French Quarter. "I can remember not being able to see the top of the bar," David said. "But, I remember eating oysters, just him and me."

Religion and the Methodist church were more important to the Dukes than ever. Colonel Duke made certain the family attended services every Sunday and that Dotti and David knew their Bible studies. Maxine tried to attend church, but she was physically unable to do so. Rising early on Sunday morning and sitting through a long church service was more than she could manage, so Colonel Duke would get the children dressed and fed and allow Maxine to sleep late.

One day, Colonel Duke taught a Sunday school class, and although David was younger than class members, he followed along with his father. He remembers that his father lectured the class on integrity. Colonel Duke stated emphatically that "no matter what you do, don't ever compromise your princi-ples. If the crowd goes one way and you know they're wrong, then you have an absolute responsibility to do the right thing. Even if you have to do it all alone."

Young David was in awe of his father. "It hit me like a wall," he said. "Everyone was silently watching my father. He made a difference to me that has lasted through my life."

At that moment, David Duke determined that he was going to be just like his father.

CHAPTER FIVE

Adolescence and Change

BY 1960, THINGS HAD DETERIORATED in the Duke household to the point that Dotti could no longer stand living at home. Mrs. Duke's illness had put such a strain on her relationship with Dotti that communication was virtually nonexistent. Dotti felt she had no family because of her inability to cope with the problems of her parents, who were now struggling with Mrs. Duke's drinking. Dotti had no close friends at school, or in the neighborhood, and found that she could not cultivate new ones for fear of how they might react to Maxine's condition. It was a time of development for Dotti and David, and their mother could not deal with their demands.

"I wanted just one time to come home from school and find my mom . . . waiting for me," remembers Dotti.

Despite Mrs. Duke's problems, the house on St. Ferdinand Street was, as David describes it, a "Leave It to Beaver house." Colonel Duke and Maxine slept downstairs, allowing Dotti and David to share the entire second floor. The upstairs bedrooms were spacious and became private worlds unto themselves. The rest of the house was relatively small, but quite ordinary and middle class. There was a large garage that David would later expropriate for his many chemistry sets and numerous pets.

Although he was busy, Colonel Duke was often at home and always awoke early. Each morning he rose at four o'clock and began working on one of his various projects. By the time the rest of the family was up, Dad had breakfast prepared and the house ready for the day's activities. Even on Christmas morning, the children had to eat breakfast before opening their presents. Saturday mornings began with a solid meal. Then followed Roy Rogers movies, other television programs, and homework or, in its absence, assigned reading. Colonel Duke is an avid reader and spent much of his time at home wrapped up in a book or working on his drafting and construction projects. There was little idle time in the Duke household.

At a time when a daughter needed nurturing by her mother, Dotti took on the reverse responsibility of taking care of Maxine. She would see that the house was kept in order and look after little David. But if Dotti tried to assume a more maternal role of rearing David, Colonel Duke would intervene. He firmly believed that brother and sister should have a sibling relationship. He made a concerted effort to give David extra paternal care, but was unable to show the same affection to Dotti.

Despite the turmoil around him, David was having an enjoyable time. He was, as his sister describes him, "a short, skinny kid with his nose in a book or out playing Tom Sawyer." David simply did not want to see the family trouble around him. As little boys will do, he turned to a world of make-believe, living a child's fantasy and acting out his heroes' lives. One moment he was Davy Crockett, blazing a new frontier; the next he was Huck Finn, destined to make each day another adventure. David was seldom at home during daylight hours, preferring to be outdoors. In grade school, he took piano lessons and did exceptionally well, but rebelled against afternoon lessons because his first love was the open air. Whenever he was inside the house, he often went straight to his bedroom to read. By the time David had completed the sixth grade, Colonel Duke had made certain that his son had read all the major classics, as well as the complete works of Shakespeare.

During this period Colonel Duke decided to have Maxine hospitalized. She improved, but only temporarily. Dotti hoped that her mother would come home from the hospital healthy and transformed into a new mom, but her wish never materialized. Because he was still young, David was kept in the dark about his mother's condition. To this day, he claims this period was not as destructive to him as it was to his sister.

While David would excel to gain his father's approval, Dotti would rebel, and the chasm between father and daughter widened with each day. Maxine was in no condition to guide Dotti, and Dotti's father could not take the place of a mother. Finally, Colonel and Mrs. Duke decided a different environment might be good for Dotti, and she spent her high school freshman year at All Saints Episcopal School, a private all-girls boarding institution in Vicksburg, Mississippi.

"Everything fell on me," said Dotti, "I thought life would be easier if I got away from home." This sounded good to a fourteen-year-old, but All Saints Episcopal did not prove to be the answer. Dotti, once again, rebelled against the strict discipline of the boarding school. Her grades were dismal. Colonel Duke intervened, pleading with the headmaster of the school to allow Dotti to remain.

Many years later, she found letters her father had sent to the principal, urging him to give his daughter another chance. It was easier for him to convey his love for Dotti through letters to a stranger than to his daughter directly. Dotti also found it impossible to express affection to her parents. In a letter to a friend she wrote she would "do anything for my dad."

Things did not improve at All Saints Episcopal, and after a year, Dotti transferred to Acadia Baptist Academy at Eunice, Louisiana. This move was even less successful than her term at All Saints had been. What Dotti needed was personal attention, but she feels she did not receive enough at Acadia. She was unhappier than before she left New Orleans. Dotti returned home at the end of the semester and attended East Jefferson High School in Metairie for her junior and senior years.

In 1961, David was eleven and was filling his days reading and spending as much time with his father as possible. Colonel Duke was devoting more free time to his construction company, and David took every opportunity to be with his dad. Maxine was not physically able to do much with or for her son, so the burden fell on her husband. Although he was busier than ever, Colonel Duke took his son along with him whenever possible. David would do anything to be with his father. Colonel Duke encouraged the inquisitive youth to join the Cub Scouts and, later, the Boy Scouts.

"I really liked Scouting, especially when I was younger," Duke remembers. "My dad liked the idea and helped me a lot with Scout projects."

The Duke household remained tense, but on an even keel, for the next year. No one wanted to confront Mrs. Duke's problem, and the Dukes lived each day waiting for a potential time bomb to go off. As a unit, the family was growing apart, and each member migrated in his own direction, rather than trying to work together to find a solution to their common problem.

Colonel Duke was successful with his job at Shell and his after-hours work with his construction company, but his real his love was the military. His knowledge about the U.S. government's missile program was invaluable and each summer he would go to Washington to work at the Pentagon. It has been suggested that Colonel Duke had secret ties to the Central Intelligence Agency, but there has never been any evidence to substantiate this theory. While he did have a background in missile research, his future work in Vietnam and

Laos would be limited to construction projects under the direction of the State Department.

Dotti was in her senior year at East Jefferson High School when she announced to the family she was getting married. Colonel and Mrs. Duke were not thrilled by the idea, but everyone attended the wedding ceremony in Texas. In hindsight, quitting high school to get married was a dreadful mistake, but at the time Dotti could not cope with her life at home. Her new husband was a soldier and she soon was living in Japan. Strikingly beautiful, she became a successful model in Tokyo. Some time later, the marriage began to deteriorate. The union ended in divorce, and she returned to the States but never again lived in New Orleans.

David now had the entire upstairs at home to himself and made the best of it. He set up a chemistry lab in Dotti's old room and became fascinated with science, especially the physical sciences. Although he was interested in sports and outdoor activities, most of his time was now devoted to experimenting with chemistry sets and reading about science. He would spend the afternoon reading and working on experiments, then wait for his father to come home to tell him all about what he had done during the day. Colonel Duke was not only David's father, but also his best friend.

Duke always had many pets, including snakes, toads, dogs, cats, squirrels, birds, and goldfish. In a story Duke loves to tell, he saved up enough money to buy two white rats. He was told they were both females, and he kept them in a homemade wooden cage in the garage. One of the rats became pregnant and David assumed the other rat must have been a male. A litter was soon born and everything looked normal for a few days until the baby rats began to move.

"They were not slow-moving like their parents," Duke said, "but crawled swiftly. When hair began to appear on the babies, I quickly noticed that they were covered with grey fur." He took the rodents to a pet shop where he was told that the original white rats were indeed females and that a wild rat must have mated with one of them.

He was amazed by the difference in the parent rats and mixed offsprings.

"It was fantastic," he remembered. "This was the first time it had occurred to me that genes make a profound difference in the behavior of animals."

His fascination with science and nature and the effects of physical biology soon replaced Tom Sawyer and Huck Finn. The little boy who lived in a world of make-believe grew into a young man with an inquisitive mind for science and the genetic differences of animals. Undoubtedly this would help lay the groundwork for his future theories about racial differences.

Colonel Duke was always trying to save money and improve his financial position. In 1963 he built a new home in suburban Metairie at 1105 Athenia Parkway and sold the house on St. Ferdinand Street for a handsome profit. The new house was larger and more modern than the one on St. Ferdinand, but the move ended David's life at Claiborne Elementary and the "Leave It to Beaver" period. David would find that life would become more serious in the future. He was enrolled in the seventh grade at Metairie Junior High School on Metairie Road. Although a public school, it is located in one of the wealthiest sections of the New Orleans area and, like Claiborne Elementary, was all white.

Colonel Duke and David were still regular churchgoers, although they attended various churches, depending on what the pastor had said the previous week. Social issues, especially integration, were a hot topic, and Colonel Duke was as politically conservative as he had ever been. Metairie was virtually all white, and he did not want to be told that moving to any particular part of the city was morally wrong. The one church they attended most frequently was Munholland United Methodist Church on Metairie Road, the same church where David's future political opponent, John Treen, is a member.

Leaving St. Ferdinand Street and the only real home David had ever known was difficult. The few friends he had were now too far away to visit on a regular basis, and he was not adept at making new ones. Colonel Duke was busier than ever with work and the military, but he still managed to spend time with his son. Maxine's health was poor, so once again she was hospitalized, and once again she seemed to recover. But the improvement did not last. David was now old enough to realize what was going on. He was alone most of the time, and the only satisfaction he found was in his reading and his science projects.

Just when the Dukes were getting settled in the new house, Colonel Duke decided to move to 235 Jewel Street in an upscale neighborhood near Lake Pontchartrain. Like the previous two houses, it was in an all-white area of the city. Once again, David had to leave his friends and begin the painful process of making new friendships all over again. On a personal level, David was very reclusive, spending a lot of time in the swampy areas around New Orleans finding specimens and hunting and fishing with friends. He always managed to have a few close friends, but he was not the type of person to be "one of the guys" or to reveal much of his inner self to just anyone.

Eventually, David would deal with the household problem by simply immersing himself in his reading, science projects, and outdoor activities. When he came home from school or play, David immediately would go to his room and read or throw himself into his science projects.

The last family trip took them to California in 1963 to visit Dotti. Colonel and Mrs. Duke, together with David and his dog Friskey, drove from New Orleans to Los Angeles. When Dotti saw David, she noticed a difference. His smile and happy outlook were no longer as effervescent. He confided to Dotti,

"I now know the kind of hardships you went through. It's now on my shoulders. I'm sorry I wasn't more understanding with you when you were at home."

Back in New Orleans, David was enrolled for the eighth grade at Clifton L. Ganus Christian School at 6026 Paris Avenue. Located in an upper-income area of the Lakefront of New Orleans, it was a progressive, all-white school that stressed strong educational achievement. With the household in turmoil, Colonel Duke felt David needed all the personal attention and guidance possible.

David fit right in at Ganus and was remembered by teachers as being a good student. He joined in sports and participated in other extracurricular activities offered by the school. He made a few friends, but still spent most of his free time outdoors, reading alone in his room, or working on a science project. Magazines such as *National Geographic, Science Digest,* and *Popular Science* filled his afternoons with curiosity about life.

"I aspired to be a doctor," he remembers, "that studied the human body in relation to space travel." His grades show that he excelled in mathematics, English, and science, but was only "adequate" in most other subjects. The problems at home followed David, and he was becoming emotionally intense.

Ganus had a basketball team, and David enjoyed being on the squad. The games were a great opportunity for the family to be together. Colonel Duke usually went to the games, although Maxine attended only a few. She was not up to dealing with other parents. By this time however, Duke was used to being on his own and tried to distance himself from her.

In 1964, the issue of integration was the major topic of discussion throughout the South. At the time, David was quite sympathetic to the plight of blacks. He was so outspoken in favor of the civil rights movement that he was given an assignment by his teacher to do a civics term paper on the arguments against integration. "I was sided [*sic*] with the civil rights movement at the time," he said. "It was sort of my way to assert myself with my father." Colonel Duke was extremely conservative and David was at a rebellious age.

At first, he thought the report would be just one more assignment, but things quickly changed. He went to the school library and began researching everything he could find on integration. Ganus' library had books and magazines dealing with current issues from a typical media perspective. David was not satisfied.

"Ganus had all the same books you could buy at any bookstore," he said. Books such as *Black Like Me* and *The Myth of Race* showed the negative effects of segregation and took a positive view of integration. When he had found enough information to substantiate the liberal side of the slate, he sought anything that could give him an opposing view of the integration issue. He took the bus to the New Orleans Public Library and then went to the Doubleday bookstore on Canal Street. Neither had the type of information necessary to support a credible argument for segregation.

"I was a bit surprised," he said, "that the only books public libraries carried were opposed to segregation. Some books even went as far as arguing that blacks were superior to whites.

"I began to assemble my paper for segregation by trying to glean [information] from the liberal books. I supposed that there just weren't any credible social scientists and others who opposed integration, and that the liberal press was correct in portraying 'racists' as ignorant and uneducated."

By chance, Duke read an article in the local *Times-Picayune* that reported a group called the Citizens Council had held a meeting at the Municipal Auditorium to oppose forced integration of public education. The next day, he rode the bus to the Council office on Carondelet Street in the heart of the New Orleans central business district.

The Citizens Council, or White Citizens Council, was a racist organization formed in the mid-1950s to fight integration. At one point, the group was reported to have had 50,000 dues-paying members. One of its founders was the late Judge Leander H. Perez of Plaquemines Parish, who gained national attention as a leader of anti-integrationist and anti-Semitic factions in Louisiana. According to *Leander Perez, Boss of the Delta,* the Judge was a frequent and popular speaker at Council rallies. So important was the Council to segregationists that Judge Perez offered trophies and U.S. savings bonds as incentives to anyone bringing in new members.

What David discovered at the Council office was about all the information anyone could hope to find on racist views. There was a staff of both paid and volunteer workers who were more than happy to help the fourteen-year-old learn the benefits of being a Caucasian. The young boy walked into the office and asked if they had any material regarding integration.

"The lady behind the desk gave me a broad smile," he said, "and motioned me to look at the twenty-foot-long bookshelves behind her which were covered with books!"

David first read a book entitled *Race and Reason—A Yankee View,* by Carlton Putnam, which offered historical, psychological, cultural, and biological reasons why integration would fail and ultimately produce crime and poverty. Duke was fascinated with it.

"I read the book carefully. I thought that I would find nonsense, but the book was extremely well written. I couldn't put it down," Duke said. "The author was sensitive and intelligent, and there wasn't a shred of the hatred that I expected to find in it. It didn't convert me, but it began an intellectual odyssey into the other side of the race issue."

Putnam argued that forced integration in education would lead to an educational and social catastrophe. He further declared that there were deep inborn differences between races that outweighed environmental factors in social, athletic, and intellectual performance.

A historian who had written biographies on Theodore Roosevelt and others, Putnam also stressed historical and archeological interpretations in his theories that race played a major role in the development of societies.

"If Putnam was right," Duke decided, "then the social implications are tremendous." He decided to satisfy his own intellectual curiosity by spending long hours in the school library and at home reading and researching everything available on the race issue from both the left and the right. Often, he traveled down to the Citizens Council office and read from their library, or borrowed books to bring home with him. Additionally, he asked a lot of questions. One of the Citizens Council volunteers remembers the young student constantly inquiring about a particular Council view on race, and more often than not, once again researching the issue.

Already having a solid foundation of readings on genetics, biology, and psychology, Duke was able to handle easily the works of many respected scientists who agreed with the basics of Putnam's thesis.

He read books by Dr. Henry Garrett, who for fifteen years chaired the Department of Psychology at Columbia University and headed the American Psychological Association for another fifteen years. Dr. Carlton Coon, a leading American physical anthropologist, introduced Duke to the view that race was a key factor in the development of modern man. Dr. Coon was the author of many prominent textbooks on physical anthropology used in American universities.

Psychologist Arthur Jensen became another of his scientific heroes. Jensen, who once held strong environmental positions on racial behavior, later came to the conclusion that intelligence was primarily a process of heredity rather than environment. Dr. William Shockley, a Nobel Prize-winning physicist who invented the transistor, had begun his first pronouncements that race vitally affects society. Duke viewed him as a hero who sacrificed his prestige in the pantheon of science to speak his mind on the most important thing in the world, the survival of the white race.

Jeanette Williams, a friend of the family from Shell Oil, often visited the Duke home during this period, helping Maxine to deal with her illness. After David learned Mrs. Williams had a psychology degree, he would initiate discussions on the subject of environment-versus-heredity. She told Mrs. Duke she was amazed that a fourteen-year-old could discuss the subject with the depth of a college professor.

"The books I found at the Citizens Council," Duke said, "had hard scientific facts about race and the origin of man . . . credible evidence that there were genetic differences between blacks and whites." What these books really had were outdated racist theories about the inferiority of non-white races and told of the doom that would befall the world if race mixing occurred.

Race and Reason—A Yankee View and similar books did not transform Duke overnight, but rather made him pay attention to a whole new area of science. "It made me think," he said, "that maybe it wasn't all environment." He went back to the books of Ashley Montague and Margaret Meade, but felt their arguments were not as cogent as those claiming racial differences.

It was not the normal reaction of a fourteen-year-old boy, but David Duke was far from normal. He spent a great deal of time on the scientific issue of race, something most young people his age could not have cared less about.

"At the time," he recalls, "I had an emotional commitment to minorities. The liberal material I had been reading gave me guilt feelings about how the black people had been treated in historical America. I had a hard time . . . between my heart and my reasoning . . . but I was totally fascinated by my dilemma."

The people who ran the Citizens Council were experts at taking in misguided people and molding them into racists.

Despite any adolescent differences with his parents, Duke was basically conservative because he was the product of a very conservative father whom he idolized. Organizations such as the Council thrive on the fears of the ignorant or less fortunate. A bright, inquisitive young kid strolling in off the streets looking for information is like a junkie tripping over a drug dealer. The sell is always easy. The Council soon made David part of its "family," and in time he became addicted to racism.

In 1964 David got his first taste of politics. The presidential race was in high gear in the fall of that year, and people at the Council were all supporting the Republican nominee, Sen. Barry Goldwater.

"He was my first political hero," said Duke. "He wasn't afraid to say things that were controversial. He was a great American . . . a real hero of mine in politics." David enjoyed going to the Goldwater campaign headquarters and helping out with telephone banks or anything else he was asked to do.

As things got lonelier at home, David began spending more time at the Citizens Council office. He soon became a regular, taking the bus after school and helping in any way he could. No longer was he spending time with chemistry sets or reading Shakespeare. He exchanged those pleasant passions for an examination of racist theology.

This was a time in David's life when he was putting the pursuits of the child behind him and turning to more serious matters. Another area he devoted more time to was his church activities. He became convinced that the fundamental Christian ideas of the Church of Christ were correct and publicly accepted Christ as his savior, with baptism by immersion following at the church on Carrollton Avenue. He also became concerned about his father's salvation and was able to convince him to be baptized as well. Colonel Duke, who had been a lifelong Methodist, was moved by his son's concerns to the point that he consented to join the Church of Christ. In this period of his life, David was developing his basic attitudes in support of both Christianity and what he called the survival of the white race.

Some may find it contradictory for a young man to believe in racial segregation and still claim be a born-again Christian. But at the time, most Christian churches in America were still segregated. Even Catholic churches in New Orleans had separate pews for blacks and whites, as well as racially segregated schools. Many Christians at that time saw segregation as not being demeaning to blacks but simply a reflection of differences God had created when he made the races.

It was during this period that Colonel Duke symbolically accepted David into manhood, recognizing that his own role had changed from solely that of father and teacher to that of a person who could learn from his son as well. "David gave me a new perspective," said Colonel Duke, "and I began to fully appreciate his own independent intellect."

The change in David brought about by the revelations found in the Council library was obvious to his teachers at Ganus. He became vocal as he read more and more racial books and began to debate anyone on racial subjects. In one year he had gone from a liberal, humanist viewpoint on race to a basic outlook that there are profound racial differences that affect the whole social fabric. Participation in the Goldwater campaign whet his appetite for current affairs and history. Over the next year, he would relate his newly found racial view to history, politics, and social policy.

CHAPTER SIX

Coming of Age

GROWING UP IN THE UNITED STATES during the turbulent era of the 1960s was not easy for many young people. It proved to be especially difficult for David Duke. Troubles at home and an almost hyperactive personality made taking life in stride impossible. His natural inquisitiveness and tendency to seek parental figures made him a prime candidate for extremist politics. In the absence of firm guidance from his family, Duke went through his teen years latched on to a racist crusade.

Duke remained at Ganus for his freshman year in high school. Most of his free time was spent at the Citizens Council office or reading books about racial issues. At school, he was remembered as just another "polite, quiet kid." The only difference between him and other students was that Duke could hardly let an hour go by without arguing race or the decline of white culture. He sought to persuade anyone willing to talk with him that his position was right.

But all of his energy was not devoted to reading and to the Council, and David lived a relatively normal life for a fifteen-year-old in 1965. He became interested in the opposite sex and had a number of girl friends. The house on Jewel Street offered him the chance to spend time fishing, swimming, and in other outdoor activities in and around Lake Pontchartrain.

The lake, at the time, was not as polluted as it is today, and the public was allowed to swim in it.

Although it has no real beach, the lake has an extended seawall that helps minimize flooding during the hurricanes that plague New Orleans. David and his dog Friskey would walk from his house to the lake. David would swim "for a mile or so," with Friskey jogging along the shore.

Colonel Duke was still working at Shell and would often leave his car at Gary's Super Service Station, located not far from his downtown office. Gary's was owned by a black man who allowed David to come in and work on engines.

"They were very nice and taught me a lot about cars," he said. "I was just another kid helping out."

At the time, Ganus had classes only through the ninth grade, so once again a change in schools would be required. In the fall of 1965, Duke began his sophomore year at Warren Easton High School, located at 3019 Canal Street.

It was all white, but had a more lower-middle-class student body than Ganus. The school has an old, large brick building, nothing like the modern classrooms at Ganus. It is best remembered for having great football teams in the late 1950s and the dubious distinction of counting presidential assassin Lee Harvey Oswald as one of its former students. Duke was not particularly happy at Warren Easton, which he found "lacking in motivation."

As had happened previously, changing schools separated Duke from any friends he may have made, putting him back on square one. By chance, he met a student from Colombia named George Cardona and the two quickly became pals. George, who came from a wealthy family, had moved to New Orleans to live with relatives and attend high school in the U.S. His girlfriend Barbara Noule remembers Duke as a loner.

"We double dated a lot with David," she said. "But we never did things with other kids, like go to football games or mingle with other kids at school."

Cardona proved to be one of Duke's best friends at Warren Easton. Barbara, George, David, and whichever girl he might have a date with would never attend school functions. "David was different from other kids," according to Barbara. "If we went to his house to pick him up, we would honk the horn and wait for him to come out. We never went inside." At the time, Barbara was not aware that inside the Duke house Maxine was most likely in no condition to meet visitors.

"David was real smart," Barbara said. "He knew a lot about politics. He and George would always have long discussions about whatever was going on at the time. But I don't ever remember him being against blacks or Jews. He was just always very polite, had a good sense of humor, and was really a nice guy."

Matters at home were at an all-time low, and Colonel Duke was busier than ever before. David devoted almost all his spare time to the Citizens Council and to his father. He was learning how to cope with his family problems by directing his energies to right-wing activism. At the same time, he discovered the Council could provide a protective shelter from his family difficulties.

That fall, Colonel Duke was preparing to go to Washington for his annual two-week stint of active duty with the Army. He was scheduled to leave on September 9, the day New Orleans was struck by Hurricane Betsy. The city sustained more than a billion dollars in damage and the loss of fifty-eight lives. Electrical power was not available to any part of the city, and Moisant International Airport was forced to close. As a result, Colonel Duke missed his trip to Washington and rescheduled plans to go in the spring. Some Army Reserve members met later that week, and someone mentioned the possibility of taking a trip overseas, an idea that piqued Colonel Duke's curiosity.

"It gave me something to think about," he said, "but the first time we talked about going overseas we never dreamed how it would work out."

Soon after the hurricane, Shell wanted Colonel Duke to move his office to Lafayette, Louisiana, about 150 miles from New Orleans. The idea of selling the house and moving did not appeal to the family.

Colonel Duke was discussing with David and Maxine the possibility of relocating the family when a friend in the military called him with a solid proposition. The Vietnam War was beginning to escalate, and the government was looking for experienced people to go to Southeast Asia to help in any way possible. Colonel Duke was informed that there was an opening in the United States Agency for International Development. The USAID is a branch of the State Department that assists under-developed countries. Among USAID objectives are the funding of building projects, such as hospitals, bridges, and other construction. With his military and engineering background, the job seemed his for the asking.

The chance to go to Vietnam excited Colonel Duke, but he could not simply walk away from his responsibilities at Shell and with the Army, not to mention Maxine and David. This was settled when Shell offered him early retirement. He had accumulated enough years with the Reserves and in military service during the war to receive an additional Army pension. Coupled with his salary from AID and his pensions, the family could do well financially in his absence.

Colonel and Mrs. Duke had grown apart over the years, and it was time for him to move on. He very much wanted to get involved in the war in Vietnam and, as he put it, "go full-time in the struggle against communism." There was nothing further he felt he could do for his wife, and he was a man driven to perform. In September of 1966, Colonel Duke said goodbye to Maxine and David. He headed for his first assignment with USAID, which took him to Da Nang, South Vietnam. His first job was working as a civil engineer, helping the Vietnamese rebuild bridges destroyed by the Viet Cong. By the end of the war, he would be gone from the U.S. a total of nine years.

He did manage, however, to visit his family back in New Orleans twenty-four times, mostly in the first four years. Leaving had been difficult, but he secretly had always wanted to be a military man. The chance to serve his country and really be involved was worth the pain of being away from the son he loved.

"There is a child-like quality to both my dad and David," says Dotti. "They always look to the bright side of everything." In this case, Colonel Duke, like so many other people involved in the war effort, believed that in Vietnam "America could help share the freedom and democracy that we enjoy in the United States."

Colonel Duke's departure took away the only stability David had ever known, for his father had wielded great influence on the household. Everything the Dukes did was a reaction to Colonel Duke. Where they lived, the way they lived, and what they did as human beings depended heavily upon him as the leader of the family. He was now living on the other side of the world, involved in a controversial war. For the first time in Maxine and David's lives, the head of the family was not there to be the pillar of strength they had always depended upon. David adored his father, who was also his best friend and confidant. Although Colonel Duke was strict with his children, David always knew his father loved him. It was not Colonel Duke's personality to openly express his love, but, as David recalls, "If I was being reprimanded by my father he might say, 'Son, I love you, but you shouldn't do that,' or 'I'm going to have to punish you, but you know I love you.' "

With Colonel Duke out of his life, David sought someone or something to take the place of the man "who never told me a lie." He immersed himself in the Citizens Council, learning all he could about racist issues. Books such as *African Genesis* by Robert Audry and *Origin of Races* by Carlton Coon occupied his reading time.

He also got caught up in the burgeoning issue of ecology and thought *Silent Spring* by Rachael Carson was one of the most moving books he had ever read.

Becoming an activist, not only racially but ecologically, Duke often attended meetings of the Sierra Club. Whenever possible, he would go with friends to the Pearl River wilderness area and camp out. He remembers "living off the land with heart of palm, fish, and wild game." He even prided himself on being able to go into the swamp with "only a few hooks and line and a good knife, and live for days in the cypress swamps and remote lakes of Southeast Louisiana." For Duke, recognition of racial differences was as natural as recognizing the three varieties of hummingbirds found in the swamps.

Duke startled some ecology-oriented meetings by agreeing that "we must preserve the threatened fauna and flora of the planet such as great whales of the Pacific and the Rocky Mountain cougar." Then at the same time, he asked, "Why shouldn't we also preserve the distinct races of mankind that add so much beauty to the earth? Why should we treasure and protect every variation in nature and then endorse policies that will destroy the unique characteristics of people?"

In reading works on the threat of overpopulation, he became convinced "that white people were the true minority on earth; that current Western immigration policies, coupled with higher non-white birthrates and racial intermarriage, would eventually constitute a genocide of the white race and an eradication of its cultural traditions and institutions."

Duke also saw a political threat from demographic changes. He soon became fearful for the political policy of the nation if whites became the minority. He had little faith that blacks could maintain the unique qualities of Western civilization he so cherished.

Reading extensively about race, Duke delved into history to see what the early leaders of the United States thought in relation to his theories. His heroes in American history included Thomas Jefferson, Abraham Lincoln, Robert E. Lee, and Theodore Roosevelt. One day when he was reading Jefferson's "Notes on the State of Virginia" he stumbled upon a passage that was pivotal in his deeper involvement in politics.

One of Duke's favorite quotes from Jefferson reads: "Nothing is more certainly written in the book of fate, than that these people [the Negroes] are to be free." The quotation is chiseled in foot-high letters in the walls of the rotunda of the Jefferson Memorial in Washington, D.C. It has been repeated in a thousand books and magazine articles, often to show that Jefferson would favor the flourishing civil rights movement if he were alive today. Duke knew the quotation well.

While reading Jefferson's "Notes" he saw it again, but in an entirely different context. The full quotation reads:

> "Nothing is more certainly written in the book of fate, than that these people [the Negroes] are to be free[,] nor is it less certain that these people equally free cannot live under the same government. Nature, opinion, and habit have drawn indelible lines of distinction between the white and black races that can never be erased."

Jefferson went on to advocate freeing slaves and repatriating them to Africa.

Upon reading these words, David Duke was dumfounded. Later, in writing about the incident, he related that he almost shouted in anger at what he saw as a great deception. He thought to himself that these were the words of Thomas Jefferson, the man who wrote the Declaration of Independence; yet anyone who uttered such words today would be bitterly condemned by the media as un-American.

He recounts finding the same distortion in the words of Abraham Lincoln. In his research, Duke discovered dozens of speeches by Lincoln condemning slavery, but unequivocally arguing against racial equality and for racial segregation and repatriation. Duke loved to quote the sixteenth president: "Negro Equality! How long in a government of God great enough to make and maintain this universe shall there be demagogues to vend and fools to gulp debauchery such as this?"

Duke wondered how many of the participants of the great civil rights march knew of Lincoln's true sentiments. "How could the speeches of Martin Luther King," he asked, "be made in the shadow of the Lincoln Memorial?"

Duke became convinced that integration, busing, affirmative action, wide-open third-world immigration, and other policies were in effect because the liberal-dominated media had simply not allowed the public to hear both sides of the story. He thought disaster loomed unless the truth were told. Until this point, however, he had not wanted to become a leader or spokesman because he was still too private, too introverted. He had wanted to be a scientist. But now that all had changed. He now knew that protecting the interests of the white race would be his calling and, as he said later, "any other career would be superfluous."

Although she had a housekeeper, Maxine found it increasingly difficult to raise her son alone. Colonel Duke decided that a sixteen-year-old boy needed more direction, and David was enrolled for his junior year of high school at Riverside Military Academy in Gainesville, Georgia. Located in the foothills of the Blue Ridge Mountains, Riverside is a strict school, but one with an excellent academic program.

Leaving home and New Orleans was not easy for Duke. Boarding school was different from anything he had known. At home, he had always had a room to himself and was able to do pretty much as he chose. But at Riverside, he had three roommates and a highly regimented program and shared a bathroom with twelve others. Students wore uniforms and their daily activities were strictly scheduled.

Reveille was at 6:15. David was expected to spring out of bed and prepare for morning inspection at 7:15. This included a check to see if his bed had been "perfectly" made. Each piece of clothing was to be arranged in military fashion. Soap, toothpaste, and toothbrush were to be in a specified order, his uniform neat, and his shoes spit-polished. There was no housekeeper to help Duke through this one.

Cadets would run to assembly and march to breakfast at 7:30, then march back to the barracks and be in class at 8 A.M. Lunch was at noon, and all cadets would assemble and march in file to a thirty-minute meal. They would then return to class for a dose of military science. This class consisted of teaching high school students such important information as the kill radiance of a hand grenade and the muzzle velocity of a bazooka. At 3 P.M., cadets assembled for one hour of drill, carrying real M-1 rifles, which one former cadet remembers "felt like they weighed a ton."

Participating in sports was mandatory for all students each day at 4:15, so Duke practiced with the school's basketball team for one hour. After practice, he once again reassembled and marched back to his room to get ready for the evening meal at 6:30.

At 7:15 P.M. he prepared for the evening room inspection. He was then allowed to study from 7:45 until 10, when all lights and radios had to be off. Weekends were the same, with the exception of Sunday, when all cadets were expected to wear dress uniforms and perform a command drill display.

The staff at Riverside made certain no cadet would ever have idle time to get into mischief. Colonel Duke had the same philosophy, but still allowed his son the freedom to spend leisurely hours reading and exploring his mind. The only time for unregulated activity available to cadets was two hours on Saturday afternoon when an officer who had collected enough merits for good behavior would be allowed to walk into town.

At first, military school was a time of rebellion for Duke. He was used to outdoor activities after school, such as swimming, playing sports with neighborhood kids, or sitting by Lake Pontchartrain. Military school ended that kind of leisure. It seemed to have an impact in making Duke more serious about his beliefs and his life's course.

During this period, he fell under the guidance of an elderly English professor named Van Houten, who came from a prominent New York Dutch family. Duke had read extensively, but under Van Houten he began to develop his creative writing skills and some of the exposition patterns that have served him in debate and in preparing racist publications later in his life.

Van Houten believed in the positive effects of creativity and often said that a young man needs to be able to lie by a river bank and dream about the world. Unable to do this freely in the structured hours of military school, Duke began to express his feelings through his writing. His love of the outdoors could not be quenched by the confining military life, but he began to spend more time in thought and reflection.

Most Riverside cadets were from the Northeast, and during the first few weeks of school some of the older and bigger company members gave Duke a lot of grief about his racist and Confederate sympathies. Sometimes he was hazed by the cadet officers in his unit. Hazing would often include the practice of striking a cadet's hands and fingers with large scrub brushes. Duke's personality is such that he always responds to adversity with defiance. The hazing he endured because of his beliefs resulted in more resolve and more defiance. This only served to strengthen a trait he still carries with him— finding solace in loyalty to his own beliefs rather than in the approval of others.

In response, Duke began to do what he has always done: use the power of his personality to win his associates over to his way of thinking. By the middle of the year, he had orchestrated a huge barracks party to celebrate Robert E. Lee's birthday. A former cadet at Riverside remembers Duke as "the kind of guy who no matter what he says or what he does, over time you just instinctively grow to like."

Although he was away from the Citizens Council, Duke still managed to make his new racist theories the main topic of discussion. Every evening, cadets in each dormitory would get together for a rap session. It was here that Duke learned he could gain someone's attention, and often their respect, by taking a stand for what he believed in. This included debating his racist ideas.

Even at conservative Riverside, Duke's views were considered outlandish. Two of his roommates were Jewish, and David's arguments against Zionism did not win him their admiration. But despite his views, he was able to gain their respect, and even friendship. Duke remembers, "I did manage to win most of the boys over to my thinking."

Duke's history teacher, a Lieutenant Bell, at first was skeptical about Duke's racist perspectives. But by the end of the year he allowed the outspoken young man to give a class presentation on the Southern interpretation of the Civil War. Bell took Duke under his wing, and when the school wintered in Hollywood, Florida, he would often take Cadet Corporal Duke with him to the beach where they skin-dived, spearfished, and girl-watched. While at the beach, Duke met a pretty high school junior and later took her to the Riverside prom. He was able to help convince her younger sister to accompany one of his roommates. At the prom, some of the older cadets began to cut in on the Jewish cadet's dances with the girl, and Duke angrily stepped in, forcing the other cadets to seek their fun elsewhere.

After the rocky period at the beginning of the school year, Duke adapted well to the military discipline of Riverside, but he still longed to be back in New Orleans, running with Friskey and swimming in the lake.

Holidays were the only time Duke was able to return to New Orleans. He did not like the regimented life at the boarding school.

"It stifled me," he said. "I was used to being free and exploring the natural environment. At Riverside, there was never time for any of that."

Cherishing his privacy, Duke missed the time spent alone to think and dream. Although he disliked the dormitory-style life of the boarding school, he was a good soldier and fully expected someday to be an officer, just like his father.

CHAPTER SEVEN

JFK and the KKK

DURING THE TIME COLONEL DUKE was in Southeast Asia, he corresponded with his son frequently. Presenting his case by mail, David finally persuaded his dad to let him return home for his senior year. However strict he was with his children, Colonel Duke always seemed to know when they really needed him.

Duke returned from Riverside for the summer, happy to be back in New Orleans. With Maxine in poor health, David was on his own. His father had arranged a summer job for him at a local brokerage firm, and David enjoyed it. Like his father, David has never been frivolous with money and can squeeze full value out of a dollar. Dotti refers to her brother as "the thriftiest man I have ever known."

The months between Duke's junior and senior years was the last of his "fun summers." He spent less time at the Citizens Council and more time with his friends. Fishing in the lake and swimming were almost a daily routine. He often went to Ship Island, a sugar-white sand-barrier island thirteen miles off the Mississippi Gulf Coast. He would "light a campfire and sleep under the stars, spearfish for my food, and let the sun bake my body and bleach my hair."

During this period, Duke began to grow taller and assert himself. With friends, he would sometimes make the dangerous trip out to the oil rigs to spearfish sharks. The trick was to spear the shark and tie the line to a piling before the beast could make dinner out of his human predator. Duke relished the excitement and the danger. Even though this was before the shark became a popular dish, the boys would always skin and filet their catch, bring the meat back, and store it in a large white chest freezer at David's Jewel Street home.

The unusual became commonplace for Duke. He loved to read biographies, with Thomas Jefferson and Robert E. Lee his favorites, and he became determined to live his life in what he regarded as a "heroic mode." But Duke's idea of heroism seemed to be nothing more than raw strength or a devil-may-care attitude. His father's admonition to the Sunday school class about going against the crowd if it went the wrong way seemed to Duke more of an imperative to be different than an ethical priority. His drive to assert himself in a unique way is a recurring pattern in his life, one that continued right through his election to the Louisiana House of Representatives.

Duke enrolled at John F. Kennedy Senior High School for his senior year. JFK was a public school, located at 5700 Wisner Boulevard in the Lakefront area of New Orleans. It was a new school, having graduated only one previous senior class, and was considered advanced for the New Orleans public school system.

Immediately after school began, Duke became active in far-right politics. Since his first introduction to racist philosophies, he had constantly read everything he could get his hands on. He was now ready to explore the realms of racism further. He continued to debate anyone on the merits of white people and the evils of new government plans for affirmative action and liberal civil rights policies. Although he was new at school, he made a few friends right away. People with strange tastes and motivations seem to migrate in the same direction, and the racists at JFK were no exception.

"There were eight or nine of us who had the same ideals," he recalls, "and we hung around together." This was the group of students interested in the Ku Klux Klan.

His year at JFK High School marked the first time he personally encountered school integration, and it only seemed to confirm everything he had concluded from an intellectual viewpoint.

"I was shocked," he said, "by the academic mediocrity that integration wrought." Duke had a couple of personal encounters at school which angered him and helped to further motivate him to become active in the Ku Klux Klan.

In 1967, most girls wore short skirts at JFK, and the school stairwells were open. During a class break, Duke was waiting for his girlfriend at the base of a stairway when he encountered a black student who was looking up the dresses of white girls as they descended the stairs. The student would grin from ear to ear and make obscene comments to some of them as they passed. The embarrassed girls scurried off to class while some white boys pretended not to see it. But David Duke became incensed.

Duke was not physically imposing, but somehow he got the better of the larger black student and pinned his left arm behind his back. He paraded the stunned young man down the hall past astonished fellow students to the principal's office, where he practically threw the student across the desk. An outraged Duke told the principal what had happened and insisted that the student be disciplined. The principal replied that since it was Duke's word against the student's, nothing could be proven. He ordered him to release the boy and return to class. Duke still alleges today that "black students are often not punished [for wrongdoing] because liberal administrators fear charges of discrimination."

The Vietnam War and the civil rights movement were dominating the political arena in 1967. Philosophically, people were either for the war or against it, for civil rights or against it. Duke felt that anyone who challenged the U.S. effort in Vietnam was directly attacking his father. He believed that the country was drifting away from the "traditional Christian American values" that Colonel Duke had taught were essential for the country's survival. In his mind, the nation was like a car driving off a cliff, and he had to do something before it was too late.

Affirmative action was becoming a big national issue, and Duke started a file at home of every newspaper and magazine article he could find on the subject. He knew names, dates, places, court cases, concepts, and arguments. He was convinced that affirmative action was reducing whites to a "second-class citizenry in the United States, proving that the civil rights movement was never about equal rights, but a racial movement that would be used in the overthrow of whites in America."

In senior papers he wrote:

> "Truly fair-minded Americans believe that the best-qualified person regardless of race should deserve the job or promotion. Yet Affirmative Action advocates who work for racial discrimination against whites continue to prattle about human rights, human dignity, and the evils of discrimination. Are whites supposed to be not entitled to human rights, or dignity? Is discrimination any less evil when exercised against a white person?"

> "When whites talk about excessive black crime and drug rates, they are informed that actions should not be taken against a race because of the actions of a few. Yet, none of those critics seem[s] to worry about the collective guilt and punishment being exacted on whites."

"Not only does Affirmative Action brutally repress the more talented individual, and creates a singular injustice, it so hurts the productivity and quality of the greater society, that it causes the general fabric of society to be eroded. Ultimately, it even hurts the quality of life of the very people it purportedly aids, those who encounter the incompetent and often corrupt Affirmative Action policemen, the less-qualified person who catastrophically pushes or pulls the wrong lever in the chemical plant that ignites it, the person on fixed income who counts his money and finds he must pay more to pay for incompetence and low-productivity."

"If hiring ratios by race are morally right on the assembly line, why aren't they in the National Basketball Association?"

". . . preferences affected by a person's hardships or conditions are not racist, but when a less-capable, middle-income minority person is arbitrarily favored by quota over a poverty-stricken white . . . it is racism in its most pernicious form."

Although the papers Duke submitted were fairly well written, his teachers were appalled by the content. His racist viewpoints were beginning to affect his grades. It was the first time Duke's beliefs, through his writings, had been challenged, and the experience left him frustrated. It was made clear that if he mellowed his racist positions he would receive higher grades.

"I was not about to change what I knew to be right," he said.

In the fall of 1967, young people were dropping LSD, smoking marijuana, protesting the war, and wearing psychedelic clothes, the Beatles' Sergeant Pepper album was number one around the world, and David Duke joined the Knights of the Ku Klux Klan.

Founded in 1866 by Nathan B. Forrest, the Klan has gained international attention as the premier white racist organization. The Klan was formed as a Southern protest group opposed to Reconstruction, but before long, however, members began terrorizing blacks throughout the South. Forrest disbanded the group in 1869, but many members continued to deny blacks their constitutional rights, particularly the right to vote. A second Klan was organized in 1915, and this new version was not only anti-black but also anti-Catholic and anti-Semitic. By the mid-1920s, the Klan claimed between four and five million members. It declined soon after and not until the civil rights movement of the 1950s and 1960s did it have any real impact. Duke naively felt that his Klan was "a Christian group of individuals dedicated to honor and non-violent rights for whites."

Duke was introduced to the Klan by one of his school mates at JFK. He considered joining for some time and finally made the decision to do it.

"I was really nervous the first time," he said. "The meeting was held at one of the members' home in New Orleans. Some of the guys from school came to my house and gave me a ride. Once I saw what was going on, I realized it was not a frightening organization."

It was at this meeting that Duke met Jim Lindsay. Lindsay, a successful real estate developer, wielded such a great influence on Duke that he eventually became almost a surrogate father. Because of the negative image of the Klan, Lindsay used the pseudonym Ed White when working with the group. A mysterious character, Lindsay was murdered a number of years later. His estranged wife was charged with the crime but later acquitted.

Compared to the Klan, the Citizens Council looked like the Mickey Mouse Club. Here were real, live bigots ready to defend the rights of white people no matter what the consequence. No one dared to question whether the country was correct about the Vietnam War. Nobody denied that blacks and Jews were getting favored treatment from the federal government. These were people who thought like David Duke.

Duke joined the Klan the first night he attended a meeting and became a member of the local "den," which consisted of "about thirty-five members, most of them Catholic." The Klan has had the reputation of being anti-Catholic, but Lindsay's Klan tried to remain true to the purposes of the original Knights of the Ku Klux Klan, and did not discriminate against Catholics.

New Orleans is 60 percent Catholic, and this was reflected in the membership. Duke was surprised by how "positive the meeting was," and he enjoyed the rituals and the secrecy surrounding Klan meetings.

"Most of the members were businessmen." Duke said. "It consisted of people who wanted to protect white, Christian values in a non-violent way."

Could David Duke be telling the truth as he sees it when he makes statements about the Klan's non-violence? He believed then, as he does now, that the causes the Klan stood for were noble and just. He refused to believe the media stories of rednecks riding in pickup trucks terrorizing blacks because "my Klan didn't."

When Duke heard the words "Ku Klux Klan," he did not conjure up images of lynching or brutality. The major Klan groups were separate and distinct, and even though the public does not normally distinguish between them, Duke repeatedly makes it clear that he hates and will not tolerate any violence. As in everything else he has ever done, Duke immersed himself in the Klan. He regularly attended bi-monthly meetings and read everything he could about the organization. Soon he became, in the words of one former Klansman, "a model member."

During the fall of 1967, Duke had a job delivering newspapers for the *Times-Picayune*. He had purchased a used 1963
Ford Galaxy for deliveries, and he used the job to save money
for his college education. His "new" car gave him freedom to
explore the outdoors around New Orleans, and to discover
the secrets of the opposite sex.

At the time, Duke had a sizable newspaper route of about
200 homes in uptown New Orleans. By coincidence, a friend
had decided to give up his route of 220 papers, so Duke took
on the added deliveries. The first time he threw both routes
together happened to be a rainy Sunday morning. Starting
at 2 A.M., he had to read each address, search for the numbers
in the darkness and the rain, then put the newspapers in a
dry place near the door or on the porch. He finally finished
about 7:30 A.M. Sleepy and tired, he drove home on the Lake
Pontchartrain Expressway to the West End Boulevard exit,
where he dozed at the wheel. The car ran straight into a huge
oak tree at forty-five miles an hour.

His head smashed through the steering wheel and wind-
shield. Taken by ambulance to Ochsner Medical Foundation
Hospital, Duke was treated and released the next day. He
spent two weeks at home recuperating. He suffered a severely
broken nose, one that required surgery twice. As luck would
have it, Duke had come within a whisper of death, which
would have precluded the next twenty years of racist turmoil.

As soon as he was able, Duke returned to class and to the
Klan. The remainder of his high school year was devoted to
his studies at JFK, odd jobs, and his new fascination with the
racist organization. He was, as his sister put it, "frustrated
and angry" with life at home. His father was fighting communism on the other side of the world, so he would have to
survive by himself—or with his new Ku Klux Klan family.

CHAPTER EIGHT

A Fighting Tiger

DAVID DUKE GRADUATED from John F. Kennedy Senior High School virtually unknown by most of his classmates. He was still a reserved, skinny kid who spent most of his time reading or debating racist viewpoints. He had not yet hit upon the tactic of taking outlandish positions to gain attention for his beliefs. Until this time, his political activities were primarily restricted to Klan activities or researching racist theories.

Duke spent the summer of 1968 working at different jobs, including selling Kirby vacuum cleaners door to door. His polite manner and driving work habits made him a natural salesman. Kirby vacuum cleaners were large machines used in homes and offices. Within two weeks Duke was the number one salesperson for the company, and management had its eye on him. He enjoyed selling for Kirby because he really believed in the product. Sincerity, whether directed toward household appliances or racist ideology, was a powerful attribute for a young man.

His door-to-door sales territory consisted primarily of middle- to low-income whites. Duke "seldom sold to blacks because their credit was usually turned down." Interestingly enough, he sold to the same constituency who find his politics most appealing.

After three weeks of record-breaking sales, Duke was promoted to sales manager for the entire New Orleans East area. Duke happened to be in a local Sears store the day before assuming his new job. The vacuum cleaners he had been selling were priced at $265, yet Sears had a model that Duke believed could serve his customers well for only $69. Duke believed that Kirby was the best quality vacuum available, but said he "felt guilty that high-pressure sales were burdening people with a vacuum they really couldn't afford."

He went to the manager and promptly resigned, protesting what he called "the exploitation of people." When Duke had a cause, his radical passion could not be restrained.

Duke had been painting houses for his father's construction company for a couple of years and decided to go into business for himself. The future Klan leader donned paint-splattered overalls and knocked on doors of homes with old or peeling paint.

"I gave them a low enough quote," Duke said, "that most of them hired me on the spot." Ultimately, he made enough money to finance his college studies and some radical politics as well.

Since David was in grade school, Colonel Duke had emphasized that a college education was "the most important means of attaining success in life." He also wanted his son to pay most of his own educational expenses. It was not because he could not afford to pay the tuition, but he felt it would enhance David's desire to do well in school.

"Many successful parents," said Colonel Duke, "have less than successful children because the children didn't have to learn self-discipline and self-reliance." For holidays and special occasions, David's grandfather, Ernest Duke, had often given his grandson money for his college savings account.

With a limited amount of money, young Duke decided Louisiana State University in Baton Rouge was as far as he could afford to go. Duke packed up all his belongings and headed off to start a new life at LSU.

Since wrecking his car the previous fall, Duke had been limited to walking or taking the bus. He bought a used Fiat just before leaving for LSU. On the way to Baton Rouge, the engine caught fire, forcing Duke to abandon the burned vehicle. He stood with all his worldly possessions piled on the side of Airline Highway. Someone took pity on the young man, and he was given a ride to LSU. His unorthodox arrival could be viewed as an ominous sign, foretelling a period of unusual things to come.

Because his budget was limited, Duke lived on campus in a dormitory under the north section of the school's football stadium. The stadium, which then held 68,000, is home to the Fighting Tigers football team. The arena has been dubbed Death Valley because of the thunderous noise fans make during a Saturday night game.

Built in the 1930s, the stadium was the most inexpensive place to stay on campus, for the simple reason that no one wanted to live there. Rooms were crowded and there was only one bathroom for the entire hall. To further accentuate the dismal living conditions, rooms in the stadium were not air conditioned, and the intense South Louisiana heat made the crowded conditions seem even worse. At first, Duke bunked with three other students. He was finally able to obtain a tiny, one-man room under the stairway, allowing him the solitude to pursue his love of reading. The conditions resembled nothing Duke had ever experienced, but for now it would serve as home.

The largest university in Louisiana, LSU was founded January 2, 1860, as the Louisiana State Seminary of Learning and Military Academy. Ironically for a Southern school, William Tecumseh Sherman, the famed Civil War Union general, served as the first president of the institution. LSU did not become a major university, however, until the administration of Gov. Huey P. Long in the 1930s. It has a large, sprawling campus, filled with ivy-covered buildings and oak and magnolia trees adjoining a beautiful lake. Located near the Mississippi River in Baton Rouge, it is a large university now enrolling some 25,000 students.

The Vietnam War and racial unrest were making college campuses across the United States a tinderbox, and LSU was no exception. Students, both liberal and conservative, were passionate in their views either for the war or against it. Organizations such as the Young Americans for Freedom and the Young Republicans staunchly supported the U.S. effort in Southeast Asia, while the Students for a Democratic Society and the Demonstrators for Peace were adamantly opposed to the war. It was the time of Woodstock and Haight-Ashbury—and the solidification of extremist views for David Duke.

One of those who remembers Duke as a freshman was Jack Glover, a journalism student from New Orleans. "David sat next to me in a couple of classes, otherwise he would have gone unnoticed," he said. "But David was different. I mean he was very intense about school and politics. You could talk to him for a minute and realize that he was just . . . different."

Duke had outgrown the Citizens Council by the time he reached LSU. The Council had served as a surrogate family, but was limited in terms of how much it could accomplish. Other than being pro-segregation, anti-black, and anti-Semitic, the Council was not addressing issues David felt were critical to the survival of America.

Even the Ku Klux Klan was failing to exhort the enthusiasm needed to fulfill his fantasies of racial purity. Remaining a member of the Klan, Duke kept in close contact with Jim Lindsay, although his inquisitiveness about different political ideas continued driving him toward a new and dangerous path.

The size of a large university such as LSU makes it easy for a student either to make friends and become part of the system or to blend quietly into the background of academic life. During his first year at college, David Duke was in a state of racist limbo. Away from the Citizens Council and disenchanted with the ordinary racism of the Klan, he sought a deeper and more defined system. He also delved more deeply into an issue that had begun to intrigue him — the Jews.

As he looked further into racist ideology, Duke became more distrustful of the news media. He felt it had lied to him and all Americans about the truth of racial differences. The news media, in his mind, was controlled by Jews and was soft on communism. He read articles discussing the Jewish domination of Hollywood and the three television networks.

In what was fast becoming an obsession, Duke noted the names of the major network chief executive officers: Sarnoff at NBC, Paley at CBS, and Goldenson at ABC, all of whom were Jewish. The Klansman became angered by the Jewish leadership in the civil rights movement, especially the head of the NAACP, Kivie Kaplan. In an article by Jewish intellectual Nathan Glazer, Duke read that "seven out of ten leaders of the SDS and other radical leftist groups were Jewish."

At that point, David Duke plunged into anti-Semitism, but not without reservations. In a letter to his father in October 1968, he wrote:

> "I don't mean to offend Aunt May. Her husband may have been a fine Jewish gentleman, but I am shocked, Father, how so many Jews seem to dominate the forces I despise . . . Martin Luther King's famous 'I Have a Dream' speech had a Jewish communist speech writer . . . those who want to stab the American soldier in the back in Viet Nam invariably appear Jewish — such as Abbie Hoffman and Jerry Rubin. . . . The egalitarian school of anthropology [is] led by Boas and Montague. Did you know his real name was 'Ehrenberg'? Gene Weltfish, Melville Herskovitz and others . . . the Rosenbergs and most of the communist spies caught and convicted in America . . . the founders of communism. I even encountered an article by Winston Churchill written in 1920 saying that

the Russian Revolution was nothing more than the capture
of Russia by the Jews.

"Yet, I respect many who are Jewish. You know how I
respected Mr. Newman at Kohlmeyer & Co. I liked working for him and listening to him. He was a good conservative. I wish you were back in New Orleans. I hate not
even being able to talk on the phone to you. It will be
good to see you at Christmas."

Over the next few months, Duke plunged deeper into books
dealing with what anti-Semites refer to as "the Jewish question." In one publication entitled *Behind Communism,* atomic
spies and Hollywood figures were pictured together on page
after page. Duke came to believe that international communism was a Jewish creation. He claimed that Jewish support
of integration was nothing more than a means employed by
Jews to "settle an old score with the Gentiles."

During Duke's freshman year, LSU was almost entirely
white. Of the more than 18,000 students enrolled in 1968,
only 296 were black. The first black undergraduate had enrolled, under court order, fifteen years earlier, but he had
withdrawn from the university after a month of campus turmoil.

If a black student wanted a degree in higher education, he
or she usually chose Southern University across town rather
than LSU. Southern was virtually all black and was considered
a major university. Nevertheless, by 1968 more black students
were enrolling at LSU.

Duke was still a devout Christian and studied many publications that railed against what they called "the Jewish war
against Christianity." These publications accused Jews of promoting lawsuits aimed at the removal of Christian symbols
from public buildings. Instead of regarding such issues in terms
of separation of church and state, Duke interpreted them as
a direct attack on Christianity and Western traditions.

Anti-Semitic publications such as *The Cross and Flag*, a newsletter published by notorious racist Gerald L. K. Smith, blamed Jews for the liberal and amoral slant of Hollywood, as well as for the spread of international communism. One student who knew Duke at LSU remembers the newsletter had a major influence on the young Klansman. "David read it every month," he said. "He would read it, memorize it, then research what the paper said at the library."

Duke developed a deep friendship with Father Lawrence J. Toups, a maverick Catholic priest whom he became acquainted with through the Citizens Council. As a freshman at Ganus High School, Duke looked to Father Toups for spiritual guidance. What he found, instead, was another racist figurehead. The priest often visited Duke at LSU to discuss "the Jewish issue."

Father Toups was virulently anti-Semitic, believing Jews were subverting Christianity and the Western world. He showed his young racist disciple a 1966 *Look* magazine article entitled "How the Jews Changed Catholic Thinking." The rogue clergyman told Duke that churches, universities, government, and the news media were being infiltrated by anti-Christian Jews who, through Zionism, wanted to dominate the West.

Colonel Duke was never anti-Semitic and had relatives by marriage who were Jewish. Therefore Duke was reluctant at first to take a stand against Jews.

"Father," he wrote in another letter, "I don't want to be bigoted or judge people unfairly, but I can't close my eyes to what this group has done to the Western world. It seems to be boiling down to who will stand up to them or will raise their voice against the true intolerance they represent."

Duke's father was halfway around the world involved in a struggle against communism. The young Duke was an easy target for a Catholic priest who was so dreadfully anti-Semitic. Father Toups used his trump card to transform Duke from an ordinary Southern racist into a traditional, hardened anti-Semite.

Like Jim Lindsay, the priest provided the support of a missing father Duke craved. The receptive young man concluded that his own racial philosophy was completely in agreement with Father Toups'. In a short tract created for Father Toups and the Citizens Council, Duke wrote:

> "God created different races and in his infinite wisdom separated them by Continents. Nature, God's handiwork, creates races by geographic separation over eons of time. Are we doing God's work to destroy the distinctions that God created? Isn't there a beauty and wonder in the variety of the life and humanity on this planet? Wasn't the Old Testament about . . . the bloodline of the Israeli people being preserved as from whence Christ would come? How can it be perfectly Christian for the church to practice segregation for one thousand nine hundred years and suddenly for it to become unChristian to believe in preserving racial integrity?"

Father Toups gave Duke books written by Catholic priests that contained inaccurate translations of the Jewish Talmud. The interpretations in the publications Duke read were certainly overzealous against Christ and Christianity. Duke read that the Talmud equated "Christ as a bastard and Mary as a whore," while another book claimed that if Christ returned they would "seize him and boil him in semen." Still another read, "The best of Christians deserves death." What Father Toups failed to tell his young proselyte about his perverted view of the Talmud was that, in truth, the book is a revered chronicle of the ages.

Duke was becoming angry. He felt a great wrong was being committed, and he determined to fight it with all his might.

Spending most of the first semester in Baton Rouge, Duke returned home to New Orleans only for the Thanksgiving holidays. For him, life on campus was a time for spiritual and mental growth he had never known before. Most young men on their own for the first time would spend days discovering themselves, meeting girls, or participating in general college hell-raising. With the exception of attending Saturday night football games, Duke could not fit into normal college life.

Colonel Duke was busy working with USAID, but found time to write his son often. He tried his best to offer guidance, but was too far away, and David was now eighteen years old. Duke related his radical views to his father, who "tried to move him toward the center." But neither Colonel Duke nor anyone else would be able to moderate David's new experimentation with extreme right-wing philosophies.

In 1968, Reserve Officers Training Corps was mandatory at LSU for all male students during their first two years. This program is offered at many colleges as a way to earn a commission as an officer in the United States military. Duke very much wanted to do well in ROTC, if not for himself then certainly to impress his father. He aspired to join the Army so he could go to Vietnam as soon as he finished LSU.

One of those who observed Duke in ROTC was Michael Connelly, president of the conservative Young Republicans at LSU. Later, Connelly would become Duke's most ardent opponent on campus. They were in the same ROTC class when Connelly first noticed the then-unknown racist.

"He was quiet, but very dedicated to the program," he said. "Nothing like the radical he turned out to be."

Before Duke began public demonstrations over radical viewpoints, he was chewing on the ear of anyone who would listen to him.

"He would follow me out of class to discuss the war or especially racial issues," remembered Jack Glover. "At the time, I was against the war and pretty much a liberal. David loved to get me in one of his discussions. He would get all riled up and try to convince me that his positions were correct. He even thought the Young Republicans were a bunch of wimps."

Duke distinguished himself in ROTC, impressing fellow cadets as well as the faculty. At the end of the first year's program, he was named the outstanding basic cadet out of a field of 3,000. The award is a two-part honor, based on outstanding academic performance in the classroom and exemplary leadership skills on the drill field. Thus, Duke had earned the highest distinction in the basic corps. It was just what the young cadet needed in his quest to emulate his father.

In the spring of 1969, Jack Glover injured his leg and had trouble walking on crutches to classes. "One day I picked up the phone," he recalls, "and it was David Duke, offering me a ride to class. I thought this was strange, because I didn't even think he knew my name. You didn't have to agree with David Duke to like him."

But Duke made making friends difficult. One student who shared a class with him was a light-skinned black girl named Felicia. Duke, not realizing she was black, befriended her. "One day she brought her baby to class with her," said Glover, "and the child was very black. David was embarrassed, and they weren't friends any longer."

One of the weekly activities offered at LSU was a public forum called Free Speech Alley. Held each Wednesday afternoon between 12:30 and 2:30 in front of the LSU Union, it had been a fixture for years at the university. It enabled students to vent whatever grievances they had, from disagreements with the school administration to political topics of the day. Students walking to lunch or class would usually stop by, listen for a minute, then move on.

Duke, however, found the idea of a public forum exciting. The thought of arguing his positions on racial issues in front of a large group was tempting, but he was not ready to take the racist pulpit yet. He attended the sessions weekly, but during his freshman year never got on the soapbox. By watching others, he learned what gained the attention of students, and thus the groundwork was laid for the moment he would step into the public spotlight.

Back home in New Orleans for the summer, Duke built his small painting business into a successful enterprise. In the hot New Orleans summer, temperatures often reached into the nineties, with humidity close to 100 percent. He would rise before sunup and scrape and paint houses until darkness fell around 8 P.M. Too tired for much social activity, he usually stayed at home alone, reading racist literature. During that summer he made enough money to buy a $400 used Nova convertible, which he kept until graduation.

Most of his freshman year was spent researching racist ideas. He was not yet well known on campus and had not made many friends. He tried to get involved by attending meetings of the Young Republicans and the Young Americans for Freedom early in the year, but found them to be "without real purpose or direction."

He did, however, make time to attend Ku Klux Klan meetings regularly while he was at home in New Orleans. Jim Lindsay and Father Toups were still around to provide some semblance of parental direction.

The remainder of the summer was uneventful. Maxine was in poor health and although Colonel Duke managed two brief visits, the house on Jewel Street was not really a home. Colonel Duke noticed that his son was "restless," so the two spent a great deal of time together.

Dotti remembers her brother was beginning "his frustrated period." He was not able to relax and enjoy life like other teenagers. Normal activities were not a part of Duke's 1969 summer program. David was serious about learning racist ideology. He was involved with the Klan, but the organization was not as political as Duke thought it should be.

"I liked what the Klan stood for, but I wanted to be more vocal," he said. His leisure activities were limited to listening to music or reading in his room.

The summer ended, and it was time for him to return to LSU for his sophomore year. This time, David Duke would make headlines.

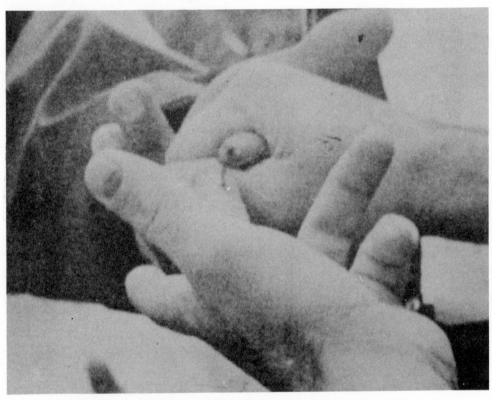

Bleeding black and white hands are compared at LSU's Free Speech Alley, 1969.   (Photo courtesy of *The Daily Reveille* and Bazuki Muhammad)

CHAPTER NINE

David Duke
and the Nazi Party

THE FALL OF 1969 was the most radical period of the Vietnam era at LSU. Campus activists, both for and against the war, mounted drives in an effort to force students into political awareness. It was a volatile time, marked by mistrust of and bitterness toward the establishment. Already primed for a revolution against the status quo, David Duke leaped into the fray. Once he publicly crossed the line into extremism, his life would forever be a crusade for racist ideas.

With the money he earned painting houses during the summer, Duke was able to move into Hodges Hall, leaving the prison-like conditions of his North Stadium dormitory. A large brick structure in the center of the campus, Hodges Hall was very much like the dormitories at Riverside Academy. Each suite had two bedrooms connected by a common bathroom, so Duke would no longer have to bathe with residents of an entire floor.

Duke had disassociated himself from the Citizens Council, which by this time no longer had any real political influence. Most people in Louisiana had adjusted to integration, making the segregationist group passé. What Duke sought was a more defined system, one that opposed communism in a deeper philosophical way. The basic racism and bigotry of the Klan was lacking in gusto, leaving him in political limbo. He needed more. He searched for a powerful ideology that could generate real solutions to the problems Duke foresaw in America.

His racist quest ended with a book entitled *White Power* by George Lincoln Rockwell, the murdered leader of the American Nazi party. The book advocates "a white, Christian nation" and is considered the Bible of hardened racists and anti-Semites. Duke long before had read Adolf Hitler's *Mein Kampf*, but *White Power* was contemporary.

"Many of the aspects of National Socialism appealed to me at the time," Duke remembers.

George Lincoln Rockwell was the best-known white racist of the 1960s. Although he was a Nazi, he was far from the stereotype. A son of the well-known vaudevillian Doc Rockwell, he grew up on the knee of such entertainers as Fred Allen and George Burns. During World War II, Rockwell served in the U.S. Navy as a fighter pilot. Although he professed a belief in the U.S. Constitution, Rockwell also believed in the John Birch Society's concepts of a communist infiltration into America's government and news media. He theorized that Jews were at the heart of this conspiracy orchestrating what he labeled "the liberal media." A confirmed anti-Zionist, Rockwell contended that the Holocaust was a wild exaggeration that had been repeated incessantly to promote Israel psychologically.

Like so many racists, Rockwell also believed the white race was doomed unless a white-power countermovement arose to fight communism. The Nazi leader envisioned a crusade with ideological roots that brandished powerful banners and symbols in opposition to the subversive manipulation by the Marxist movement.

The theme Rockwell repeatedly stressed was Jewish media control. He consistently maintained in the "Rockwell Report"

that the "favorite tactic of the media was to blackout all opposing viewpoints." Rockwell's solution was to display the swastika, the world's most hated symbol, to create enormous
publicity that would foster a forum for his views.

Frustrated and angry, Duke came to believe the white race
was headed for extinction. He believed Rockwell was right in
using radicalism to polarize and stimulate discussion on the
issues he thought crucial. Duke discovered the National Socialist Liberation Front, a group created for college students
and supported by the American Nazi Party. Since the day his
father departed for Vietnam, Duke had become a lost ship
looking for safe harbor. To him, Colonel Duke was in Southeast
Asia doing his part in the fight against communism. The
extremist books he read explained in detail that Jews founded
communism and were the chief promoters of integration. In
Duke's mind, the NSLF held revolutionary ideas that could
offer a compelling response to the dangers of the time.

The few students who shared Duke's extremist views followed
his lead without question. These five or so members would
be his first fanatic supporters known as "Dukies."

The racist apostles formed a corps of "Dukies" who were
always seen, but never heard. Duke's in-depth knowledge about
racist and anti-Semitic issues was enormous. At first, he spoke
on Nazi issues only to people he knew. But soon he attracted
a small number of student intellectuals who found his articulate arguments seductive. With only a handful of fellow neo-
Nazis, Duke was unprepared to become a campus radical. So
his activities were restricted to reading and formulating what
path he would take with the NSLF.

Early in the school year, the Vietnam issue was reaching
fever pitch. Because the topic was in the forefront of the news,
a local talk show on WJBO radio was sponsoring a forum.
Mike Connelly, the vocal president of the Young Americans
for Freedom, was there to represent his conservative views.

David Duke, an unheard-of member of an unknown group, also showed up to join in the discussion. He became a participant by simply telephoning the station and requesting to be added to the program. The host figured Duke might provide a new angle to the issue, so he gave the NSLF member an opportunity to speak without knowing what to expect.

"We were getting ready for the broadcast when David Duke showed up," said Connelly. "No one at the station knew what the National Socialist Liberation Front was. I knew a little about Duke, and what I knew was bad."

Program host John Camp remembers that Connelly had warned him that Duke was a radical, but Camp thought he could handle anyone on the show. He had recently interviewed black radical Stokley Carmichael, among others. But he had never seen the likes of David Duke.

"The show got out of hand from the start. Duke just jumped in, saying that Jews were causing all the trouble in the world," Camp said. Connelly, Camp, and the radio engineers were stunned by Duke's performance.

"I couldn't believe this was the same quiet kid from my ROTC class," said Connelly. "Here we were, supposedly having a discussion about whether or not the U.S. should be involved in Vietnam, and Duke spends the entire show attacking Jews and blacks and communists."

After the show, everyone left the control booth, only to discover two "Dukies" or, as Connelly remembers them, "goons," waiting for their leader in the lobby. They were with Duke for his first public appearance, but as always, he spoke and they listened.

"I was trying to get the message across that I didn't feel that the U.S. made the right decision to get involved in Southeast Asia," Duke remembered. "But since we had made a commitment to fight communism, we should support our troops 100 percent."

Duke had grown to believe that Jews, especially Secretary of State Henry Kissinger, had locked the country in an "Asian war." He saw the government's position as "not in the interests of the American soldiers, bogging them down in a war [with] no real intention to win."

Kissinger would become a favorite whipping boy of Duke for years to come. "The Zionist Kissinger," he often said, "cannot truly represent the interests of the United States by putting the interests of Israel first."

A number of sponsors called the radio station and threatened to cancel future advertisements on WJBO if Duke were ever allowed back on the air. "Until that time we had never worried about what format the show took," remembered Camp. "David Duke changed all that."

Duke immediately returned to Free Speech Alley, this time not as an observer but as the major attraction. The previous year, the Alley had been dominated by members of the Students for a Democratic Society, a far-left, anti-Vietnam War group, and Connelly of the YAF.

But after Duke stood up the first time to speak, the Alley was never the same. Before Duke, no one would have dared to say the things he was preaching. Like no one else before him, Duke attacked the Nixon administration for selling out in Vietnam, blamed deteriorating conditions in America on black criminals and welfare cheats, and assailed Jewish influence in the news media.

"I was just saying things that other students felt inside," he said. "But nobody [else] had the courage to stand up and tell the truth, in fear of censorship or retribution."

Prior to Duke's ascension to the soapbox, a crowd of fifty was considered large at FSA. But once David Duke got up to speak, hundreds stayed to listen or to hiss.

A large national anti-war demonstration called Vietnam Moratorium Day was scheduled for October 15. An organization calling itself the Vietnam Moratorium Committee was working with the school administration to make the event official. A meeting between the VMC and LSU Chancellor Cecil G. Taylor took place in the Vieux Carre room of the LSU Union. Duke heard about it and showed up with fellow NSLF disciples.

Although his extremist opinions were without support among the liberals present, Duke was tolerated. He was allowed to become part of the process, legitimatizing him as a participant. The planned protest was endorsed by such liberal groups as the Young Democrats, the Episcopal Chapel Council, the University Christian Chapel, and the Baton Rouge Society of Friends. But Duke, who was opposed to everything those organizations stood for, made his opinions known at the meeting so others would learn who he was and what he stood for.

As expected, a counterdemonstration called Victory in Vietnam Week was planned by Mike Connelly and the Young Americans for Freedom. Scheduled from October 12 through 18, it was staged in the hope of overshadowing the anti-war rally by encouraging more conservative students to become involved in supporting the war. On October 3, a resolution was adopted by the YAF denouncing the Moratorium and urging everyone to participate in its own effort.

By now, practically everyone on campus was getting in on the act. On October 9, more than 300 people gathered in the Royal Ballroom of the LSU Union to plan the anti-war demonstration. This was quite an achievement, as the first meeting was attended by only twelve people. Students handed out Moratorium pins and white armbands to volunteers as a show of protest against the war.

That same day, the Young Republicans, who were having a hard time convincing their own members to sponsor a counterdemonstration, were finally able to pass a resolution denouncing the Moratorium, but only after forty-four motions.

The final, watered-down motion simply stated, "We cannot endorse a program that does not have confidence in President Nixon."

The YAFers were frustrated by the enthusiasm generated by the anti-war group. To compound matters, Duke had stolen Connelly's place in the spotlight as campus spokesman for the conservative side.

"We were the guys defending what the country was doing in Vietnam," says Connelly, "and David Duke was jumping up and down attacking everybody and his brother as being communists."

Crowds as large as 500 were now commonplace at Free Speech Alley as the debate over Moratorium Day intensified. Connelly and the YAF appeared each week, prepared to defend President Nixon's policies, while those in opposition railed against the war on moral grounds. But overshadowing the debates was David Duke, who immediately upon stepping onto the public podium began to shock everyone in attendance with tirades against Jews and blacks. Even students from the conservative Young Americans for Freedom were appalled by Duke's outlandish behavior. But the crowds continued to grow larger each week as Duke took to the stage with his new racist show.

Duke knew he had found a home for his extremist views at Free Speech Alley. It also gave him a forum to further organize his campus crusade for the NSLF. His attention shifted from the classroom to preparing for his next speech or converting additional students into "Dukies." He was totally committed to the program he believed offered the only defense to the end of white, Western Christian culture.

"You have to remember the time," Duke says now. "I had a lot of support from kids at LSU and at a number of high schools. It wasn't just me against everyone. Things were more radical then."

The next six months would be a time of intense paranoia for Duke, who was quickly learning to trust no one except his close friends and his mentor, Father Toups.

"You couldn't be in the same room with David at that time," said Dotti. "He was so against communism, almost like an intense crusade . . . it was frightening."

The day preceding the Moratorium was highlighted by a debate in the Union Cotillion Room attended by more than 400 people. Featured speakers were Mike Connelly and associate professor David B. Johnson representing conservative viewpoints, and law professor Benjamin Sheiber and student Hampton Carter expressing opposition to the war.

Duke was outraged that he was not allowed to participate in the war of words. As would be his custom in the future, Duke and his band of "Dukies" arrived at the Union early, getting seats as close as possible to the speakers. When it came time for questions from the audience, Duke was ready with a combination of questions and rhetoric. For no apparent reason, he would launch into a tirade about Jews, their domination of the news media, and the negative impact they were having on winning the war.

His irrelevant comments left everyone bewildered. But he relished the role of spoiler and, although Connelly got the only standing ovation of the night, Duke was satisfied he had made progress in advancing his NSLF ideas.

Even at the height of the anti-war movement, LSU was still a very conservative institution. Of the almost 20,000 students enrolled at the time, only about 1,200 participated in the Vietnam Moratorium Day rally. A student vote conducted by the Young Republicans revealed that 65 percent of the students opposed the Moratorium while 59 percent were in favor of U.S. involvement in the war. This decisively weak showing by the anti-Vietnam groups ended the anti-war issue's domination of the news columns in the student newspaper, the *Daily Rev-*

eille, and in Free Speech Alley for the year. It also resulted in a free forum for David Duke to express his racist ideas.

Each Wednesday, Duke took to the soapbox at the Alley, and students kept coming back to listen to his tirades. Many were angered, some were gawking, but almost everyone on campus knew about Duke and what he stood for. On Tuesday, November 11, he made his first splash in print. The *Reveille* carried an editorial about "David Duke and his LSU Nazis." The editorial abhorred what Duke was saying but acknowledged his right to say it.

On November 13, Duke made headlines on the front page of the *Reveille* in an article entitled "Jews, blacks lambasted at heated Alley." The debate the previous day had begun with discussions about the environment and criticism of the athletic department, the latter being a fairly common target. But Duke soon stood up and alleged that Jews, such as Abby Hoffman and Jerry Rubin, were leaders of the pro-Viet Cong Movement. He claimed that "85 percent of the communist traitors convicted of spying in the United States were Jews." Duke then identified himself as a National Socialist. There was an outcry from the audience as Duke declared, "Whites are the master race, in that we should have the right to keep the white race white." It was not Duke's style to shout, but his firm, confident tone made shouting unnecessary. He was quickly losing his shyness and becoming "the big racist on campus."

Later that same session, a black student named Carl Tickles took to the soapbox to vent his frustrations. Angrily, he asked Duke to explain the difference between their hands. The racist replied emphatically his were white and Tickles' were black. That response only angered the black student more. He immediately solicited a knife from a spectator, slashed his own hand, and challenged Duke to compare their blood. Duke declined.

But another white student, John Hart, accepted Tickles' offer and cut his hand as well.

As the silenced crowd of students looked on, Duke lectured the bleeding Tickles, "It [doesn't] mean a thing. I could walk across the street to the science lab and get a big, hairy rat and his blood would be just as red. Any good blood pathologist could instantly tell the difference between white and black blood."

This brought a combination of boos and laughter from the excited FSA crowd. It also prompted the *Reveille* to print a front-page photograph of a black hand and a white hand, both dripping blood. At no time had anyone except David Duke created such emotion at conservative LSU.

Duke continued to attack Jews and the news media at every opportunity. He would use this format for years to come as a way to convince others that white Christians have something to fear from Jews. "In this country," he would say repeatedly, "the press is controlled by Jews. You are victims of suppressed news."

In increasingly more hostile attacks, Duke declared that "Jews who hold allegiance to Israel over America should not be allowed to hold high government positions." He further insisted that "the negative influence of Jewish culture must be limited." At first the message evoked boos and hisses from the audience. But slowly his hostile ideas drew cautious acceptance, and some students began to applaud.

On one occasion at FSA, Connelly got up to speak and reminded Duke of the debate on WJBO. He said that during the radio program Duke had expressed full support for National Socialist party leader Frank Collins. Duke vehemently denied making the remark. The YAF leader then asked if it were not true that Jews were among many of the capitalist leaders of the country. Duke answered, "I am not trying to defend the system because the capitalist system is almost as corrupt as the communist one." Duke believed the free enterprise system was being stifled by international banks, which he claimed were controlled by Jewish interests and large corporations.

The Alley session ended with cheers and boos being directed at both Connelly and Duke. Connelly, who was very conservative, had to defend issues Duke made appear liberal. Members of the Young Democrats, as well as other left-wing groups, sat back and gave Duke the opportunity to control the direction of the debate.

At Free Speech Alley, Duke often handed out copies of the NSLF newsletter, *The Liberator.* The publication was filled with propaganda that influenced Duke to take increasingly more radical positions. The paper carried advertisements for such products as tear gas, described as "negro control equipment, guaranteed to drop the most vicious buck in his tracks."

The pen is mightier than the sword, and David Duke used a pen as least as sharp as a razor-edged cutlass. Angered by what he felt were personal attacks by Mike Connelly, Duke composed a letter to the editor of the *Reveille* on Wednesday, November 19. In it, Duke proceeded to elaborate on what he thought were the finer points of National Socialism:

> "Exterminate all Jews, and with more efficient methods than Hitler used! Ship all the Negroes back to Africa in cattle boats! Exterminate all people who politically disagree. According to Mike Connelly these are the aims and objectives of the National Socialist Liberation Front. What has Connelly been reading—*Argosy* Magazine? If he or anyone else can prove that this is what I and the NSLF have advocated, I will quit.
>
> "The NSLF has different views from the run of the mill groups on campus, whether they support the right or the left. Their approach to the problems confronting our civilization is completely mechanical, economic, and materialistic. National Socialism, on the other hand, is unique! Instead of stressing materialistic economic dogma as democratic-liberalism has in its Eastern version or West-

ern version, we believe that the quality and spirit of our people are by far the most important issues of our time.

"What are the goals of the NSLF? Our first goal is to break through the communication barrier in this country and to let the people know exactly what we stand for instead of what certain people say we stand for. Then we will express to them why we believe as we do. Once the people hear both sides, we are confident that they will choose ours; then we can proceed to build the leadership we need to liberate our people so that they can determine their own destiny."

DAVID DUKE

The letter shocked most people, but further confirmed Duke as the right-wing leader on campus. He remembered what his father had taught years before in Sunday school: "If the crowd goes one way and you know they're wrong, then you have an absolute responsibility to do the right thing, even if you have to do it all alone." Duke was now involved with the unpopular philosophy of National Socialism. All he needed was a crowd to give life to words from the silent pages of racist literature such as *White Power*.

On Wednesday, December 18, Duke headed to Free Speech Alley for one of the most highly emotional sessions ever held at LSU. He was handing out literature when a black student appeared at the speaker's stand carrying a burning copy of *The Liberator*, the NSLF newsletter. The crowd, which was largely black, cheered the student, who shouted, "I'm sick of all this." He then grabbed the NSLF pamphlets from Duke and set them afire. With his voice quivering, the agitated student asserted, "There is more politics than thinking about humanity in this country."

Shaking with anger, he stared at Duke as he related how he had just dissuaded two North Baton Rouge blacks from killing the racist. He concluded that Duke nevertheless would probably meet a violent end.

It was just the type of reaction Duke could exploit. Taking his lead from George Lincoln Rockwell, he had succeeded in creating the kind of emotion that made people listen. Only a relatively few students agreed with the racist ideas Duke was espousing, but no other speaker representing any ideology could match his fervor and oratorical skill.

Standing like a martyr, Duke claimed liberals and communists were trying to suppress literature that questioned the idea of racial equality. He displayed a copy of Rockwell's *White Power* and complained it could not be sold in the campus bookstore, while books advocating black power were readily available. "Like it or not," said Duke, "the white man built Western civilization."

He then launched into his favorite topic, blaming Jews for spreading the false theory of the equality of races. The crowd tried to shout him down, but Duke persisted.

"The way to show me that I am wrong," he demanded, "is not to beat on me or burn my papers, but to persuade me in a debate."

As soon as Duke left, so did the crowd.

Duke regularly received threats from black and radical liberal students. One threatening call described a plan to pour gasoline under his dormitory room door while he slept and burn him to death. Threats would become common as Duke moved down the road of radicalism.

In late March 1970, three black LSU students were arrested for allegedly plotting to kill Baton Rouge Mayor W. W. ("Woody") Dumas. The Alley of April 1 centered on whether or not District Attorney Sargent Pitcher was playing politics in arresting the men. Tempers flared when black students used the soapbox to raise legal defense funds for the three accused. Various black students took turns blasting Pitcher as a racist, while no one responded in defense of the district attorney.

No one, that is, until Duke stood up and for more than an hour delivered a tirade against the three suspects. Although

the audience did not agree with the racist orator's NSLF philosophies, the majority of the students did agree with his position regarding Pitcher. This made Duke appear as the only
white speaker willing to stand up to black pressure.

"That was the first time a large number of students came
up and said I was right in what I was saying," remembers
Duke.

During this radical period, there was never an organized
chapter of the National Socialist Liberation Front at LSU.
Although he read a great deal about National Socialism, David
Duke was never a member of the Nazi party. From September
1969 until Christmas of 1970, however, Duke spouted Nazi
ideology.

It was during this "Nazi period" that Duke made the political statement he regrets most. In the early spring of 1970,
Tulane University was sponsoring a lecture by left-wing lawyer
and anti-war activist William Kunstler. Duke became so incensed by the idea of "Viet Cong Kunstler" being allowed a
forum at Tulane he decided to make his own protest at the
lecture. In the midst of Kunstler's three-dozen Black Panther
supporters, David Duke, alone and dressed in a Nazi uniform,
carried a sign that read "Gas the Chicago 7" and "Kunstler
is a communist Jew."

It turned out to be more than Duke bargained for. The
next day a picture of the young racist, in uniform and wearing
a swastika armband, appeared in the newspaper.

"I was trying to show that Kunstler was a flag-burning anti-
American," he said. "I was young, and I may not have been
right for wearing the uniform, but I was right about Kunstler."

Undaunted by the photograph, Duke continued his crusade.
The *Reveille* of April 2 printed a front-page picture of Duke
and an unidentified black student in debate. Duke was holding
a copy of *White Power*. The picture was titled "Put Up Your
Dukes" and carried the caption, ". . . whites are mentally su-

perior to Negroes." There was also an invitation for critics to debate him on the issue.

Thus, Duke had accomplished what he had set out to do just a matter of months before. His radical views were now known to just about everyone.

In the same issue of the *Reveille* was a quarter-page editorial by student Patrick De Rouen defending Duke's right to speak at Free Speech Alley and chastising those who opposed it. This was significant because even though Duke had not modified his words, people were beginning to listen.

Even though Colonel Duke was half a world away, his son's growing radicalism was not going unnoticed. The colonel returned to New Orleans to speak with David and was particularly furious about the Kunstler incident. While in Vietnam, Colonel Duke had received a copy of a newspaper displaying a picture of his son dressed up like Adolf Hitler.

"It made me want to get the hell back to the States," he said, "and talk some sense into David." Being adamantly anti-Nazi, Colonel Duke wanted to give his son the perspective of someone who had lived through the tragedies of World War II. Probably the only thing that exceeded the young activist's ideological devotion was his love and respect for his father.

"My son was convinced," Colonel Duke said, "that there were differences in races, but he really began to see that the repressive nature of totalitarianism far outweighed any philosophies that he was examining. I could tell that I had reached him when he cried and told me that he would always be dedicated to the white race. He knew he was wrong for wearing the swastika and espousing Naziism."

Duke heeded his father's advice. He began to combine his views on race with the philosophy of radical libertarianism.

After the stern rebuke by his father, Duke began to publicly distance himself from the NSLF, but still investigated its extremist ideology. He believed that racial survival was the most important objective and continued promoting various groups such as Nazis, the Klan, the Christian Nationalists, the Minute-men, and the John Birch Society. Although he was still extremely radical, he began to form a world view quite different from that of his early days at Free Speech Alley. Love for his father superseded any dedication to National Socialism. By the close of 1970, David Duke had abandoned the Nazi party, but not its racist and anti-Semitic philosophies.

David Duke carries a copy of *White Power* at LSU's Free Speech Alley. (Photo courtesy of *The Daily Reveille* and Bazuki Muhammad)

CHAPTER TEN

The White Youth Alliance

DUKE HAD BEGUN TO DEVELOP a closer relationship with Klansman Jim Lindsay. Lindsay shared Colonel Duke's view of Naziism but still promoted a strong white and anti-Zionist position, as did many Klansmen. Due to the influence of his paternal mentors, Duke decided he would not support any Nazi organization. He told friends in New Orleans that he no longer supported the NSLF, but, in truth, he joined a group called the White Student Alliance, known for its close association with the Nazi party.

Headquartered in Arlington, Virginia, the White Student Alliance was a youth arm of the NSLF. Although it was considered separate from its Nazi cousin, it embraced the same ideological principles. The WSA was never a national political power, but managed to organize chapters on numerous college campuses.

In the fall of 1970, David Duke's life began to change. He moved off campus into a small apartment on Chimes Street, a few blocks from LSU. The meeting with his father months earlier had forced him to seriously question many of the tenets of National Socialism. The university's best-known racist thus embarked on a new crusade: converting students sympathetic to the NSLF to the WSA. And his nine or ten devout supporters willingly followed.

As soon as the first Free Speech Alley of the semester began, Duke returned to attack passionately familiar targets, such as Jewish control of the news media and integration. Students came to watch their favorite bigot blast the "Jewish communist conspiracy" and race-mixing. But this time, there was no more defense of the Nazi system from Duke. Duke did maintain, however, that even though he was opposed to the institution of Naziism, he believed Americans were not allowed to hear both sides of the issue because of "Zionist media control."

Duke denies he ever used the term "Jewish communist conspiracy," but the phrase was attributed to him numerous times throughout his student career. Because of in-depth research and extensive preparation, Duke would sometimes tie up the discussion at FSA for more than an hour. No matter what the topic of the day, he found some way to interject Jews and blacks into the debate.

WJBO had the most popular AM-radio call-in talk show in Baton Rouge, hosted daily by John Camp. As with most talk shows, a wide variety of listeners called each day, giving their thoughts and opinions. A regular caller was Mrs. Babs Minhinnette, who had gained fame—or notoriety—in the Baton Rouge area for her many years of right-wing activities.

She had created such groups as Females Opposed to Equality to fight the Equal Rights Amendment; the Concerned Parents Association, which sought to curtail any form of sex education in schools; and the Taxpayers Education Association, a group which opposed any new taxes for schools. She also created the Citizens for Pure Water, which successfully stopped Baton Rouge from fluoridating the public water system because of fear it was part of a "large conspiracy by the federal government."

The Student Government Association sponsored numerous speakers who came to the campus to discuss various issues of

David Duke with friend Babs Minhinnette. (Photo courtesy of Barbara Wilson)

David Duke pleads for white rights. (Photo by Michael P. Smith)

the day. One was a black woman named Julia Brown from the extremely conservative John Birch Society. Babs Minhinnette and her ten-year-old son went, as usual, to the sparsely attended program. Brown offered the usual anti-communist remarks and propaganda of her organization, then fielded questions from the audience. David Duke stood up and took command of the program for the next two hours.

"He knew far more about the issues of the day," said Minhinnette. "We were all impressed that David knew more about conservative issues than the lady from the John Birch Society."

From that moment on, Babs Minhinnette became the leading "Dukie" in America.

Immediately, Duke became a hero to Babs Minhinnette and the Concerned Parents Association. In one evening he had expanded his following from 20 or so college students to a group of more than 250 adults. So impressed were they with the young racist that many devoted every spare moment to causes supported by Duke. These people formed the core of support which remained with Duke throughout his college years. For the first time in his racist career he had access to people with money and the wherewithal to help promote his platform.

From that night on, the thirty-seven-year-old Minhinnette became a kind of surrogate mother to Duke. "He was really a pitiful sight that first night at LSU," she said in a slow, soft Southern drawl. "He was so skinny and his shirt had buttons missing. But I remember he stood up for what he believed in, no matter what the cost."

Duke began spending a lot of time with Babs and her husband, Virgil, at their home. They ate supper together, watched television, and acted very much like a family. The Minhinnettes were members of a private club where Duke spent many afternoons swimming with them in the pool.

"David would loan us some of the books he had on problems facing white people and the truth about what the FBI and what the government [were] trying to do with forced integration," Minhinnette said.

The Minhinnette house became a base of operation which helped launch Duke's political career. It was here the young racist was able to formulate plans. Before meeting the Minhinnettes, Duke could only show people material from books he found or speak at Free Speech Alley. But now, through his new family, he had access to a typewriter and a copying machine, two simple items vital for disseminating information for any movement.

With money raised from WSA dues, combined with donations from Babs Minhinnette's Concerned Parents members, Duke was able to publish a newsletter entitled *The Racialist*. *Webster's Dictionary* defines racialist as "one who advocates or believes in racism."

Although Duke did not consider himself a racist, he did consider himself a "racialist." To Duke, racialism is a contraction for racial idealism, meaning pride in one's own heritage and its potential, not someone opposed to other races.

The paradoxical nature of David Duke's racism has eluded explanation. He conveys sincerity because he believes his racist ideas are honorable and true. On one hand, Duke alleges he believes in the right of Israel to exist, but on the other, maintains he is a staunch anti-Zionist. David Duke will argue this position is not contradictory. He is convinced his philosophies are correct and has no reservations about making outrageous statements about Jews and blacks.

The Racialist was circulated at LSU and many high schools. Within a month of meeting the Concerned Parents, Duke had distributed thousands of the pamphlets throughout the capital city. The booklet was appropriately subtitled "The White Power Program," by David Ernest Duke. It outlined goals of the White Student Alliance, as well as the group's ideology. On the front page was a picture of Duke at Free Speech Alley holding a copy of George Lincoln Rockwell's *White Power.*

Although the White Student Alliance was not directly aligned with the NSLF, it promoted many similar tenets. *The Racialist* stated that its platform was "directed primarily to the white student, who believes in the greatness of his race, and who wants to be protected against his enemies." Sending out an alarm to readers, Duke further wrote that the main objective of the group was to defeat adversaries of the white race, whoever they may be. It claimed whites were "losing their schools to black savagery, their hard earned pay to welfare and their culture to no-win [R]ed treason and Jewish and black degeneracy."

Duke told students that only "through strength and idealism [can] the white race that built America survive." Duke defined racialism, or racial idealism, as "the idea that a nation's greatest resource is the quality of its people."

Expanding his anti-black and anti-Semitic agenda, he became anti-capitalistic as well, calling capitalism an "unfortunate system by which the United States is run." Although he agreed with some of its principles, Duke maintained that capitalism was controlled by international bankers who limited true competition and free enterprise. He reminded readers that "our nation was not founded for any economic doctrine."

He denied that communism, capitalism, or any materialistic doctrine could save the white race. He suggested whites could survive only through "racial idealism," which meant "a raising of the Christian ethics, hard work, honesty and excellence."

A ten-point racial program was outlined, urging the "Protection, Preservation and Advancement of the White Race." This first point would form the credo of the White Student Alliance. The other nine were simply extensions of this statement.

In this first point, Duke acknowledged that to achieve true white protection, white majority rule would eventually have to be established. He asserted that black crime had made it difficult for the races to live together.

"Jewish-controlled . . . motion pictures, radio and television," he wrote, "have plainly become mass propaganda machines which are feeding every imaginable kind of filth and lies to our people." There was no way, he continued, that the two races could be successfully mixed. Separation would be the only solution — separation of schools and neighborhoods.

Duke attacked "anti-white" foreign policy-makers for bogging down American fighting men in an "Asian war." He called for aid to other white countries, such as South Africa and Rhodesia, and demanded an end to sending billions of dollars to "non-White, communist nations."

Duke's messages were peppered with populist beliefs. He advocated a system in which a working person would no longer have to work "one-third of his life just to pay interest on his home." *The Racialist* called for an end to high interest rates, which were "economic robbery." *The Racialist* contended people had a right to feel as secure in their jobs as they did in their homes. Duke foresaw a plan whereby every American would be awarded a decent standard of living as long as "he did work efficiently and to the best of his ability."

Protecting the environment and the educational system of America were the sworn duties of all members of the WSA. "Our race must not be sacrificed to technology," he wrote. "Instead technology, as all things, must serve the interest of our race." Duke has always included a broadly based platform to delineate his racist theories. To that, he added non-racist issues, such as the environment.

He railed against much of modern art, which he labeled "anarchistic garbage created by Negroid and Jewish degeneracy." He proclaimed that a Jewish-controlled press had perverted the news media, and a free press was no longer available because they had "blacked out the Racialist arguments from the American people." This anti-Semitic theme has appeared time and time again throughout Duke's career. He portrayed Jews as a racist group banded together to advance the cause of Zionism.

The Racialist called for a pro-white government so people could once again have "new faith based on Racial Idealism." This meant separation of the races in order to maintain "racial consistency by one's pride in one's racial identity, purity and heritage." The newsletter outlined reasons why the WSA was important to the survival of all white readers. It claimed that no other college organizations were devoted to white causes, and that only by uniting could the country be saved. The group would be "neither left nor right."

It further noted that "half the white people [are] Republican or Democrat, Southern or Northern, rich or poor, labor or management or Protestant or Catholic. It is time to band together to further the common interests of whites. It is time for an end to infighting by whites, by the formation of a united front for Racial Idealism."

Duke closed the issue by urging Alliance members "to use every means possible to convey the ideas of the white majority."

Across the top of the newsletter was a "White Power Message." Duke had arranged for a taped telephone recording, which would play twenty-four hours a day, giving racist messages to whomever called. Whenever someone felt the need for a bit of racism, all he had to do was pick up the phone and receive an earful.

No matter what Duke did, the White Student Alliance was unable to attract more than a handful of members. Duke had already told the WSA members he could no longer support Naziism, a stand that many radical elements resented. Things were moving toward a showdown. Taking the advice of his father, Duke wrote a letter to WSA headquarters in Arlington stating:

> "You know that I am totally dedicated to the survival of our race and our Christian Faith, but I have told you that I cannot support the policies of National Socialism. Although Adolf Hitler was pro-White and anti-communist, he is to the racial movement as the Inquisition is to Christianity. Excusing his crimes by pointing out Soviet and [A]llied war crimes does not lessen his culpability for crimes that were committed, exaggerated or not. The truth is that whatever his motives, he was the greatest disaster ever to befall the white race. . . . I am sorry if my opinion will cause our friendship to be severed, but I must act honestly on my convictions in this matter."

Duke immediately sent a copy of the letter to his father, who keeps it to this day.

The break with Naziism ushered in a new era of closeness and mutual respect between Duke and his father. It seemed as though a heavy millstone had been lifted from the racist's neck, opening up opportunities to grow and evolve. He was still a radical, but was beginning to temper his extremism. Babs Minhinnette believes that after his withdrawal from National Socialism Duke seemed "to flower and grow."

To fill the void left by his defection from the WSA, Duke and his mentor Jim Lindsay formulated a new organization modeled after the Knights of the Ku Klux Klan. Lindsay was delighted with its less-radical policy. He convinced his racist apprentice to modify his hardened positions, and the path was paved to create the White Youth Alliance.

Duke saw the White Youth Alliance as a modern Klan without the Klan trappings. To give the WYA an identity, he chose the symbol of a cross inside a circle. This was the original Klan symbol, called a cross-wheel, which Duke found in an old book. Members would often brandish armbands sporting the cross-wheel, which looked very much like a swastika. No matter how much Duke attempted to distance himself from Nazis, he still wore the scar of the Kunstler incident.

Duke was looking forward to joining advanced ROTC so he could follow in his father's footsteps and become an officer. When he went to register, LSU's highest-ranking cadet was denied entry into the program because of his radical activities. It was the most devastating setback Duke had ever experienced. He had always expected to become an officer. Rejection by the Army at this point ended any chance he may have had to serve in the military.

The commander of LSU's Army ROTC program at the time was Col. James May, who said of Duke, "He had fine leadership qualities but his philosophy was different from ours and that of our country. His affiliation with Naziism precluded Duke's getting a commission in the military."

"Hell," May declared, "we couldn't tolerate such a thing."

Both Duke and his father tried in vain to get the rejection overturned but were unable to persuade the university to reconsider its decision. This only solidified Duke's belief that he was being singled out by the Army for speaking up for the causes of white people. The decision to deny Duke advancement in ROTC strengthened his determination to "get things going with the White Youth Alliance."

Once again Free Speech Alley became the David Duke Show. But there was a difference. He now had an established organization of more than 275 members on campus and the support of the Concerned Parents Association. Duke began to hear cheers along with jeers at the Alley.

The Reveille once again made Duke a regular news item. One issue devoted two photographs and almost a half-page editorial that ironically claimed too much time had been focused on the radical leader.

"It always gets back to a commie Jew plot by the black lovers of America, against the good ole white folks," the editorial lamented. "But do not try to argue with David Duke.

He's no fool. Every bit of information he has is backed up with facts and figures. The facts, as often as not, are from a Who's Who of World Jewry and the figure is usually 85 percent of anything."

Dr. Benjamin Spock had been invited by the LSU Lyceum Committee to speak on September 30. Dr. Spock had gained fame as a pediatrician, writing bestselling books on child care. By the late 1960s and early 1970s, he had become a leading opponent of the Vietnam War and the policies of President Nixon.

Spock had been arrested a number of times for protesting the war and the military draft. Duke loathed Spock's philosophies as much as he detested William Kunstler's. He decided to use this opportunity to move the White Youth Alliance into action.

Working with Babs Minhinnette and the Concerned Parents Association, Duke planned for both groups to picket Spock's speech together. In a letter to LSU officials, the Concerned Parents urged that Spock be denied the right to speak. They claimed it should be illegal for any tax-supported agency to provide a platform for pro-communist speakers to voice their views. The request was immediately turned down, and the program proceeded as scheduled.

Duke and some of the members of the WYA met at the Minhinnettes' house early in the day. They made signs and planned strategy for the evening.

"I wanted to draw attention to the fact that Spock was hurting our soldiers in Vietnam," said Duke. "If he was going to speak, then we were going to peacefully show that we disagreed with what he was doing."

The speech took place at 8 P.M. in the LSU Union Theater. It was a sellout, with more than 1,300 people in attendance plus an additional 300 students watching on closed-circuit television in the Union's Colonnade Theater.

Another 300 protesters gathered outside the Union at seven o'clock. Duke, the White Youth Alliance, and the Concerned Parents Association were greeted by a group of Spock supporters. The WYA members were carrying American flags and signs such as "Spock is a dirty old doc" and "Spock's Philosophies Create Monsters." A Baton Rouge newspaper, the *State-Times*, printed a picture of Duke holding a sign reading "Students for America — Free Lt. Calley not Spock." There was a great deal of name-calling and anger, but the protest remained non-violent.

Duke and a few WYA members paid the admission price of fifty cents and went to hear Dr. Spock deliver his speech. Spock spent the entire speech attacking the government's position on the Vietnam War. He said students had an obligation to protest.

"I'm opposed to violence," Spock insisted. "But I never claimed to be a pacifist." The famed baby doctor also added, "We have a moral right to go to violence as a last resort." He was well received by the mostly liberal audience, winning a standing ovation.

After the speech, Spock fielded questions from the audience. Duke got right into the picture. Most students supported Spock, so when Duke got up to speak the entire hall groaned.

Duke used Spock's anti-war sentiments for his own purpose. He asked Spock if sending "young men to die in Vietnam is wrong?" The anti-war activist answered yes. Duke then asked him if it were "not then reasonable to believe it was just as wrong to have the United States become involved in the Middle East? Nothing can bring back the 40,000 Americans who have already died in Vietnam, but there is still a chance to prevent a new Vietnam in the Middle East."

Spock replied, "It is impossible to correlate the Vietnam War to the Middle East."

Continuing the cross-examination, Duke asked emphatically, "Doctor, you have advocated the redistribution of wealth

in America from the rich to the poor. You say, in your own
words, that we need a revolution in this country. You also say
that there are people starving right now in America and facing
repression. Doctor, if you are really sincere, I want to know
if you are willing to give up your island and your yacht voluntarily, here and now, and give them to the poor . . . something you want the government to force on everyone else."

A flustered Spock ducked the issue, responding, "I am not
a Communist, and I wish you would tell the Concerned Parents
Association that!"

Duke's brief performance that evening solidified the White
Youth Alliance and made him an even bigger hero with the
Concerned Parents Association. The WYA had, in a matter
of weeks, grown into a recognized group on campus.

Being something of a star at LSU, Duke attracted a certain
type of girls. But he was looking for something else. He received
a phone call one day from a coed named Chloe Hardin. She
lived in Herget Hall, one of the newer girls' dormitories at
LSU. Her roommate was Marilyn Memory, who later married
Duke's archenemy Mike Connelly.

"Chloe was taken by David from the very beginning," Marilyn remembers. "She really believed in what David was saying
at Free Speech Alley. She was very conservative and was active
in the Young Americans for Freedom and the Young Republicans with Mike and me."

Chloe was the product of a conservative, upper-middle-class
upbringing and was described as "an attractive blonde who
was very polite and always dressed nicely." Although a relatively
shy person, Chloe wanted someone whom she could believe
in. She saw Duke as a maverick and a leader of the conservative
agenda who was not afraid to stand up for what he believed.

The White Youth Alliance would sometimes meet outside
the LSU Union, handing out literature to students going to
class. One day, Chloe passed by the Union and stopped to see
for herself if the talk she had heard about David Duke were

true. She was given some information and borrowed a few books. Using the excuse of returning the books, Chloe phoned the racist leader. Duke was so impressed by her knowledge of right-wing issues that he asked her for a date. They spent their first evening together eating hamburgers and talking about politics.

"From that time on," said Duke, "I guess we were girlfriend and boyfriend."

Marijuana was becoming popular on college campuses and the issue found its way to Free Speech Alley. On October 7 a number of students defended legalizing pot, claiming it was a harmless drug. Duke was the only speaker to support strong anti-marijuana laws. The *Reveille* quoted Duke as saying that 25,000 people die each year in traffic deaths as a result of drunken drivers. "Legalizing marijuana would add 10,000 more deaths a year," he declared.

Duke returned later that same session and launched another attack on Jews. He claimed they were the chief supporters of the Black Panthers and that "Jews have promoted race-mixing in the press."

Interestingly enough, during this radical period Duke was able to maintain friendships with some Jewish and black students. He saw what he called "wide group differences," but did not let them affect his personal life. Despite his outrageous speeches at Free Speech Alley, he was still able to cultivate relationships with students who opposed him. This peculiarity in his personality was, to say the least, disarming.

Duke was dating Chloe on a daily basis. They would go either to the Minhinnettes' house or to his apartment. Chloe was attracted to Duke and quickly became his steady girlfriend and chief supporter among the White Youth Alliance.

Until meeting David Duke, Chloe had spent most of her time with other girls in the dorm. She often went with Marilyn Memory to her parents' home in New Orleans for weekend visits. But Chloe was dating Duke and Marilyn was going steady with Mike Connelly, so a strain developed between the two roommates.

"She was so sweet, and we were always so close," remembered Marilyn. "But once she met David, I hardly saw her anymore."

People who associated with Duke found his causes took priority over everything else in their lives. Because he had such a strong commitment to his racist ideology, Chloe soon joined "the struggle."

Civil-rights leader and comedian Dick Gregory was the next scheduled lecturer sponsored by the LSU Union Lyceum Committee. Gregory was a controversial left-wing, anti-war figure, even more to the left than Spock. As expected, Babs Minhinnette, the Concerned Parents Association, and the White Youth Alliance were geared up to hold a counterdemonstration.

The Concerned Parents Association wrote a letter to Gov. John McKeithen asking him to stop Gregory from speaking at LSU. The letter, published in the local newspaper, accused Gregory of being "pro-communist" and therefore "guilty of treason." McKeithen refused to get involved, setting up a repeat of Dr. Spock's appearance.

Concerned Parents President Mrs. Claude Groves said it would be useless to picket because it had done no good during the Spock lecture. It was announced, however, that David Duke and the White Youth Alliance would meet to organize a protest at 7:30 P.M. in the Colonnade Room of the Union, just before Gregory's speech.

"If we can't prevent our student fees from being used to finance the black revolution," Duke said, "the least we can do is let people know that we disagree with Gregory."

The day of the Gregory speech was filled with tension across campus. Duke spent the entire day planning with his fellow members of the WYA. They met at Babs Minhinnette's house and made such signs as "The Black Revolution is Red," "Gregory is a Riot," "America for Whites—Africa for Blacks," "White Power," and "Race Above All." The signs included the familiar letters WYA, complete with the Klan symbol of a circle with a cross in the middle.

Gregory was as radical as expected, and the overflow crowd gave him a mixed reception. He attacked the Nixon admin- istration and the Democratic party. His rhetoric was as anti- white as Duke's had been anti-black and anti-Semitic. Outside the LSU Union, Duke and twenty WYA members staged a silent protest.

But other than front-page coverage in the *Reveille,* nothing much came of it. Unlike the Spock protest, response to the Gregory speech was calm. There was only so much attention Duke could muster from his demonstrations. For the first time, he began to lose interest in the White Youth Alliance.

CHAPTER ELEVEN

A Cul-de-sac

POLITICAL GROUPS WERE ALLOWED to set up portable tables in front of the LSU Union to give out literature endorsed by their particular organizations. Duke enjoyed the opportunity to speak to students who stopped by the WYA table. Almost everyone on campus was curious about the fiery racist. Groups such as the Young Republicans, Young Americans for Freedom, and Young Democrats were milquetoast compared to the WYA. The natural inquisitiveness of people drew them to Duke, and he used that to further his cause.

Free Speech Alley found Duke receiving more support each week. He soon turned his attention to the Nixon administration's handling of the Vietnam War. He said Nixon's foreign policy "does not safeguard the American people, but feeds someone's lust for power, money and personal gain." This time, not only WYA members but anti-war students as well applauded Duke's comments.

"American soldiers go to battle with confidence and are cheated out of that confidence," he told the crowd. "Nixon is not out to achieve a military victory over the enemy. Nixon has his political finger in the wind. We should be willing to bomb all Hanoi for one American prisoner. If you want to do something about it, join the White Youth Alliance."

Someone from the crowd asked Duke if he would bomb Hanoi if the prisoners were black or Jewish. The young racist replied, "Blacks will agree that they have no business in Vietnam because they are not part of white culture."

With the exception of the Young Republicans, the crowd applauded. A smiling Duke stepped down from the soapbox like a valiant gladiator. He enjoyed the role of whipping boy and he reveled as the underdog.

Duke was envious of friends who had been promoted to advanced ROTC. His lifelong dream had always been to become an officer like his father. He had become a dedicated anti-communist and wanted to fight in Vietnam, not just in the streets of Baton Rouge.

Although Duke was still dating Chloe, the two went their separate ways for the Christmas holidays. They were reunited in January and became closer than ever. It was the first long-term relationship Duke had ever known. "She was everything I thought a woman should be," he said.

The United States Agency for International Development had transferred Colonel Duke from Vietnam to Vientiane in central Laos. He returned home for one of his regular visits at Christmas and noticed his son was "discontented with what he was doing with his life."

The two Dukes spent most of the holidays together. Colonel Duke suggested to David that he might take some time off from school and visit him in Laos. He knew his son was still crestfallen over his rejection by advanced ROTC. As a dependent, young Duke qualified for USAID to pay all his travel expenses, and since Colonel Duke had a two-bedroom house, living costs would not be a problem.

There were a number of positions available with various U.S. government agencies operating within neutral Laos.

"I told him to just think about it," said Colonel Duke, "and he could give me an answer in a month or two. There would be a job waiting for him."

Duke asked his father to "help him find a way to assist in the fight against communism."

Little was changing at LSU. The editorial section of the *Reveille* of Tuesday, March 2, carried a headline reading "Duke of Dixieland." It referred to Duke as "LSU's racist in residence" and criticized his monopolizing of Free Speech Alley. It said that Young Americans for Freedom President Mike Connelly had to spend most of the conservative group's time refuting statements by Duke.

The school paper was under pressure from the faculty and the administration because of the attention it paid Duke and the WYA. But the WYA was good press, which made it difficult for the paper to totally dismiss the young racist leader.

The editorial, written by *Reveille* editor Charlie East, alleged that the White Youth Alliance had spread to junior high schools and high schools through pamphlets announcing an upcoming white power rally. East closed by saying, "Maybe a whole new generation of David Dukes will be produced through this indoctrination process, although the thought is rather frightening. But right now, the ugly banner of white supremacy [will] be handled by Duke." Everyone on campus knew what Duke was trying to do, but no one did anything about it. Students continued coming to Free Speech Alley to listen and watch.

The *Reveille* of Thursday, March 4, gave the WYA additional publicity. There was a large headline reading "White Youth Alliance opens big campaign," followed by a news release from the WYA urging students to sign a petition to stop a "new Vietnam in the Middle East." The article said the petition would be available in front of the LSU Union on the following Monday and Tuesday.

Duke hoped the petition would help restrain the "tremendous forces at work in the country trying to railroad the U.S. into a military commitment to Israel in the Middle East War." The announcement added that "unless intelligent concerted action is taken immediately, there will be another bloodletting of American youth similar to Vietnam." It closed by boasting that the WYA hoped to gather five million signatures and deliver them to the president at the 1973 inauguration.

The idea of gathering five million signatures was not out of the question in Duke's mind. If he got the ball rolling at LSU, then the rest of the country could very well follow. He set up a stand under the oak trees in front of the Union and talked to every passerby who would listen. With Chloe at his side, he tried to get the petition signed.

But the Duke publicity machine was about to grind to a halt. A quarter-page letter to the editor from George Tully, Jr., appeared in the *Reveille*. He criticized the newspaper for publishing so many stories about Duke and accused it of promoting the WYA to increase readership. If the *Reveille* would stop making Duke a media star, he contended, then the racist would soon fade away. It was just the excuse some of the newspaper staff had been looking for. Duke had made great copy, but the *Reveille* had allowed itself to be used. It was time to stop. After March 9, 1971, David Duke's name was never mentioned in the *Reveille*.

Frustrated at LSU, Duke wrote to his father in March and notified him that he planned to go to Laos as soon as the semester ended. The idea of leaving Chloe saddened him, but any chance of serving with the military was too tempting for the racist ideologue to pass up. Still angered by the ROTC rebuff, Duke wanted to show those who rejected him that they were wrong in denying him military advancement. He longed to take action on his anti-communist beliefs and play out his right-wing fantasies. With the strong repudiation by the Army at LSU, Laos seemed the only solution. Besides, Duke missed his father terribly and wanted to be with him.

Once Duke decided to go to Laos, he moved away from racist and anti-Semitic attacks and focused his attention on patriotism. At Free Speech Alley he now addressed the issue of winning the war in Southeast Asia. Duke secretly had plans to join the war personally, with or without ROTC.

U.S. Army Lt. William Calley had been convicted of murder for his participation in the killing of Vietnamese civilians at My Lai in 1968. Many conservatives thought Calley was acting in the line of duty. Duke had long used the Calley issue in an attempt to discredit the government's handling of the war. He was now more vocal than ever on the issue.

Many students agreed that Calley was a scapegoat for the Army, and a number of marches were held to protest the lieutenant's conviction. Such diverse groups as the liberal Progressive Students Association, the Young Americans for Freedom, and the radical White Youth Alliance all denounced the Calley conviction.

May 5 had been chosen as the date for another national day of protest against the Vietnam War. A committee calling itself the Baton Rouge Peace Action Group was sponsoring a series of activities. A "Night Peace Vigil" on campus was planned for May 4. A demonstration would be held at 1:30 the next afternoon in the Memorial Oak Grove featuring various speakers and music. The vigil was to be followed by a march to the state capitol and an anti-war rally where organizers hoped to ratify a "People's Peace Treaty."

The Young Republicans and the YAF planned a counterdemonstration in support of the war effort. The young conservatives were unaware that another counterprotest was being formed by the White Youth Alliance, Babs Minhinnette, and the Concerned Parents Association. Everyone was getting ready for a showdown. The anti-war groups planned to march, the YAF and Young Republicans planned to march, and the WYA and Concerned Parents planned to march. The Baton Rouge police department was in a quandary about what to do with all the groups marching at the same time.

Duke and the WYA met at the Minhinnette house to make signs for the protest. They began the march on campus, doing their best to offset the larger liberal demonstration. Walking to the capitol, the WYA members were heckled by onlookers lining the streets. The racist group was shunned by both supporters and opponents of the war. Although there was a great deal of shouting, authorities made certain that enough police were present to maintain order.

By the time the three groups reached the state capitol, the mood had turned hostile. Speakers from the left unloaded a barrage of verbal attacks on the Nixon administration, the YAF countered with patriotic recitations, and Babs Minhinnette and Duke burned a Viet Cong flag. A total of about 2,500 people were involved in the protests.

The anti-war rally of March 5 marked Duke's last major activity with the White Youth Alliance. The group had served its purpose. Duke had learned how to organize people who shared the same racist beliefs. But he knew the WYA would never be anything more than a small, racist college club. The real problems of white people were far more important than picketing left-wing speakers. Anyway, Duke was preparing to leave for Laos as soon as the semester ended. His focus had been diverted from the present to what lay ahead.

Before he left Baton Rouge, Duke said goodbye to Babs and Virgil Minhinnette. It was the last time they would see each other for more than six months. The Minhinnettes had provided Duke with the influence of a strongly supportive second family.

There was a small going-away party at the Minhinnettes'. The White Youth Alliance and the Concerned Parents bid farewell to the young man who had galvanized their ideas about racism. Chloe had already headed back to Florida for the summer, so Duke went straight to New Orleans to pack for Laos.

In retrospect, the transition from high school to college had proved turbulent for Duke. Away from the Klan and the Citizens Council, he had experimented with far-right radicalism, which in the end only left him frustrated. Duke was a racist, not a Nazi. An obsession with maintaining the white race and western Christian heritage would dominate his future.

CHAPTER TWELVE

Wanderlust

WHEN HE ARRIVED HOME, Duke found a Pan American Airlines ticket waiting for him on his bed at his parents' house on Jewel Street. He would be home for only two days before the first part of his journey was to begin.

Duke had been able to make contacts with many far-right extremists around the world through his many connections with the White Youth Alliance and the Ku Klux Klan. With help from Jim Lindsay, he had arranged to meet with them along the way. Most of them were college professors, writers, politicians, or students who were members of racist or far-right organizations. Duke may have abandoned the White Youth Alliance, but he was still intrigued by the far right. The time spent with his father in Laos was intended to be a period of reflection. But Duke had spent too many years studying racist ideology to totally disassociate himself from radicals altogether.

Duke left New Orleans in mid-May for his first stop enroute, Honolulu, Hawaii, where he found an inexpensive room at the Young Men's Christian Association. The YMCA would prove to be a favorite place to stay throughout his trip.

He spent his first three days sightseeing around the island on a rented bicycle, climbing Diamond Head, visiting Pearl Harbor, and touring local museums. But Duke wanted to meet with other right-wing extremists at the University of Hawaii, and Lindsay's connections helped set up such meetings. They allowed the inquisitive student of racism a chance to interact with racists from different cultures.

This would be his method of operation for the next seven months as he traveled the world. Hawaii was more of a vacation for Duke than an educational experience, and he spent most of his time swimming in the ocean and learning to surf.

His next stop was Tokyo. "I'll never forget the sight as we flew in over Tokyo Bay," said Duke. "There was a line of ships and barges as far as the eye could see. I knew then what an impact the Japanese would have on the economic future of the world."

He found a room at the Tokyo YMCA and toured as much of the city as possible the first day. "I was very impressed by the Japanese people," Duke said, "and by the cleanliness of the country and the lack of crime. Japan was the first mono-racial [*sic*] country I had been to. I could see what a country could do if its racial heritage is preserved."

Touring Japan by rail during the next week, Duke visited historic landmarks and museums. He took time away from traveling to meet with ultra-conservative advocates at universities. It was in Japan that Duke found there were many advocates of other racist theories.

He recalled, "I met people in Tokyo who felt that the Japanese culture was being threatened, just as I see the white culture being decimated in America." The exchanges opened up a new dimension of racism for him. The realization that racist societies existed across different racial boundaries excited the young traveler, further heightening his curiosity.

Duke left Japan after a week. He made a brief two-day stopover in Hong Kong, but was taken aback by the mass of people living there. "I got my first real visual sense of what overpopulation was and what the effects might be on us in the future," he said.

The last stop before arriving in Laos was Thailand. Duke was impressed by the antiquity of the country. "I began to understand Asian people [while] in Thailand," he said. "When I visited my first Buddhist temple, it made a great impression on me. The difference in culture was amazing."

Duke spent his last two days in Thailand by himself. He read on the beach and tried to unwind from the past two years at LSU. He then took a train to his next adventure, Laos and the administrative capital of Vientiane.

Laos is an ancient culture that has existed for almost five thousand years. It has been invaded by primitive tribes, Siamese warriors, the French, the Japanese, and finally by its surrounding neighbors during the Vietnam War. A part of French Indo-China, Laos was recognized as an independent nation by France on July 19, 1949. Laos has continually been divided because of the ethnic differences of its people. With a population of almost 3.5 million, Laos is a backward country that has never known a stable government.

Because of the political turmoil within its borders, Laos remained neutral during the Vietnam War, making the country a haven for Chinese, Cambodian, Thai, and North and South Vietnamese trying to avoid conflict. The official position of Laos was one of non-alignment with communist and non-communist factions fighting in Vietnam. Both the United States and the Soviet Union maintained active embassies in the country. In 1961, the U.S. had sent military advisors to help train the Royal Laotian Army, which maintained ties with the U.S. until the Lao government collapsed in 1975.

The American presence was strongly felt throughout areas held by the Royal Army, although officially there were no U.S. troops in Laos. Anti-communist forces occupied about one-third of the country, and Vientiane, like most other large cities, was still free. The USAID had transferred Colonel Duke from Vietnam to Vientiane, where he lived alone in a rented house in the international section of the city.

Half the people of Laos are ethnic Lao, who are descendants of thirteenth-century Thais. Mountain tribes of Sino-Tibetan and Thai ethno-linguistic heritage live in the northern part of the country, while Vietnamese and Chinese descendants predominate in the central and southern areas.

There were no trains in Laos, so Duke could ride only as far as the Mekong River, which separates Thailand and Laos. Standing alone on the bank of the river with only a duffel bag and a carrying case, he realized he was a long way from home.

Vientiane was directly across the river from where the train stopped, so Duke hitched a ride on a small boat used by locals as a water taxi.

"I was taking this boat across the Mekong River," Duke said, "and the driver had a radio playing very loud. The radio announcer was speaking Lao, so I didn't pay much attention until I heard a song by Credence Clearwater Revival called 'Born on the Bayou.' I was amazed by the backwardness of the Mekong River halfway around the world and at the same time listening to music about Louisiana."

Duke's father was waiting when he arrived. They went straight home to a small stucco cottage with a garden. Colonel Duke preferred to eat his meals at home and he had a full-time cook and housekeeper named Mythyng. She was a small, middle-aged Lao who spoke very little English. During the plane trip from New Orleans, Duke had read as much as he could about Laos. He learned a few sentences in Lao, which endeared him to Mythyng, and the two soon became the best of friends.

Because Laos had been a part of French Indo-China, the city of Vientiane might be called a small version of Paris. Colonel Duke was glad to have David living with him. Since most of the USAID work was outside of Vientiane, Colonel Duke was out of town about half the time. When he was home, the two Dukes often would go to a French restaurant for dinner.

"Some of the best memories of Vientiane were images from the relatively brief period of French occupation of Laos," recalls Duke. "On one hand, I enjoyed a culture that was so dramatically different from that of the United States. Then on the other hand, as a lover of animals, I saw a country where small animals such as cats, squirrels, and dogs were never seen because they were eaten by the local populace."

Colonel Duke had applied for a job on his son's behalf with the American Language School in Vientiane, and David was accepted for a position teaching Lao military officers basic military English. Although he had been refused advancement in the ROTC program at LSU, no one at the State Department bothered to investigate Duke's recent past.

"It's very easy for things to fall through the cracks with government bureaucracy," he said. Teaching class would be as close as Duke got to being in the military during the war. But it nevertheless provided him with a means to "fight communism."

Classes were held in a large, white stucco building, which resembled a junior high school. The small classes were made up of only twelve students each. The officers would repeat phrases that the teacher thought were necessary to converse in simple military English. It was not uncommon for instructors to teach their charges obscene phrases, passing them off as acceptable English. Rather than say good morning, for example, the unsuspecting group would sometimes begin class by shouting, "Your sister is a whore."

Working for the State Department, Colonel Duke and David held red diplomatic passports which helped cut through the local bureaucracy. Colonel Duke was often invited to parties at various embassies or at the homes of high-level diplomats. "There was not much to do in town," Colonel Duke said, "and David enjoyed meeting people from different countries." There was a private country club for the use of Americans, and David spent most afternoons swimming.

Duke was serious about "joining the struggle against communism" and worked extra hours with the Lao troops. He was given a military award by the Lao officers as their their most respected teacher.

Although he was hired to instruct students in proper English, Duke could not pass up an opportunity to preach a little racism. Each group had interpreters and the class would often have open discussions. One day the topic turned to the differences in ethnic groups and the effects of the homogenization of Southeast Asia. Duke tried to explain his philosophies about racial differences in the United States, which prompted one officer to comment, "A black person must be like a water buffalo. Very strong, but very little brain." Duke did not argue the point.

The classes Duke taught were attended not only by purely ethnic Lao officers, but also by troops of Cambodian, Thai, Chinese, and Vietnamese ancestry. In class, he noticed the way the soldiers reacted. "Shades of race made a difference," he noted. "That taught me about race and the impracticality of mixing people from different cultures. Although they were all Lao citizens, the fact that their ethnic background was different set them apart from each other. The officers I taught reinforced the idea of race, because I saw different patterns, even among the different nations of Asia."

Colonel Duke owned a 1968 Chevrolet station wagon, and David used it to explore as much of Laos as possible. Occasionally, his forays took him into territory held by the communist Phat Lao. He would climb mountains or crawl through caves along the Mekong River. Not only was there danger from enemy fire, but also from the ever-present cobras which infest the area. Twice the venomous snakes were found in Colonel Duke's house.

One day while driving to school, Duke accidentally ran the station wagon into the rear of a Russian diplomat's vehicle while trying to avoid a bicyclist. "I didn't know who I had hit," Duke said, "until a big, blond Russian got out of the car."

The damage was not extensive. The Soviet understood English and talked with Duke for an hour. After he saw Duke's red passport, the discussion turned to politics. President Nixon had just announced he was planning to visit the People's Republic of China to open dialogue with Chairman Mao. That prompted Duke to ask the Soviet what his thoughts were regarding the Nixon trip.

"He said that white people should stick together," said Duke. "He said the Soviet Union had more ethnic troubles than the Americans had." Only David Duke could get into an automobile accident with a Russian halfway around the world and find a friend with whom to discuss racist ideology.

The United States was officially neutral as far as allowing American soldiers to engage in combat or supply materials for the Royal Army directly. But independent pilots were contracted by the CIA to deliver materiel at night to Lao soldiers fighting in the countryside. These flights were known as "rice runs" and illegally used American men and money to supply small bases in the jungle.

Duke was offered a ride on one of the airlifts after being in Laos for a month. "I wasn't home at the time of David's first ride with the Air America planes," remembers Colonel Duke. "Otherwise, I wouldn't have let him go. It was very dangerous and was also illegal for him to be on the missions. But he wanted to participate in any way he could."

The pilot would head to a predetermined destination as soon as the sun had set. When he spotted an airstrip, the plane would fly about ten feet off the ground, and the co-pilot would push out the cargo to people waiting below. By the time he left Laos, Duke had participated in twenty flights, with only one close call. On a mission to Ban Houei Sai, in the mountains northwest of Luang Prabang, Duke's plane was hit by mortar fire.

"I heard a noise, then felt a hard push on my side," he said. "A piece of the mortar lodged in my belt." When Col. Duke heard of the incident, he forbade his son to join any more of the illegal missions.

The original purpose of Duke's going to Laos was to take a new look at himself. He had begun to attend church less frequently, but Colonel Duke insisted they both go to church each Sunday. The Duke family had always attended Protestant churches, but in Laos Colonel Duke regularly attended mass at a Catholic church. An American priest named Father Menger ran the church, and he and the younger Duke became friends.

"He was really a great guy," said Duke. "He was very anticommunist and taught me a lot about Catholicism."

Teaching at the American Language School was not a fulltime job, so Duke found he had a great deal of spare time. He began writing articles that were not totally racist or anti-Semitic. "[In] Laos," he said, "was the first time I got a magazine article published back in the States." Since age three, he had been an avid reader, and writing provided him an outlet to express his ideas.

After five months, Duke prepared to leave Laos for an extended return trip to the United States. He had corresponded with Chloe, who was about to graduate from LSU. The White Youth Alliance had quickly dissolved in Duke's absence. The WYA had been created by David Duke and no one at LSU had comparable racist skills. But he did not abandon his extremist ties and kept in touch with Jim Lindsay and others in New Orleans.

With time on his hands, Duke read volumes of racist material he brought with him or found along the way. The experiences encountered on the trip only reinforced his belief in the superiority of the white race.

The Dukes were traveling in the countryside on the day David was to leave when they encountered five thousand villagers fleeing a communist attack. The picture of peasants desperately running for protection, with their sole possessions on their backs, made Duke a more staunch anti-communist than ever before.

"The whole Laos experience gave me more opposition to communism and more respect [for] those who oppose it," he said. "Liberals were wrong in not standing up to the international communist threat."

Duke packed his duffel bag with all his possessions and said goodbye to his father. He then took off for the first stop on his journey back to New Orleans. Going to Laos had given Duke the chance he needed to be with his father, who was the only man who could really influence his radical son.

"I knew when David left Laos," Colonel Duke said, "that he was a better man." He tried to persuade his son of the importance of working within the American system.

The young Duke had been able to accumulate extra money while working with the American Language School, so he mapped out an extended return trip that began in Rangoon, Burma. Rangoon would only be a brief stop, however, because "Burma was a shut-down country." After only one day, he was ready to move on to India, a stop that permanently influenced Duke's commitment to racism.

India was first settled by Aryans, a warlike nomadic tribe. Many people believe they produced the purist white race in the world. The name India comes from the Sanskrit word for Aryan, and during the reign of the Third Reich, Germany glorified the early conquests of these conquerors and claimed the white people of Western Europe were directly descended from them.

On arriving in Calcutta, Duke was astounded by the conditions of the city. "The backwardness of the people and the incredible poverty made a tremendous impact on me," he said. "The dirt and trash on the sidewalks, children with bloated bellies . . . it was like looking at a nightmare." Duke stayed in Calcutta just long enough to visit some Hindu temples before taking a plane to New Delhi in the north.

Duke located a room at an inexpensive hostel, and found New Delhi much more to his liking. "New Delhi was a mess, but much better than Calcutta," Duke remembered. Unlike Laos, New Delhi was filled with cats, squirrels, rats, pigeons, and other small animals. "It was not that the Indian people were any wealthier than the Lao," he said, "but the Hindu religion taught them to respect animals, not to eat them."

New Delhi was filled with libraries, museums, and universities, where Duke researched racist philosophy. He had made arrangements to meet with a right-wing Indian politician and numerous college professors. They agreed with Duke's theories that the white race would be lost to race mixing in America, just as they thought it had been in India. Duke was glad to see members of other races felt the same threat he saw in the United States.

"I wondered why a civilization would rise and fall," said Duke. "India was once a great and powerful country, ruled by Aryans. Now it's a nation of starving, racially mixed people."

While traveling in India, Duke made friends with a student from England named Rodney, whose father was a pilot for British Airways. After meeting with people and seeing the sights of New Delhi, Duke wanted to visit the Taj Mahal, located in Agra, only a few hours by bus from the city.

David and Rodney met at 4 A.M. to take the bus to Agra. They searched for a cafe so Duke could eat breakfast, but when they saw how unsanitary the conditions were, they decided to wait.

"People with dirty hands would take a plate or cup someone had just used, wipe it once with a filthy rag and put it out to be used again," Duke observed.

Duke's English friend found a taxi driver who would take them to Agra for twelve dollars, which sounded like a bargain.

And with a private driver, they would be able to stop along the way. Duke ordered the driver to stop at the next place serving food so they could eat. Finally, they found a small bazaar on the side of the road that included a cafe. The street market was filled with snake charmers, fakirs, and other live acts. But Duke got to eat an egg sandwich.

They watched an animal act as they were preparing to leave. There was an emaciated trained bear, which was being beaten by its owner. "I wanted to do something to help the animal, but Rodney and the taxi driver said the local authorities would frown [on it]," said Duke. "I felt it a little strange that on one hand these people could worship cattle and rats, then on the other hand be so cruel to [other animals]."

About halfway to Agra, near the town of Mathura, they noticed an ancient temple that had been reduced to ruins by the ravages of time. They told the driver to stop so they could get out of the car for a better look. The two walked off the main highway for twenty yards and came across an old road paved with perfectly cut stones.

"The road had obviously been made a long time ago by very special craftsmen," Duke said. "You could see how level and straight it had been engineered."

As they approached the temple, they could see it had once been a great edifice. Duke was amazed by the beauty of it, especially up close. "You could see that there [were] once inlaid precious stones, along with carved artwork in every stone block," he said. Duke and Rodney took a few minutes to view the temple and take pictures, then Duke went around back to further explore the ruins. Over the centuries, the temple had virtually collapsed, leaving only two main walls standing. He walked around one wall and was startled to discover an Indian girl about eight years old sitting alone.

"She was skeleton-like," he recalls. "She had been sitting on the ground and slowly stood up when she saw me coming. I'll never forget her big brown eyes and her bloated belly. She had a huge sore on her shoulder that was covered with flies, and she would try to brush them away but they would come right back."

Duke put some rupees in the little girl's hand, and, without saying a word, she turned and walked away.

"My eyes swelled with tears," Duke said. "This made every study I had ever made come alive in flesh and blood. I realized then that the preservation of our heritage was life or death. . . . We should live the same way as our fathers. If I didn't do something, someday our descendants in the United States could be sitting in a dilapidated Lincoln Memorial, begging for handouts from foreigners."

The experience at the temple convinced Duke that what he believed all along about race was correct. "I realized my life would be dedicated to the cause of protecting the white race," Duke said. "I knew then that there was no turning back. I knew exactly that the struggle was represented in that forlorn little girl."

The two travelers continued on to Agra and the Taj Mahal. Completed in 1648, the Taj Mahal was built by the Mogul Emperor Shah Jahan as a mausoleum for his wife Mumtaz Mahal, who had died in childbirth. "The visual impact of the sunlight on the Taj Mahal made it look skull-like," Duke said. "It reminded me of the art of Aryan Indo-Europeans."

His three-week tour of India was climaxed by three days in Bombay, which Duke described as "thoughtful." He spent time meeting with a number of racist professors and political figures. He also did some shopping in marketplaces which sold every imaginable type of reading material. Duke purchased some anti-Zionist literature that he said "could not have been sold openly in the U.S. because of Jewish pressure."

He next flew to Karachi, Pakistan, which Duke felt was "dirty, decaying, and offered nothing of interest." He flew out before sunup for a two-week trip to Israel. Duke hoped the experience would crystallize his views of world Zionism.

Duke was traveling alone, and it was easier for him to carry his clothes and personal items in a large duffel bag. As the jet approached Ben Gurion Airport in Tel Aviv, the flight attendants handed out instructions for passing through Israeli customs. Because of the conflict in the Middle East, Israel has developed one of the strictest-controlled airport security systems in the world.

Suddenly, Duke remembered the anti-Zionist books purchased in India. He almost panicked at the idea of explaining the pro-Palestinian books to Israeli soldiers. "When you're twenty-one, you just don't think about a country having 'forbidden books' but that's the way it is in a very repressive state like Israel," Duke emphasized. "I knew the [Anti-Defamation League] had files on my activities in the U.S. I'm sure they passed [them] on to Israeli officials."

Customs officers were checking luggage and strip-searching everyone. As he moved closer to the front of the line, Duke imagined what the inspectors might do when they discovered his duffel bag was filled with anti-Zionist books. "There was absolutely nothing I could do at this point," Duke recalls.

The customs officer asked Duke for his passport, which he politely handed over. To his surprise, the officer looked at it, wrote down his name, issued him an entry visa, and told him to proceed. What luck, he thought! It then dawned on Duke that his red diplomatic passport had saved him from probable arrest or immediate deportation as an undesirable.

It is interesting to note that if Duke attempted to enter Israel today the story would be much different. In today's computerized world, Duke's reputation as an anti-Zionist would not be overlooked. After he wore a Nazi uniform to protest the William Kunstler speech in New Orleans, the Anti-Defamation League began following his anti-Semitic activities and notified Jewish organizations throughout the world about him. Duke is one of the most detested political figures among Jews, not only in the United States but throughout the world.

Duke took a room near the city of Jaffa on the Mediterranean Sea, not far from Tel Aviv. He toured the country, taking in as much of its ancient history as possible. But he was not satisfied with just looking at Israel. He wanted to know first-hand what the country and the people were all about.

"They were building a Nazi society," he contends. "As a Christian, I felt the persecution that the Zionist government was conducting."

Time not spent visiting historic places was devoted to conversations with Palestinians and some Israelis. "I was very impressed with the people I met and the racism I saw," he said. "When I spoke with the Palestinian people, it softened my positions about Jews and blacks in America. By looking at the oppression of the Palestinian people in Israel, I saw what blacks had been through back home."

Nevertheless, he had hardened his positions against what he calls the advantageous treatment Israel gets from the United States and the rest of the Western world.

The night before he was to leave, Duke returned to his hotel after an all-day outing at the beach. The woman at the front desk informed him that two men from the Israeli government had wanted to look in his room so she had let them in.

"It was not messed up, but I could see that someone had been digging through my things. My airline ticket was on top of the dresser, and I could tell that someone had looked in it." Without bothering to eat dinner, he went to bed, deciding there was not much he could do about the Israeli government at that time.

The next morning Duke went for a final swim in the Mediterranean Sea before leaving for the Tel Aviv airport to catch an El Al flight to Istanbul. When the jet finally took off, Duke was happy to leave Israel. He wondered about the government visit. Surely they must have known about his background as a radical racist.

On the El Al jet, Duke had a chicken salad sandwich and a soft drink. The jet arrived in Istanbul about 9 P.M. Duke was too tired to eat and went straight to a hotel to get a good night's sleep.

"I woke up the next morning with a terrific headache, but I was only planning to be in Turkey for a couple of days and I wanted to see all the sights I could, so I caught a bus for Bosporus," Duke recalls.

Duke headed for the nearby rocky straits of Bosporus for a day of sightseeing. His headache grew worse and he became nauseous. The bus driver stopped at an Esso gas station so Duke could get to a bathroom. He could hardly sit and suffered from diarrhea, vomiting, and a high fever.

"I thought I was going to die," said Duke. "I knew I was in a life-threatening situation, and I was determined to get medical treatment in Athens, Greece, at the American naval base" 350 miles away across the Aegean Sea.

Dizzy from the fever, Duke left the bus and found a taxi to drive him back to his hotel. "I knew I was sick, but I also knew that I didn't want to go to a hospital in Turkey." He grabbed his duffel bag and took another taxi to the airport, where he was able to catch a flight to Greece. In Athens, Duke was barely conscious and collapsed in the back seat of a taxi after asking the driver to take him to the U.S. naval base.

Duke was unconscious for three days. After he was admitted, the hospital notified Colonel Duke in Laos of his son's condition.

"The doctors phoned me at my office in Vientiane and gave me the news that my son was in critical condition in the naval hospital in Greece," said Colonel Duke. "They told me he had a very rare and sophisticated poison and that if he had not gone to a modern hospital with their toxicology equipment, he would have died."

A twenty-one-year-old American tourist's dying of food poisoning in Turkey would have gone virtually unnoticed outside of his immediate family. The local authorities would have notified the American Embassy, which would have notified the deceased's family, and the matter would have been dropped.

Duke surmises that the Israeli government became aware of his past and sent the two men to his hotel room the night before he left Israel.

"It would have been very easy for them to have disposed of me by poisoning my sandwich on the Zionist El Al flight to Istanbul," Duke claims. "I don't know if the Mossad poisoned me, but I think it is very possible."

The theory that Israelis may have poisoned Duke was greeted with great skepticism by Yigal Bander of the Washington-based American Israel Public Affairs Committee.

"I don't think Israel would have found David Duke a great threat at that time," he commented. "It's just not something the government would do. If the Israeli government was at all interested in disposing of David Duke, he wouldn't be here now."

After five days in the naval hospital, Duke was released but suffered from severe stomach cramps for weeks. He traveled around Greece for five days and saw as much of Athens as he could.

"The Greek culture was the high point of the artistic world," he said. "I would lie for hours between the Doric columns of the Parthenon and gaze upward at the temple and the blue autumn Greek sky."

The next stop on the trip back to New Orleans was Rome, where Duke stayed in a convent. He had arranged to meet a number of right-wing Italian politicians and devoted most of his time in Rome to visiting with them.

"The people I was meeting with agreed with what I had been saying the past few years," he said.

While in Europe, Duke found a number of extreme right-wing politicians who had heard about him and gave him encouragement "to get home and [continue] the struggle." It was not difficult for Duke to find people with similar beliefs once he had established himself as an extremist.

His lasts stops were in Munich and London. He was able to meet a number of established racist groups and investigated the possibility of forming a worldwide youth group. Both Germany and Great Britain have large numbers of right-wingers with whom Duke established contact for the first time.

Duke headed back to the United States for Christmas. He had kept in contact with Chloe the entire time he was away. She had just graduated from LSU and had moved to New Orleans to wait for her racist boyfriend.

When the jet arrived in New Orleans, Duke was glad to be back in the United States. He had grown emotionally during the journey and was ready to fulfill his destiny.

"I remembered that little girl at the temple in India," said Duke. "I was anxious to get to work."

David Duke displays a copy of the *Crusader*. (Photo by Michael P. Smith)

CHAPTER THIRTEEN

Commitment

THE BLACK PRISONER STARED Duke straight in the eyes, not three inches from his face. "I'll have your ass tonight, white boy," he said in a low, angry voice.

The man was a giant, at least six-and-a-half-feet tall. He stood so close that Duke could smell the inmate's foul breath.

Accenting the misery, the sweltering June heat made the tiny jail cell feel like an oven. Duke and his two young Ku Klux Klan associates stood motionless in the Orleans Parish Jail and wondered what lay ahead. Standing up for racist ideas in the past had been as simple as opening their mouths and saying what they believed was right. But now the young Klansmen were silent as six black prisoners waited for Duke's response.

As he was about to answer, a jailer suddenly entered the cell, ordering the three white youths out for further processing. Relieved, they quickly left the cell, but not before the large man gave Duke one last menacing look. It was Duke's second arrest and would prove to be life-threatening.

Duke had spent the previous seven years searching for direction in life that could fulfill his drive to achieve. He was convinced that the standard of living of the white race was rapidly declining because of government programs and a news media tilted toward non-whites.

As soon as he returned to New Orleans, Duke had busied himself preparing for his life's work as a racist leader. Mrs. Duke's illness had forced her to leave Jewel Street and move to Oregon to live with Dotti. Because the family home was empty, Colonel Duke had leased it, so Duke was forced to seek new lodging. He found a small, inexpensive apartment in Metairie. He also bought a used Ford Fairlane sedan and set out to work.

Chloe had graduated from LSU and taken a job teaching at a black Catholic girls' school in New Orleans. She wrote Duke throughout his travels, remaining in Louisiana to be with him when he returned. She was still in awe of him from his outspoken days at LSU and had become another "Dukie" devoting her life to "the struggle."

While on his trip, Duke devised a plan to form another group that could accomplish more than the White Youth Alliance. He wanted to be involved in racist politics, but LSU and Free Speech Alley were not a large enough forum. With Jim Lindsay's help, Duke created his next organization, the National party, which was intended to be the political youth group of the Ku Klux Klan. Lindsay and other right-wing-extremist businessmen from across the country funded the venture. They opened an office on 3210 Dumaine Street in New Orleans in early January of 1972.

Young Klan members from across the country moved to the city to help Duke put the National party together. Louis Darn of New York, Hamilton Barrett of San Francisco, and David Duke formed the nucleus of the newly founded organization.

Their salary of two hundred dollars a month was barely enough to live on, so the two newcomers moved in with Duke in his apartment. Money was not a major factor at the time. They were twenty-one years old and devoted to the goals of the Ku Klux Klan and the cause of white racism. Members in positions of authority within the Klan have always seen Duke as a future leader who would transcend the traditional stereotype of an ignorant redneck bigot.

The structure of the National party was the same Duke has used throughout the years to further his racist theories. He would be president of the group, formulate policy, and become editor of its monthly publication entitled *The Nationalist.* It was modeled after the Ku Klux Klan newspaper, *The Crusader.* Like the White Youth Alliance, the National party used the Klan symbol of a circle with a cross in the center. And like all white racist publications, *The Nationalist* warned of imminent danger unless whites acted to stop the growing nonwhite population in America.

Within a month of its formation, the National party had almost six hundred members in the south Louisiana and Mississippi area, as well as on college campuses across the country. Duke tapped into former members of the White Youth Alliance by working diligently to recruit high school students.

"The National party was geared to young people, high school and college students," Duke explains, "but we had a good number of older working people who joined the cause. The idea was to get the racialist message to young people before their philosophies were molded by a biased media."

On Christmas Eve, a seventeen-year-old high school senior was raped and murdered by a black man in the New Orleans area. Duke used this tragedy to form the first protest by the new group. It was billed as a torchlight parade to be held on Friday, January 21, 1972. To promote the event, Duke composed a leaflet with a picture of the murdered girl, along with the headline, "White people . . . what does it take?"

The flyer was aimed at white students, and Duke hoped to motivate them to join his cause by cultivating their innermost racist fears.

"Does it take the rape of your own girlfriend or daughter by a black savage on the rampage to make you become involved?" the leaflet continued. "It is time to stop the black plague now. . . . Join arm and arm with other whites who have suffered from Black Terror in our schools and in our streets." The flyer urged interested parties to contact "David Duke, Leader of the National Party," and listed the group's telephone number.

Because the Klan had been watched closely by the New Orleans police intelligence squad, Duke made certain all city laws were obeyed and that the demonstration would be non-violent. He had requested a parade permit, which was granted by the city. A motorcycle police escort was hired to lead a protest march from City Hall to Jackson Square in the French Quarter for a final rally.

Two meetings were held at the National party headquarters on Dumaine Street, on Sunday, January 9, and on Friday, January 14, to organize the march and make certain that police did not have any reason to arrest marchers.

"Certain members of the New Orleans Police Department were terrorizing us," Duke alleges. "They would come to meetings and photograph everyone entering the headquarters and went so far as ticketing cars that were parked legally."

On the morning of the march, Duke, Louis Darn, and Hamilton Barrett were making kerosene lanterns out of old Coca-Cola bottles. "Louis and I went and found dozens of old Coke bottles and brought them back to the headquarters to use for lanterns," said Duke. "Hamilton bought some kerosene and we filled a bottle up and put a small rag in the top and lit it to see if the idea would work."

The idea worked fine, but unbeknownst to Duke and his confederates, the NOPD intelligence squad had them under surveillance. The three were quickly arrested and charged with filling glass containers with a flammable liquid, which is against the law in New Orleans because such containers can be used as molotov cocktails in a riot.

The three were taken into custody and booked at central lockup in downtown New Orleans. It was Duke's first encounter with police, something he looks back on with a sense of pride.

"Not being afraid to be arrested while standing up for your rights is what this country was founded on," Duke said. "People from our Founding Fathers right up to the present day have had to endure hardships from repressive authorities to get the justice they deserved. If you are not willing to sacrifice for what you believe in, then there is no use in being free."

The Klansmen pooled their money, which was just enough to meet bail for two of them. Duke volunteered to stay in jail while the other two went to find Jim Lindsay.

"I was put into a holding cell with five black prisoners," said Duke, "and I did the best I could to keep them occupied until Hamilton and Louis could come back to get me out. I gave the prisoners a lecture on black pride and we really got along okay." Darn and Barrett found Lindsay and he immediately gave them money for Duke's release.

Before the young Klansmen could be arraigned, Lindsay's lawyer met with the judge. He explained that the charge against the young radicals was bogus. Because kerosene is not considered a Class A flammable liquid, it can be legally stored in glass containers. The judge agreed and promptly dismissed the counts against the activist. The arrest made Duke painfully aware that the road before him would not always be smooth. In the future, he would have to be careful.

The rally proceeded as scheduled. About three hundred young people carrying Coke-bottle lanterns marched alongside Duke and his two racist partners. Jackson Square was crowded with onlookers when Duke delivered a racist speech denouncing the establishment for "failing to protect hardworking people from black savagery." The audience of protesters shouted, "White power!" Duke had won a private victory over the police intelligence squad. It later proved bittersweet, at best.

Chloe remained with Duke throughout the march. She was now as active in the National party as he was. She was steadfastly devoted to him, following his lead without question, something he demands from all who are close to him.

One of the older high schools in New Orleans is Francis T. Nicholls, located at 3820 St. Claude Avenue. The school nickname originally was the Rebels, in honor of the Civil War general and former governor whose name the school bears. Over the years, the school became predominantly black. Many of the black students were opposed to being identified with a Civil War hero. Some students wanted the name changed to Panthers to coincide with the radical Black Panthers. When the issue came to a vote at the school board, Duke and several hundred high school students picketed the meeting, attracting local television coverage and the further ire of the police intelligence squad. The school board finally settled the dispute by changing the nickname to Bobcats, which allowed both sides to claim victory.

1972 was a presidential election year. As could be expected, Duke and his National party members were campaigning for Alabama Gov. George Wallace. Wallace, a segregationist, had run for president in the Democratic party in the past and in 1968 had formed a third party which carried much of the Old South.

Since the National party already had an office, its headquarters easily doubled as the Wallace for President campaign center. Working with Wallace aides in Montgomery, Alabama, Duke organized kids who went door to door campaigning for the segregationist governor. They distributed bumper stickers, tee shirts, and other campaign paraphernalia in white areas of New Orleans.

Duke raised money to keep the campaign going, with all the proceeds put into a separate account from the National party. The police intelligence squad contacted officials at the Wallace headquarters in Montgomery and asked them if their

New Orleans office was being run by Ku Klux Klansmen. The representative at Wallace headquarters apparently said the Wallace organization had nothing to do with the KKK and disavowed any knowledge of Duke or the National party. This was just what the intelligence squad had hoped to hear.

The police immediately arrested Duke, Darn, Barrett, and Chloe, charging them with theft by fraud for illegally collecting campaign contributions.

"I felt so helpless," said Duke. "The police handcuffed us all with our hands behind our backs like common criminals."

They were taken once again to central lockup, booked, fingerprinted, and placed in a small holding cell. They separated men from women, so Chloe was not able to draw support from Duke. Unlike the first time they were arrested, none of the group had much money, and Jim Lindsay was out of town.

"We were put into a cell that was no more than six feet by nine feet," said Duke, "and left with six black criminals." It was late June and very hot, and Duke was dressed in a short-sleeve shirt and a pair of slacks, which he would soon give up for prison clothes.

There was a telephone in the cell and Duke tried numerous times to contact Lindsay or his attorney, but to no avail.

"I was using the phone trying to find Jim Lindsay," said Duke, "when this big black prisoner was put in the cell with us. He walked right over to me and told me to give him all the money I had. I was taught by my father to stand up to bullies, but I thought this was one of those places that the rule didn't count, so I just told him that I couldn't help him."

The black prisoner just stared at Duke. The door opened and two trustees came in to escort the Klansmen to their next destination. As Duke was leaving the cell, the black prisoner walked over to him and snarled, "I'll have your ass tonight, white boy."

Duke rejoined Darn and Barrett in a larger cell on the second story of the prison which was being used as a holding area for drunks. "It was getting late and there were no chairs and it was real dark. So we sat on the floor that was soaked in vomit from drunks that were there before us," Duke said. They waited in the sweltering heat.

Finally, the young racists were given a meal of cold cuts, bread, and coffee. It was not much of a meal, but at least they were together.

"As I lay on the floor," said Duke, "I could smell the vomit. Suddenly we realized that the place was crawling with roaches. I thought about Chloe and what she must have been going through and how helpless I felt not being able to help her."

Duke figured someone must have gotten word to Lindsay. It was 3 A.M. and Duke was beginning to worry. Maybe no one knew the four Klan members were sitting in parish prison. "I didn't know what the Wallace people would do," said Duke. "If they didn't recant and tell the truth, that we were acting on their behalf, then we could all be in jail for a long time."

Arraignment was held the next morning. Duke and his followers were taken in chains, along with accused murderers and rapists, to court. "This is what our government does to kids who try to change the system," Duke remarked bitterly. The Klansmen had slept in the filth the previous night and certainly looked like criminals.

The magistrate asked them how they pleaded and Duke responded, "Not guilty." Since none of them had any money or relatives living in the area, they were turned over to the jailer for processing. Chloe did not phone her parents for help because they would not have approved of her getting arrested with Duke. Anyway, she would rather have stayed in jail than be separated from the man she idolized. Duke asked the judge if they could be released on their own personal recognizance, but the request was promptly denied.

The Klansmen were taken to a holding area in the courthouse. It was a large room containing three smaller cells.

"I was put in a cell with eighteen Negroes," said Duke, "and I could see Chloe in the next cell being mistreated by black women. They were cursing her and threatening to hurt her later, but she was a lady the entire time and never spoke back to them. I wanted to help her, but we were separated by steel bars."

After about an hour, the racists were taken to the processing room to check their belongings and prepare to start serving real jail time. Orleans Parish Jail is notorious for being a tough prison, and the prospects looked dim.

Duke contends that while in jail Chloe was offered drugs in exchange for sex.

The racist inmates were all sprayed for lice with an insecticide, then separated. Chloe was led away to the women's section while Duke and his friends were put in a large room with fifty prisoners. The room contained only one toilet, which was broken, and the floor was awash with urine.

"When the guard slammed the steel door, I had a feeling of hopelessness that I had never known before," said Duke.

Most of the inmates were black career criminals, so Duke and his clean-cut friends stood out in the crowd. There was a metal table where a young white prisoner sat staring with an expressionless gaze. "I asked him what was the matter," said Duke, "and he told us how the black prisoners had raped him the night before while [several people] just turned their backs."

The cell leader, a large black man, walked over to the table, pointing at Louis Darn. Darn was young-looking, even for twenty-one. He had bright red hair, which led the black inmate to call him "Cherry-top." The black prisoner then informed the rest of the prisoners to leave Darn alone because he was going to make the young Klansman his "wife."

To make matters worse, one of the inmates had a radio tuned to a local black station. Things had calmed down for a few minutes when a newscaster announced that four members of the Ku Klux Klan had been arrested for stealing money from the George Wallace campaign.

"The entire room turned all at the same time," Duke said, "and looked straight at us without saying a word."

This was not the place for the blonde, blue-eyed Klansman to be, but there was absolutely nothing Duke could do about it. The cell door opened and the guards brought in another white detainee. He had shoulder-length hair, which made him stand out even from the Klansmen.

It was not long before the inmates began to harass the newcomer, calling him "girly" and threatening to rape him when the sun went down. Duke and his two friends by this time feared for their lives.

"The trustees knew that there was going to be trouble between [the long-haired inmate] and one of the smaller, loudmouthed blacks." said Duke. "They made everyone except eight Negro inmates and him leave the cell. . . . But once the whites were locked in the next cell, it was shocking to realize that eight Negroes were still in the cell with [him]."

One of the black inmates pulled a crude, homemade knife and shook it in the youngster's face. He wrapped a towel around his hand to defend himself from his attackers. According to Duke, the other prisoners took turns beating the young white inmate with a mop handle until his thumb was broken and his face was covered with blood.

"We just stood with our hands gripping the bars and watched in horror what was taking place," Duke remembered with anguish.

As soon as the battered youngster collapsed on the floor, the prisoners who attacked him backed off. Duke and the rest of the inmates were returned to the cell as though nothing had happened.

"I rushed to [his] side and tried to clean his wounds," Duke said. The prisoners harassed Duke, but Duke quietly continued, shaking all the while. The black prisoners continued to threaten the smaller Klansmen with talk about making them slaves and calling them bitches.

On Thursday afternoon, a social worker came by for his biweekly check on the condition of the prisoners. "The social worker was a guy who tried his best to help us," said Duke. "The first thing he did was to get [the inmate who had been beaten] out and get him some help."

Duke related to the social worker what had happened but was informed there was nothing he could do to help. Duke thought that if he and the others caused enough trouble, the guards might put them into solitary confinement. The social worker warned Duke that solitary would be just a smaller cell with three or four of the worst blacks in the prison.

"By now, I thought we were idealistic kids who were ulti- mately going to die for our beliefs," said Duke.

Duke and the others made a vow that no matter what in- timidation or physical torture they faced, they would never allow themselves to be sexually abused. They would "fight to the death, if need be."

It was now 7 P.M. and the sun would be setting soon. Duke could not think of anything worse than being in jail. Suddenly, the door opened. Duke looked up in horror at the same black prisoner who had threatened him the day before. He was an escaped murderer who had been recaptured the night of Duke's arrest. He walked straight over to Duke and laughed. He grabbed the Klansman by the shirt and again snarled, "I told you, your ass is mine tonight."

"I was absolutely desperate by this time," Duke said. "I had to think of some way to get us out of that cell, and soon."

He had an idea and asked to speak to the social worker. Duke told the man about the new prisoner and the danger he and his comrades would face unless they were separated from the population. The social worker repeated that there was nothing he could do. The Klansman lied and said he had gotten in touch with his attorney. Duke told the social worker that if he did not help them, he would be held responsible for the actions of the other inmates.

The social worker thought for a moment, then agreed to do what he could, but made no promises. About an hour later, a trustee brought the three Klansmen to meet with the head jailer. He said they could be segregated from the other inmates, but only for one night.

Duke, Darn, and Barrett were taken to the original holding tank they had been put in while being processed. It still reeked of vomit and roaches scurried everywhere. But they were relieved at least to be away from the other prisoners.

The three were finally able to reach Lindsay the next morning, and he arranged bail for the bewildered activists. "I was never so happy in my entire life," Duke said, "than when I walked out of Orleans Parish Prison."

Lindsay contacted people at the Wallace for President headquarters. They sent a telegram admitting that Duke had worked for the Wallace committee, and all charges were dropped against the four defendants.

"It was a terrifying experience for me," Duke emphasized. "I did a lot of soul-searching during that period and realized just how high the stakes were going to be if I was going to continue the struggle for white rights."

The affair only strengthened Duke's beliefs and made him more convinced than ever that his beliefs were correct.

"The experience made me understand that America truly needed to reform its prison system," said Duke. "And that white prisoners must be protected from being raped by Negroes, even behind bars."

Duke realized at that point that if he intended to become a racist leader, he would have to get a college degree. "I knew I would [then] have the credentials to meet any new challenges which lay ahead," Duke said.

If the prison experience helped to further solidify Duke's commitment to racism, it also made him realize just how much Chloe believed in him as a person.

"Here was this beautiful Southern belle who was willing to go through the hell of jail for me," said Duke. "I had never thought about getting married until after we got out of jail and I saw Chloe again."

Chloe Hardin became Mrs. David Ernest Duke in a small Presbyterian service in West Palm Beach, Florida, on September 9, 1972. None of Duke's relatives was in attendance.

With $150 between them, the Dukes spent their honeymoon in Key West, then headed for Washington state. The two traveled in Duke's Ford and camped along the way at Yellowstone and Glacier National parks. Duke remembers, "We had the world by the tail."

In Seattle, the couple stayed with Duke's sister, Dotti. She remembers her brother had become a changed person.

"They were both so happy," she said. "They were just like any young couple."

Duke was proud to be married and planned to stay in Seattle to look for a job.

Since her health had deteriorated, Maxine had been living with Dotti.

"I wanted to become close with my mother again," said Duke. "I wanted to spend time we never really had when I was growing up."

The Dukes both found employment at the Sea-Tac Motel near the airport. Chloe worked as a waitress while her husband was the bellhop. Dotti let them stay with her until they found a small single-room apartment.

The newlyweds worked double shifts and saved their money for college. Duke tried unsuccessfully to get a job with Boeing. He considered attending the University of Washington, but because they were non-residents it was too expensive. After a few months, the two decided to return to Baton Rouge, where Duke once again enrolled at LSU.

Following the incident in New Orleans with the Wallace campaign, the National party was disbanded.

"The others were demoralized," Duke explained. "It was hard for young kids to keep fighting when the police would continually harass us."

Louis Darn went home to his family in New York, and Hamilton Barrett returned to California. But Duke had not thrown in the towel. He kept in contact with Jim Lindsay and maintained his affiliation with the Klan.

"Seattle gave me a lot of time for reading, writing, and deep reflection," Duke said. "I wanted to go back to Louisiana and the Klan and get to working for the principles I believe in."

With a two-thousand-dollar downpayment borrowed from Colonel Duke, the newlyweds purchased a home at 1195 Swanee Drive in the Eastgate subdivision in Baton Rouge for $11,500. It was a modest brick house that was to serve as a Klan center for years to come.

Chloe rented space from the Woodlawn Baptist Church and started a day care center. The center and Duke's occasional writing provided sufficient income for the two. It was a good arrangement, and the couple was very happy.

Being back in Baton Rouge, they frequently saw their old friends, the Minhinnettes. Duke had matured. He was not as outspoken as he had been in Free Speech Alley days, but was still committed to the same racist ideology he had always espoused. From now on, David Duke would channel his ambitions through the Ku Klux Klan.

CHAPTER FOURTEEN

Off to Be the Wizard!

DUKE RE-ENROLLED AT LSU in January 1973, but was no longer active politically on campus. He immediately got involved with the Klan. Within days of returning to Baton Rouge, he had made contacts with old "Dukies." It would be only a few months before Duke was elected grand dragon of the Louisiana chapter of the Knights of the Ku Klux Klan, as well as national information officer. He knew exactly what road he would follow and where it would one day lead, and he was eager to get started.

Like his father, Duke could not sit back and patiently wait for things to happen. He quickly began formulating the program he hoped would expand the Ku Klux Klan beyond its historical borders as an outcast racist group. He foresaw a political force that one day could elect candidates to public office from within its membership.

Jim Lindsay had secretly been grand wizard of the Knights of the Ku Klux Klan. But he was molding his racist apprentice to one day take over the reins of leadership. Duke's job during the next three years was to increase visibility and membership of the group so it could bring about the desired social changes.

There were only two or three hundred Klansmen in the Louisiana and southern Mississippi area who were members of Lindsay's organization. The group merged with a couple of smaller ones in New Orleans in 1971, but Lindsay had done little to promote it. He devoted most of his time to his rapidly growing land business. Once he could convince Duke that the Klan should be packaged in a new and modern format, Lindsay felt that they would have the key to white victory.

Duke became active with the Klan, and within a year he had increased its numbers to 3,000 by actively seeking college and high school students. Traditionally, the Klan had been composed primarily of rednecks and bigots, but Duke reached out to people the racist organization could have never attracted before.

Extremist groups such as the Ku Klux Klan drew support from all kinds of people, and Duke associated with radicals far more dangerous than himself.

Bill Wilkinson and Jerry Dutton were a couple of traditional Klansmen who would later prove to be among Duke's strongest enemies. Dutton became grand wizard after Jim Lindsay's death and ran the organization for five months before falling out with Duke over the direction of the organization. An ally of Wilkinson, Dutton was part of the old guard who wanted to maintain the Klan's traditional role, while Duke was trying to change the Klan into a strictly political force.

As one Klansman said, "David Duke has always been lookin' for what he could get out of the Klan. Bill and Jerry were interested in lookin' out for whites."

This disagreement in philosophies would one day cause a breach so great that Duke would leave the Klan. But that would come later. In the beginning, everything seemed to be going Duke's way, and he made the most of it.

Duke rented a building at 6667 Airline Highway in Baton Rouge for the Klan's first headquarters. It was a large building with a huge sixty-foot sign that read "Knights of the Ku Klux Klan," with the group's insignia of a circle with a cross in the center. Duke did not draw a salary from the Klan, so the office was run by volunteer workers who were more than willing to devote time to their new leader.

As grand dragon of Louisiana, Duke opened Klan chapters throughout the state in Monroe, Lafayette, Lake Charles, Shreveport, and New Orleans. He also created "units" on many college campuses and high schools. This was the same tactic he had employed with the White Youth Alliance and the National party. But he was more successful with a known commodity such as the Klan.

"At first it was a real struggle," said Duke. "We had to start from scratch. We would live from month to month, barely making enough money to pay the light bills. But it was a really exciting time."

Duke took on the task of publishing a newspaper. Like *The Racialist* and the *The Nationalist, The Crusader,* which was originally called *The Klansman,* used Duke's talents as writer, publisher, and editor. It averaged twelve pages an issue and bore the slogan, "The Voice of the White Majority." The paper contained articles on racial demographics, affirmative action, international communism, and Zionism, as well as the virtues of "hard working white Christian Americans."

Early issues sought to make the Klan appear as a middle-class conservative group, appealing to people who had previously been turned off by its emphasis on racism. Such articles as "Klan Fights Busing" and "Support Farmers" were deviations from strictly anti-black formats of past Klan programs. That is not to say the issues were not filled with some old fashioned "black baiting."

Monthly the paper carried cartoons depicting blacks assaulting whites or blacks as watermelon-eating Uncle Toms unable to function without the direction of the anti-white federal government. There was one cartoon entitled "Where will it all end?" depicting a white taxpayer, shackled by six blacks clamoring for money from government programs. Blaming the problems of whites and blacks on the federal government has been a tactic Duke has always used to give credence to his extremist political ideas. Making someone else the scapegoat has been a convenient way for him to promote normally unpopular ideologies.

As an example, in one issue in 1976, there was a crudely superimposed picture of presidential candidate Jimmy Carter kissing a black woman, with the caption, "Acting in his normal fashion." Although he knew better, Duke produced many blatantly bigoted articles aimed at ignorant people who could not follow the intricate racism of Duke's own extremist philosophies. If he cannot explain his racist ideas about blacks and Jews in an intelligent way, Duke has never been afraid to lower the standard of the conversation to terms the average bigot could understand by use of cheap racist slurs.

In an article in *The Crusader* entitled "Science Exposes the Equality Hoax," writer R. Arthur Armstrong claimed that, on average, blacks are intellectually inferior to whites. He went even further, contending, "It is doubted by some that the Rhodesian negroid even belongs to Homo Sapiens stock." The author repeatedly referred to blacks as Negroes and black children as pickaninnies, but still attempted to pass off the article as scientific fact.

Unlike the previous newspapers Duke had been associated with, *The Crusader* sold advertising space. These were not the usual cigarette or automobile ads found in most magazines. They hawked racist items such as record albums entitled *Ship Those Blacks Back* by Odis Cochran and the Three Bigots. The ad promised, "When you hear these Mississippi boys a-pickin' and a-grinnin' their musical hate and prejudice, you'll have more fun than a nigger in a watermelon patch!"

The periodical also featured Klan merchandise such as Klan robes and white-power shirts for sale. Willing buyers could also purchase 8-by-10 color photos of everybody's favorite Klansman, David Duke, available for just four dollars. Along with Klan garments and shoulder patches, a reader could buy

American, Confederate, and KKK flags and "Klan Calling Cards, Racial Purity is America's Security."

As he would later do in the NAAWP newspaper, Duke began selling hard-to-find racist books through Patriot Press, his bookstore in Metairie. Along with his own writing, selling anti-Semitic and neo-Nazi books has been a major source of income for Duke over the past seventeen years. Some books, such as *Race and Reason* by Carlton Putnam, had strongly influenced him as a student working at the Citizens Council. The books covered subjects ranging from fundamentalist Christian views to traditional conservative positions.

But a few of the publications were extremely racist or blatantly anti-Semitic. *The Hoax of the 20th Century: Did Six Million Really Die?* and *Six Million Reconsidered* were anti-Semitic books that attempted to disprove the Holocaust. Of course, Hitler's *Mein Kampf* and George Lincoln Rockwell's *White Power* were available, along with other books with such incredibly tasteless titles as *The Hitler We Loved and Why.* One could also purchase *Herman Goering—The Man and His Work.*

Duke has maintained that neither he nor the store were responsible for the information sold and "[do] not necessarily . . . endorse . . . everything found in them." A disclaimer further declared, "This material is offered in each case because, properly read from the racialist standpoint, it contains something of value and importance for a more thorough understanding of the forces and events which affect and have affected the vital interest of our race."

Duke has steadfastly denied he helped neo-Nazis by selling anti-Semitic literature and contended that he was only allowing a free flow of ideas.

"This is America," he emphasized, "and people should have the right to read anything they so desire. Although I condemn many of the things that Nazis did, there really hasn't been free access to material from both sides. It's the Nazis who want to burn books. You can go into any bookstore in the United States and find copies of communist books or pro-Zionist material, but I'm criticized for allowing free speech to occur."

But all of Duke's time was not devoted to writing *The Crusader* and organizing the Klan. He was a full-time student at LSU. The Duke's home on Swanee Drive was in need of repair so he did minor painting and other work until the house looked the way Chloe wanted it to be. She had been raised in an upper-middle-class family and, like Maxine, found it difficult to live the spartan life her husband had chosen.

This incredible devotion to "the struggle" later proved to be the downfall of their marriage. But in the beginning, Chloe traveled with Duke to Klan meetings and speaking engagements. They lived like any other newlyweds.

"It was a busy period," he said, "but Chloe was with me most of the time at the headquarters or when I traveled on weekends. She was active with the Klan and was a tremendous spiritual help."

Duke began writing for a living during this period. He found it was impossible to find a publisher willing to print anything by such a well-known racist writer. This forced him to use pen names, which he tried to keep secret. It worked in the beginning until his *nom de plumes* began to be known.

One of Duke's friends at LSU asked him to help write a book entitled *Finders-Keepers: Finding and Keeping the Man You Want.* Using the pseudonym James Conrad, Duke helped write the book, which sought to teach women how to "successfully meet and maintain a relationship with a man."

Finders-Keepers was a "how-to" book that contained helpful hints regarding what clothes women should wear to attract men, what diets they should use to keep slim, and the best way to find "intimacy through conversation." One chapter entitled "Toward a More Fulfilling Sex Life" detailed how men and women could best pleasure each other sexually.

Another piece of interesting Duke literature was a book entitled *African Atto*. It was a manual for blacks "concerned with fighting to win, fighting in the streets without any rules besides winning." Duke used the pen name Mohammed X in this guide, which gave elaborate explanations of how black power could be achieved through physical confrontation with "whitey." The author urged black attackers to use various kicks, chops, and punches against the evil white man. It further advised, "When you attack whitey, be sure that you racially insult and psychologically attack him, in addition to physical assault."

Duke defended writing *African Atto*, calling it a "spoof that was written to show that blacks were violent enough to buy this type of book."

As the Klan's national information director, Duke traveled throughout the country speaking at rallies and organizational meetings to an extent never before seen in the Ku Klux Klan. He was relentless in getting the word out that the "new Klan" had arrived.

"I wanted to get away from the stereotype of all Klansmen being ignorant bigots," he explained, "so I always wore a coat and tie to show that the leadership of the Klan was serious about making the organization grow. However, the Klan today doesn't exist simply as a memorial to the past accomplishments it made, but as a living instrument for the ideals of Western Christian civilization and the one element that makes them possible, the white race."

Duke believed the Klan had been founded as a civic group to help suppressed white Southerners. He thought that by hard work the new Klan could be cleansed of its history of lynching and terror. Once again, Duke's sincere naivete overshadowed his intellect.

In an attempt to modernize the racist group, Duke publically repudiated actions of "rogue Klan groups who engaged in illegality." He initiated as part of the Klan oath pledges of non-violence, along with the vows of brotherhood.

After he had established chapters throughout Louisiana and Mississippi, Duke got the idea to send press releases to as many media markets as possible. Radio, television, and newspapers were targeted so the public could get to see and hear Duke, who might possibly persuade some to join the ranks of the Klan. With a handful of volunteers, including Babs Minhinnette, Duke stuffed and mailed thousands of envelopes with letters touting himself and the Ku Klux Klan.

Duke was still unknown nationally and only one or two radio stations called wanting to hear the grand dragon. He was asked to make a few speeches at selected colleges, and one Baton Rouge television station asked for an interview, but nothing really big happened. That changed when the Klan office received a call from NBC's "Tomorrow" show. At the time, "Tomorrow" with host Tom Snyder was one of the most popular talk shows on television. It gave Duke a chance to be heard and seen by millions of people.

"Tomorrow" scheduled Duke to appear in early January 1974, sending round-trip tickets for both him and Chloe. Just the excitement generated from the pre-show hype would have been considered a public relations victory for Duke. No grand dragon of any Klan organization had ever been given a full hour of national exposure—and this dragon was only twenty-three years old! It was the break Duke had been waiting for since he first stepped onto the soapbox at Free Speech Alley.

Before leaving to do the show, Duke met with Chloe and a few Klan members at the Minhinnettes' house for a practice session. Someone took the role of host Snyder and ridiculed Duke's views on every issue imaginable. By the time the make-believe "Tomorrow" show was finished, Duke was ready.

"We worked for hours with David," remembers Babs Minhinnette. "We knew that Tom Snyder and the rest of the

Jewish liberals were going to try to gang up on David, so we asked every question we could think of that they might ask."

As the Klan couple left for the NBC studios the day of the show, they were excited about the prospects of David's being on national television with a late-night audience of seven and a half million viewers.

"We were pretty nervous," said Duke. "But I was prepared to present my ideals for the first time and to let the people of America see and hear viewpoints that, up until that time, had been suppressed by the media."

For a number of reasons, the "Tomorrow" show was important in understanding David Duke as a person and what he really believes. From the outset, he shocked the show's host, who was expecting an ignorant redneck. "You are intelligent, articulate, young, and charming," Snyder said. Duke has used his appearance, which is non-typical of a Klansman, to his benefit throughout his career. He immediately gained the attention of the "Tomorrow" audience simply by looking like a normal person instead of a moron in a pair of overalls.

Snyder was expecting the grand dragon to talk about the history of the Klan and attack blacks, but the discussion was dominated by Duke's personal philosophies. The Klansman has always transcended the organizations he has been affiliated with, making himself and his beliefs the main focus of attention.

The show began with Snyder introducing Duke as the youngest grand dragon in the history of the Ku Klux Klan. The host asked him if the group was a fringe organization. Duke did not answer the question directly, but rather gave a dissertation on why the Klan was needed.

"The government," he said, "has intimidated Klan members. They have intimidated people who have associated with the Klan. The Klan is an organization [that] has been working for power for the white majority in this country. And we feel the government of the United States, the leadership of the country, will not act in the best interest of the white majority."

It was not the type of answer Snyder had expected. Fumbling, he asked Duke why it was so important that the white majority be protected.

Duke answered in a calm, rehearsed voice, "The most important things to us are the great white Western Christian civilization and the ideals which subscribe to that. We want a decent country. We want a society where children can grow up to be all they can be. A good school system. A society where men and women can walk the streets of America without fear. We want a society that will reflect the very highest ideals possible."

At the beginning of the telecast, Duke was noticeably nervous and his answers seemed almost prerecorded, but he loosened up as the show progressed.

The subject then turned to Klan treatment of blacks, whom Duke referred to as Negroes until Snyder called it to his attention. Duke said that Martin Luther King, Jr., and many people in the civil rights movement were communists or associated with communists.

Duke accused the media in America of being anti-white. He said television personality Ed Sullivan had once embraced Fidel Castro, calling him the George Washington of Cuba.

Snyder never tried to pin Duke down on anything he was saying. At one point in the program, Snyder even went so far as to say, "It's difficult to argue [with] your points." It was exactly the type of response Duke had been hoping for. Snyder had prepared for the show with questions directed toward someone much less articulate and intelligent than Duke.

After a commercial break, Snyder reintroduced his guest as "Dave" Duke, which made the Klansman appear to be almost a family member. Snyder seemed taken by Duke's charm, and the show belonged to Duke from that point on.

When Duke said "we feel" when speaking on behalf of Klan members, he was referring to himself. His philosophies are far more sophisticated than those of the people who follow him. Although he speaks as their leader, the vast majority of them really cannot comprehend his complex racist ideologies. Duke has his agenda, which reflects David Duke. The Knights of the Ku Klux Klan was molded to fit his needs and aspirations, not the other way around. Duke is mentally far superior to the people that surround him and is looked upon by some as a racist messiah.

Snyder asked if Duke would want blacks to live separately from whites. "The black race does exist," Duke said. "It is not a myth. The white race does exist. It is not a myth. And they are two distinct peoples. They each have their own culture and heritage. I want them to become all that they can become. And the only way they can really do that is to be among their own people, because they have a different makeup." Duke contends today that he favors the libertarian position of not forcing either integration or segregation, but allowing individual choice. Duke does not elaborate on how civil rights could be protected in such a situation but stands by his theory that races and ethnic cultures are generally better off living separately and having their own schools.

When asked about the United States' policy regarding Israel, Duke responded with a statement that clearly describes his attitude regarding Jews: "This is my belief," said Duke. "I think that it is obvious our policy [is] slanted. I think it is very one-sided. I think that America does not need to get involved in another Vietnam-type of war . . . that we should be concerned with the interests of the majority of the American people and not this tiny Jewish minority which has such a disproportionate control over the media in this nation — television, newspapers, movies. I think our policy in the Mid-East is quite indicative of the Jewish power in this nation."

Duke may not have thought his statements unreasonable. In an article in *The Crusader* entitled "Why Oppose the Jews," he spelled out "why the Klan has always been opposed to the Jews." Duke tried to link Jews and communism with the black civil rights struggles of the twentieth century and accused former Supreme Court justices Louis Brandeis and Felix Frankfurter, both Jews, of compromising the safety and well-being of white Americans.

Blaming the news media for troubles in America is nothing new for politicians, but Duke based a large part of his political platform on alleged Jewish control of the press and the entertainment industry. An article entitled "Masters of the Media" by Dr. William Pierce in *The Crusader* charged that Jews dominate the major television networks and newspapers in the United States.

Duke came across on the "Tomorrow" show as about as intelligent as someone with his beliefs could be. The things Duke said that night reflected the same philosophies he had been preaching since his days at Free Speech Alley. The show offered an excellent opportunity for viewers to see the real David Duke.

The response Duke received from national television was enormous. "We bested Tom Snyder," Duke boasted. "The show gave me national exposure and made it much easier to get my ideals across to many more people. And that's what it's all about."

The show did more than increase Duke's name recognition. It brought more than five thousand new dues-paying members into the Knights of the Ku Klux Klan. "It was incredible," remembered Duke. "When Chloe and I got back to Baton Rouge, we received a heroes' welcome."

In one night, Duke had become larger than the Klan. It was David Duke, the person, not the grand dragon of the Ku Klux Klan, who would be invited to speak on television and radio shows. Duke may have become America's number one racist, but it was just what he wanted. He turned on the steam in an effort to make himself a major force for white power.

For years to come, *The Crusader* offered cassette copies of Duke's appearance on "Tomorrow" for five dollars, billing it as "one of the finest racist presentations."

Calls and letters came pouring into the Klan office asking Duke to appear on radio and television shows and offering college speaking dates. Over the next couple of years, Duke would receive paid speaking engagements at such varied places as the University of North Carolina, Harvard, the University of Southern California, the University of the Pacific, and Vanderbilt University. Duke never drew a salary from the Klan, but was compensated for his speechmaking. He was paid $800-$1,200 per engagement, plus expenses, which was not bad, considering the lifestyle he and Chloe were accustomed to living.

"Most of the money I made giving lectures went back into the Klan," Duke claims. "Chloe and I were dedicated to the struggle, and I traveled so much that there was never much money left to save."

Even with the Klan activities and traveling, Duke managed to complete his final year of college. He carried a heavy load of twenty-one hours of credit plus a three-hour credit exam in sociology. His last semester at LSU resulted in an A or B in every subject. After six tumultuous years, he finally had enough credits to graduate. On May 17, 1974, David Duke was awarded a bachelor of arts degree from LSU.

Colonel Duke was in Laos and Maxine was too ill to travel, so his parents were not able to attend the graduation ceremony. But Duke's new family, including Babs Minhinnette and Chloe, were there to cheer their racist leader as he climbed another rung on the ladder.

"I knew when I was sitting in jail in New Orleans," said Duke, "that unless I got my degree, I would never really be able to accomplish the goals I had set for myself."

The grand dragon was now a racist celebrity of national stature. He was spending most of his time away from Baton Rouge and Chloe. College speaking dates were combined with local radio and television talk shows. Duke was fast becoming proficient at public speaking. Unlike the early days at Free Speech Alley, he was now cool under fire and much less caustic.

"It wasn't that I had changed what I was saying," he explained. "I just had matured, and people began to see me for what I was, a person who stood up for his race, as Jesse Jackson stands for his, one who struggles for his faith and heritage, as Menachem Begin does for his. My arguments [attracted] more and more attention."

Duke always has been someone who inspires feelings of either love or hate, with not much in between. The response he received on college campuses was no different. At Indiana University, students were expecting a hooded goon but found Duke to be quite different.

"They came to hate me," he said, "but gave me a standing ovation. They really cheered me on." However, wherever he went there were always those who fanatically opposed what he stood for, which forced him to continually deal with hecklers.

Normally, Duke would give a speech which was followed by a question-and-answer period. At Vanderbilt University in Nashville, Tennessee, four white girls welcomed him on stage by chanting "David Duke is puke! David Duke is puke!"

There was a microphone set up at the foot of the stage so students who wanted to ask Duke questions could simply walk up to the mike and speak. A white female student and a black male student walked up to the stage, arm in arm, and kissed each other.

The woman took the microphone, smiled, and asked, "Well, Mr. Duke, what do you think about this?" The crowd waited silently for Duke's response.

The grand dragon looked at the black student and asked, "What is a gentleman of your caliber doing with white trash?" The audience went wild with laughter, allowing Duke to carry the day.

Most students disagreed with Duke's racist ideas. But the fact that he had the courage to say the things he did made him a folk hero to many. It was a larger repeat of Free Speech Alley. Seeing David Duke is similar to going to a freak show at a carnival. The more outlandish his remarks are, the more curious people become.

Time spent at Klan rallies and on college campuses and talk shows were the best moments of Duke's life.

"They were good times," he remembers. "I really enjoyed the programs, being in debates, reaching people with ideas. We were the total underdog. There was so much prejudice against me and the Klan. But a great number of people were able to hear the truth."

Duke has loved debating racist issues ever since his junior high school days at Ganus. He was now proficient in speaking and had developed his debate skills into an art. He had been reading and studying racist literature for more than eleven years and was an expert on the subject. He saw the Klan as an organization built upon honor. He looked upon himself as a knight defending the rights of oppressed whites.

Duke regards debate as a form of jousting. "To meet with hateful and biased people and debate freely, to see the power of ideas in action, and to walk out a winner is the greatest thing in life."

Speaking at rallies and appearing on talk shows was only part of his regular routine. As his exposure grew, so did the demand for his time. He debated Black Panther Bobby Seale, Ralph Abernathy of the Southern Christian Leadership Conference, columnists Carl Rowan and Jack Nelson, and the Reverend Jesse Jackson.

In addition to debates, he frequently appeared on television programs, including "The Donahue Show." Nationally syndicated radio talk-show host Michael Jackson invited Duke to appear on his program in Los Angeles.

"He was very clever," remembered Duke. "It was the toughest interview I ever did."

Duke did so well on the "Lou Gordon Show" in Detroit that Gordon allegedly apologized for having him on the air. "The mail was overwhelmingly critical of me and pro-David Duke," he told the *Sunday News.*

It had gotten to the point that Duke was in greater demand than all the other Klan officials combined. Although he was only the grand dragon of Louisiana, he was always the choice for interviews and speeches, rather than the present grand wizard Jerry Dutton. Duke used the office of national information director to supersede everyone else in the movement. Dutton was from the old school and represented the Klan Duke wanted to forget. It is difficult to imagine that the racist David Duke could find another racist obnoxious, but Dutton never fit into Duke's plans for the Knights of the Ku Klux Klan.

In 1974 the city of Boston was going through a difficult time over federal court-ordered school busing to achieve integration. There was sporadic violence and even death in the city known as a bastion of liberalism.

"I got a call from two men from South Boston," said Duke, "and they asked if I would come up and help."

Duke flew to Boston, followed by Klansmen Greg Durel and Ken Terry, who drove up from Baton Rouge.

"The reception we got was absolutely fantastic," Duke said. "It was the first time I realized that average people across the U.S. were interested in what I had been saying."

Duke stayed with local Bostonians at their homes in the predominantly Catholic-Irish section of the city.

"It was just amazing," he said. "I would walk down the street and strangers would yell, 'Thank God you're here' or 'We need your help.'"

Duke tried in vain to obtain a permit to hold a rally in the Boston Common, the same place where the Revolutionary War had begun. He was able to hold an outdoor rally at a park which newspaper accounts estimated drew a crowd of over two thousand people.

"I think the white people all over the country have a little more hope," he told the crowd. "We showed people there is opposition to busing in Boston. I think Boston will be the turning point in the fight. You are an inspiration to millions who want to be free of an oppressive judiciary that takes away your right to vote and replaces it with judicial fiat."

The crowd in South Boston loved what they heard and followed Duke around the area. The grand dragon stopped at every pub and was cheered on by the Bostonians.

A young husband and wife in South Boston invited Duke in for coffee the morning after the rally. They had a nine-year-old daughter who was affected by the busing order, which forced her to attend school in the all-black section of Roxbury. When the mother showed Duke the judge's order, tears filled her eyes. "What has happened to America, Mr. Duke?" she asked plaintively. It was a story Duke repeated often long after he had left Massachusetts.

The Boston Police Department could not wait for Duke to make a mistake. "I was very careful," he remembers, "not to advocate school boycotts or anything remotely illegal. I didn't want to give the Boston police any reason to arrest me."

But according to accounts by the Associated Press, Duke was partially responsible for an anti-busing demonstration that tied up Boston traffic for hours.

After he had stirred things up for over a week, Duke returned to Baton Rouge. The Boston incident was important because, at age twenty-four, David Duke had become the leading white-rights activist in America.

On a personal level, Duke had found the purpose in life he had searched for since childhood. "Boston had been the cradle of American liberty on the continent," he said. "I saw it now as the cradle of white resistance to busing that included the values and freedom that this country was founded upon."

Duke had become the defacto leader of the Knights of the Ku Klux Klan. It would not be long before he, Jerry Dutton, and Bill Wilkinson would part ways over accusations about a stolen mailing list. Dutton and Wilkinson split with the Knights of the Ku Klux Klan and started their own organization called the Invisible Empire of the Ku Klux Klan.

The November 1976 issue of *The Crusader* carried the following bulletin about Dutton: "After his attempt to take over our movement failed, he . . . attack[ed] our organization and the very best leader the white race has in America, Mr. David Duke."

The Crusader had been Duke's creation. Any attempt at a takeover by Dutton or anyone else would have proved to be fruitless. Duke had become larger than the Klan. Neither Dutton nor Wilkinson would prove to be any real threat to Duke's domination of racist leadership.

Finally, Duke was granted his longtime wish, and he was elected grand wizard of the Knights of the Ku Klux Klan. From now on, he would be known throughout the world as the leading spokesman for racism, anti-Semitism, and white power.

CHAPTER FIFTEEN

Making the Klan Work

ORGANIZING THE VARIOUS GROUPS Duke had been associated with had never been difficult. The Klan would be no different. Before David Duke, Ku Klux Klan meetings were held in secret at out-of-the-way farms or quietly at someone's house. It was not illegal to be a member of the Ku Klux Klan but very few people wanted to be publicly associated with the racist group. Duke boldly advertised rallies in newspapers and on radio.

One of these early rallies was held outside Baton Rouge at a famous country-and-western hall named the Old South Jamboree, near the town of Walker in Livingston Parish. It was a perfect location for a rally because the area had been a hotbed of Klan activity for many years.

More than three thousand people turned out to hear Duke and other racist "celebrities." Men dressed in white Klan robes diverted heavy traffic off the main highway onto empty fields surrounding the hall. Uniformed state troopers lined the highway, looking in disbelief at the number of cars and trucks arriving. Spectators from grandmothers to infants came to see "the biggest Klan rally ever."

Before the rally began, the audience milled around, talking and browsing at merchandise booths filled with Klan paraphernalia. The stage was adorned with Confederate flags, the

Klan insignia of the circle and cross, and a large banner reading "White Power." Finally, the band struck up "Dixie" and the evening's program began.

A lengthy invocation was delivered by a Baptist preacher dressed in a white Klan outfit, complete with matching white shoes. During his fifteen-minute prayer the preacher asked God to "deliver us from the heathen communists, the money-hungry Jews, and the enemies of this land, the Congolese welfarites [sic]." Each time he asked the Lord for help, the crowd responded in unison, "Amen!"

He then relinquished the stage to local Klan hero Bill Wilkinson. The good ole boy commended the preacher for a wonderful invocation and then introduced the luminaries for the evening.

The first speaker was a young lady who had developed flourishing careers in two disparate fields and had appeared on the covers of numerous magazines. While working in New Orleans she had contacted Duke and expressed a desire to help the Klan.

"Before she spoke," Duke recalls, "we carefully went over [her] speech to make certain she didn't say anything that might cause her embarrassment. We were happy to have her help, but we knew that if she said too many controversial things, it would come right back to haunt her."

When it was time for the petite beauty to address the crowd, she was visibly nervous. After all, this was her first speech at a Klan rally.

"The speech we had prepared went right out the window," remembers Duke. She was warmly received by the assembly, and although her speech consisted of only one sentence, it was more than enough to get her in hot water.

"Maybe when your wife or daughter or neighbor gets raped by a Negro," she declared, "you'll get smart and join the Klan."

As a result of that statement, the young lady soon found it impossible to work regularly in either field in which she previously had excelled. Doors were closed, and a large contract with a major corporation went down the drain.

The evening proceeded on schedule with a speech by Duke's ally, "Dr." James K. Warner of the Los Angeles White Christian Movement. Warner then introduced Duke, who entered from the rear of the hall to a standing ovation by the entire audience. As he walked to the stage, "Dukies" lunged from their seats to shake his hand or just to touch the grand wizard. Duke was mastering the art of arousing large numbers of people, and this rally would be similar to the hundreds that followed in years to come.

Dressed in a suit and with Chloe on his arm, Duke resembled a presidential candidate campaigning for votes. He sported a broad smile as he began slapping backs, kissing babies, and waving to the enthusiastic crowd. The chief difference between this meeting and a presidential rally was that the hall was filled with white-robed Klansmen.

Duke approached the microphone, looked across the room, and waited for the crowd to finish its applause. "Isn't it wonderful to see 2,700 people in one room together," he asked excitedly, "and all of them are white?" Thunderous applause followed. It was just what the audience had come to hear.

The grand wizard immediately attacked Washington for its Middle East policy and the "communist sellout in Vietnam." Duke continued by reminding everyone "how much you have lost because of integration." It was typical David Duke. He delivered the same racist message as the preceding speakers, but captured the attention of everyone present, including the police and the news media. He doled out tales about the resentment of "hardworking white Christians" who struggled to make ends meet despite "federal government interference." The audience wanted more.

The mood of the crowd changed from sociable to angry as Duke continued his barrage of accusations against Zionist domination of American culture. Everything from high unemployment to high interest rates was blamed on "Jewish interests."

He followed his anti-Semitic oration with a string of statistics about black crime and the decline of the standard of living of whites.

"The trouble with white people," Duke told the crowd, "is that we never stick together. No white person has the right to complain about being passed over for a promotion in favor of less-qualified blacks, no white has the right to complain about his child being attacked in an integrated school, or paying outrageous taxes for minority welfare to finance massive reproduction of illegitimates, unless they are willing to stand up and fight for our basic human rights!"

The audience peppered Duke's speech with chants of "White power!"

By this time the audience was becoming a mob. "This world is not meant for cowardly people," he continued. "Courage flows from our blood as heat is emitted from the sun. The real question is whether you as an individual will join in the struggle to save our people."

The audience was spellbound as Duke recited his racist litany. Instilling fear and paranoia into those receptive to his message has been a key to Duke's success.

Duke then led the wildy excited audience out of the hall into a nearby field for a final prayer and cross-lighting. The Ku Klux Klan claims it never burns crosses, but instead "lights the cross against the darkness." As the crowd gathered around the burning cross, Duke closed his speech with a tale of the early days of Reconstruction:

> "The white Southerner lay prostrate at the heel of tyranny. Most of the war was fought on Southern soil and there was tremendous devastation. Sherman's march to the sea was one of the most infamous acts of war in the history of this continent.

"Even the British in the American Revolutionary War did not burn the farms and homes of women and children to starve their opponents into surrender. Almost every Southern family lost family members in that great war.

"Then, after the assassination of our true friend, Lincoln, the radical Republicans came to power and decided to use the South like a vassal state to continue their political corruption and control over congress.

"Every Southern man who fought with the Confederacy or who served in any civil or state government was denied the right to vote. The great bulk of the voting population was disfranchised while the Negroes, who were 99 percent illiterate and who had no political history or experience, had total political power.

"Law broke down, barns were burned, men were robbed and murdered, women were assaulted. Sound familiar? Hordes of carpetbaggers descended upon the South, joined by the traitorous scalawags who were ready to exploit the politically immature Negroes and the powerless whites.

"At the last possible moment for white survival in the South, a handful of courageous men met in Pulaski, Tennessee. They were educated men. They created the Ku Klux Klan. In no time, they were 500,000-strong. They defeated the forces of tyranny and restored civilization to the South and, indeed, preserved it for all of America.

"And now, it is time again for a great movement for our rights and liberties, for now there is a new Reconstruction that this time is not just facing the South but all of America. Look around. Look at the changes in your neighborhoods, in the schools you once attended. You are losing the nation of your forefathers and mothers. Your children will grow up and walk as strangers in their own land, a land that will far more resemble Haiti or Guyana than the land of Jefferson, Washington, Lee, or Lincoln.

"We ask not to suppress anyone. We only seek to preserve our own rights, our own heritage, the things that make our hearts beat with joy and pride. We say that we have the right to survive.

"Listen to the call of the blood that flows in your veins. Can you remember the struggles your ancestors fought for your freedom that you now enjoy? Join with me in a Christian brotherhood that stands uncompromisingly for your rights, the Knights of the Ku Klux Klan!"

After the rally, Duke spent time recruiting potential members among the spectators. Most people in attendance were Klan members, but many came out of curiosity to see the man who had become a national spectacle.

There were booths staffed with volunteers ready to sign up anyone willing to "join the struggle" as soon as he parted with fifteen dollars.

"The rallies were always a tremendous way of letting people know the truth," Duke said. "Once they realized that they could make a difference, they became involved."

The Walker rally was just one of countless Klan meetings Duke sponsored across the United States, Great Britain, Canada, and Europe. He almost always spoke extemporaneously, so his speech was different at each stop. But the racist message he delivered never changed, and he always managed to find an audience. Although still in his mid-twenties, Duke was the biggest racist draw in the world.

Chloe became pregnant in late 1974. "It was just one more reason to keep working for the struggle," said Duke. "Knowing that I was about to bring another person into the world made me more determined than ever to see that my child had the same right to do and be all that he or she could be."

They had both wanted children, and Duke was elated at the thought of being a father. Because she was pregnant, Chloe no longer traveled with her husband to speaking engagements. Duke was out of town most of the time, speaking either at colleges or at Klan rallies. He was not really much help to Chloe during that period.

"It wasn't that I didn't want to be with her," he said. "I had a commitment elsewhere."

Chloe gave birth to a girl christened Erika Lindsay (named after Jim Lindsay, Duke's late Klan mentor) on August 30, 1975. Duke was out of town at a Klan function and did not arrive at the hospital until after the birth.

"Like most men," Duke said, "I wanted a son. For one second . . . well, you know . . . I wanted a son. But once I saw her pink feet, white tuft of hair, and her beautiful face, I was never happier."

It was a very important moment in his life, but soon he was back on the road promoting the Klan. Babs Minhinnette stayed with the mother and baby while dad was busy saving the white race.

In the fall of 1975, Louisiana was preparing to hold elections for all state offices, including legislative seats. Duke felt he was ready to run for office.

"The time was right," remembered Duke. "I looked for a race that I could not only air my views [in] but also win."

The seat Duke sought was for the 16th senatorial district held by a respected one-term incumbent, Kenneth E. Osterberger. Located in a very conservative area of Baton Rouge, the district contained some of the wealthiest people in Louisiana, as well as many middle- and lower-income neighborhoods. More importantly for Duke, it was almost all white. Another attractive point was that the district included LSU. Duke felt his connections with college students could be used as a base of support. Although many students were registered to vote in their hometowns, a large number voted at precincts near campus. With the help of his many Klan friends, Duke hoped to make inroads into Osterberger's conservative constituency.

Amiable and conservative, Osterberger was in the real estate business and was extremely popular with voters in his district. As was the case with many conservative Southern politicians,

Osterberger at the time was a Democrat, but has since switched to the GOP.

"We knew there was no way I was going to lose the election to the grand wizard of the Ku Klux Klan," Osterberger said in his soft Southern drawl. "So we decided to just ignore him."

Ignoring David Duke has always been easier said than done, and this campaign would prove no exception.

Since this was Duke's first run for office, he had to learn the political process from scratch.

"I was extremely naive about politics," he admits. "I had a wealth of beliefs and ideals but I didn't know the mechanics."

The campaign was run out of his house with the aid of friends such as the Minhinnettes and others. "We had a few Klan members helping us," Duke said, "but our real support came from students from LSU and New Orleans."

This would change as the election grew nearer and carloads of Klan supporters descended upon Baton Rouge.

Osterberger and Duke were the only candidates to qualify for the District 16 seat. "Since it would be just David and me," said Osterberger, "I decided to have a 'mini race' and not raise too much money."

This made good sense because Duke was known publicly only as a crackpot from Free Speech Alley or as the grand wizard of the Ku Klux Klan. The incumbent would prove hard for Duke to attack because his record in the legislature was so conservative.

"I felt I had done a pretty good job of reflecting the views of my constituents," Osterberger said. The voters would echo that sentiment.

The campaign material Duke used in his first race in 1975 was almost identical to that used in his winning campaign in 1989. His paid advertisements announced that he opposed "all attempts to increase taxes" and favored "halt[ing] the expansion of the welfare state." Ads further noted that Duke was against gun control, forced busing, and "reverse discrimination against white people in employment, scholarships, and promotions."

The grand wizard listed among his qualifications being a graduate of LSU as well as "working for the U.S. State Department in Laos." The Klan was never mentioned. Duke knows when to downplay his past and, for that matter, his present affiliations. He did say, however, that he had the experience to be a senator through "extensive legislative lobbying against bills discriminating against the White majority."

Duke's campaign material read like an article from *The Crusader*. Under the headline "Give the Majority a Real Voice," the Klansman noted that black legislators worked openly for the interests of their constituents and that many white politicians were "slaves to the black vote." He repeated his warning that whites needed a spokesman "to actively work for our interest and principles."

He attempted to shield his anti-Semitism by warning that white politicians who did anything significant on behalf of whites "will be called racist or incur the disfavor of the powerful political forces and the media."

It is almost impossible for Duke to pass up any opportunity to blast "the media masters."

He wrapped up his platform by proclaiming he was not ashamed to "stand up for the white majority." Duke prided himself on "openly talking about what most politicians are afraid to even whisper about." He insisted, "My most important qualification is my proven courage in standing up for my convictions."

Duke was trying to position himself as a mainstream candidate, but he said the same things in his campaign literature that he had been printing in *The Crusader*. One can even see the same racist message as far back as *The Racialist*. The idea that government should reflect the "heritage, traditions, and ideals of the white Western Christian civilization" remained Duke's philosophical foundation.

The Dukes—David and Chloe—appeared in ads as the perfect blonde, Aryan couple. He was convinced he had a real chance to win the election and wanted the public to regard him as a stable family man. Although he never mentioned the Klan in any of his campaign literature, he made no attempt to hide his racist affiliation. The Baton Rouge *Morning Advocate* carried numerous articles dealing with all Senate races. Whenever he was mentioned, Duke was identified as the grand wizard of the Klan.

In a press release supplied by Duke, he billed himself as "National Director of the Knights of the Ku Klux Klan, publisher of *The Crusader* and lecturer." He would not show his Klan affiliation prominently on his campaign material, but was proud of his position when speaking to the press.

Debates for all legislative races were sponsored by local television station WBRZ. When it came time for the candidates from District 16 to meet, Osterberger declined to appear with Duke.

"We thought it would be demeaning to appear on the same platform with the grand wizard of the Ku Klux Klan," said Osterberger.

Duke jumped at the chance for television exposure. The program was aired on Sunday morning. Since Osterberger had declined to appear, WBRZ was able to hype the event even more. The set was staged with two chairs, with Duke sitting in one and the other, labeled "Ken Osterberger," vacant. Duke was dressed in a conservative coat and tie and spent the entire half-hour delivering his standard racist message in his most sincere manner. Calm and well prepared, the Klansman was able to avoid his racist affiliations and have his own show, unimpeded by a cross-examining candidate.

Rather than spend air time defending his role as grand wizard of the Klan, Duke gave the audience a chance once again to hear him denounce liberals, blacks, and "the media."

The show was one more opportunity for Duke to use the news media, which he claims maligns him.

Supporters of Duke were not above political dirty tricks. It is the nature of racist politics to draw from the worst types of people. Two weeks before the election, Duke supporters from across the nation descended upon Baton Rouge to help their hero in the election.

"It was not uncommon," said Osterberger, "to see cars with Pennsylvania, California, and New York license plates covered with Duke for Senate signs."

Standing at busy intersections, "Dukies" could be found waving signs to passing cars. The help Duke received was one thing, but the intimidation his supporters dished out was another.

Osterberger's campaign office was located on Jefferson Highway in a busy part of Baton Rouge. Crank telephone calls to the office became frequent. Almost daily, the master power switch to the building would be turned off, causing the air conditioning to stop. More than one time a stink bomb was set off in the air vents, making it necessary to vacate the building. Of course, Duke was never anywhere near these occurrences, but one can suspect he enjoyed hearing about them.

A week before the election, Osterberger received a strange visit.

"My secretary," he recalls, "told me two men and a woman wanted to interview me for a documentary on the Klan."

One of the men claimed to represent the major newspaper in Lake Charles, the *American Press,* and the other two said they represented some television station. When they insisted on conducting the interview then and there, Osterberger decided something was amiss.

"It didn't seem right," says Osterberger. "For one thing, one of the men wandered around the room checking his light meter, even after I told them to call back the following day to request an appointment. And the woman kept asking questions that didn't have anything to do with the Klan."

After the trio left, Osterberger noticed that one of the windows to his office was unlocked. He then called the *American Press* and was told that no interview with him had been scheduled. Informed of the incident, Howard Kidder, Baton Rouge chief of police, initiated a check on the three and recommended that security measures be taken. For a brief period, police were stationed at Osterberger's office and his campaign headquarters. When one of the group called the following day, they were advised that Osterberger would not consent to the interview.

Osterberger suspects they were part of a scheme to photograph him in a compromising position, and since the election was only a few days away, there would have been little time to counter the ploy.

Being a gentleman did not prevent Osterberger from getting in a jab or two himself. Five days before the election, the senator took out an ad in the *Morning Advocate* entitled "Don't be hoodwinked." Voters were urged to "Re-elect Osterberger," but Duke was not mentioned by name.

"I didn't want to get into name-calling," Osterberger laughed, "but some of my supporters wanted to let everyone know about Duke's Klan ties."

The public attention Duke was getting as a Klansman running for office caused a great deal of resentment among a number of his detractors. Jerry Dutton and Bill Wilkinson had split from Duke, but were still bitter.

One day toward the end of the campaign, Wilkinson visited Osterberger, offered assistance in the campaign, and said he had information that would be damaging to Duke's candidacy. Osterberger decided to take the high road and declined the offer.

"I didn't want to get in the middle of a Klan feud," he said, smiling. "Besides, I knew I wouldn't need it to win."

Although he was busy campaigning, Duke continued to give speeches across the country on behalf of the Klan. He used every opportunity he could at rallies to raise money for the Senate race.

Since the birth of daughter Erika, Chloe had been unable to work regularly, so Duke made as many paid college appearances as possible to supplement their income. "He never was around the house very much anyway," Chloe said. When he was in Baton Rouge, Duke spent most of his time either at Klan headquarters or campaigning. Even during the busiest time of the campaign, Duke still managed to write and publish *The Crusader.*

The election was held on Saturday, November 1. To no one's surprise, Osterberger won, compiling 22,287 votes, or 66.8 percent, to the Klansman's 11,079, or 33.2 percent.

The *Sunday Advocate* described the election as "a strong showing by a young Ku Klux Klan leader." At the time, Duke was the youngest person ever to seek the Senate office. "We really ran on a shoestring," the challenger insisted. Duke's tally would prove be the most votes ever against Osterberger. Four years later, the Senator once again would face a Klan supporter, but this time it would be Duke's longtime friend, Babs Minhinnette.

Campaign finance reports showed that Osterberger outspent Duke by only $10,718 to $6,386. As would be the case in the future, most of Duke's contributions came from outside the district. The two largest donations were a $500 gift from a California woman and a $1,000 loan from Colonel Duke. The report revealed Duke had contributed $4,800 of his own money.

As a racist, Duke made the campaign something other than what it should have been. Ken Osterberger was, and remains, one of the most conservative members of a very conservative Louisiana Senate. But according to the *Sunday Advocate,* Duke "waged a campaign which made race an issue once again in

local politics." David Duke always makes race an issue. Whatever he does is based on race.

The Senate race of 1975 was important because it set the
stage for other bids the Klansman would make for public office. Proud of his racist ideology, the grand wizard was hardly
devastated by his first political defeat.

Duke waited for the election night results at his home with
supporters and close friends. "I learned from it," he declared.
"It was a great victory to know that over 11,000 people went
to the polls and voted for my ideals. The movement has just
started. We've just begun. This is not the ignorant redneck
from the hills voting for me. The voters are just about ready
for us."

State Sen. Ken Osterberger, Duke's first
campaign opponent. (Photo courtesy of
Ken Osterberger)

CHAPTER SIXTEEN

The Knights of the Ku Klux Klan

UNDAUNTED BY HIS LOSS to Osterberger, Duke trudged along, claiming victory of a sort.

"Making the public aware of my ideals," he argued, "was worth the time and effort we made in the first Senate race. We raised issues that never could have been talked about before."

The Crusader contended that the election defeat would be "the impetus for others who believe as we do to seek public office." In Duke's way of thinking, the failed election was one more step toward public acceptance.

Duke now had a wife and a daughter and was quickly becoming a racist celebrity. He had become the self-styled grand wizard of not only the Ku Klux Klan, but of most racist-minded people. Through his personality he would elevate the discussion of racism and anti-Zionism from whispers in back rooms to the forefront of international news.

The Ku Klux Klan rented an auditorium at Belaire High School in Baton Rouge for a Klan rally to be held Saturday, November 22. Duke went through the normal procedures required for permission to use school facilities. The East Baton

Rouge Parish School Board had approved the rental of the building at an open meeting, signing a contract with the Klan. The board was of the opinion that since the school was a public building, anyone, including the Klan, could have access.

Prior to the rally, someone contacted Dr. John A. Bell of the the U.S. Department of Health, Education and Welfare regional office in Dallas, Texas, and complained about the school's being used by the group. On November 20, a telegram was sent by HEW to the board declaring that all federal funds to the school system would be cut off if the Klan were allowed use of the building. At the time, the federal government was contributing eight million dollars annually, so the board immediately cancelled the contract.

Duke felt he was being treated unfairly by the government because of his racist ideology. He claimed his First Amendment rights had been violated and sought legal assistance from the American Civil Liberties Union in Baton Rouge the following day. The ACLU is known for supporting unpopular causes, but the Ku Klux Klan would prove to be a hard pill for even the most liberal members to swallow.

"It was purely unconstitutional," Duke said. "I had an obligation to protect [the right of] our group and any [other] group to use a public facility. Just because one leftist in Baton Rouge disagreed with our philosophies didn't mean we had to subjugate our rights of free speech."

The ACLU does not handle legal matters internally, so Duke was directed to one of the watchdog group's outside attorneys, Lawrence A. Anderson. Fresh out of law school, Anderson seemed an unlikely counsel for a racist such as Duke. He had attended LSU when Duke was making headlines at Free Speech Alley but occupied the other end of the political spectrum. Anderson had never met the outspoken racist, but "was well aware" of the Klansman's radical past. A political opposite of his new client, Anderson had been one of the major organizers of the Vietnam Moratorium Day event years before and was a liberal campus crusader.

"Although I was in ROTC in college," said Anderson, a Southerner, "I became liberal and was very opposed to the war."

A member of the Baton Rouge board of the ACLU, Anderson remembers receiving a request to look into the case from the local chapter president.

"I got a call from Duke," Anderson said, "asking if he could see me. He said he thought the Ku Klux Klan was being denied their constitutional rights and briefly explained the Klan's predicament with HEW. I told him to come to my office and we'd discuss it."

Duke went alone to meet with his new attorney, carrying the contract cancelled by the school board. "I didn't want to use a Klan lawyer," Duke said, "because they didn't have experience with First Amendment rights law."

Political opposites, the two men got long very well on a personal level. Before applying for the permit to rent the auditorium, Duke made certain all the necessary paperwork was in order. He wanted to make sure the case would not be lost on a technicality. After speaking with the grand wizard and hearing the facts, Anderson decided to accept the case. "I felt it was a gut check," he said.

Neither the Klan nor the ACLU had much money to pay attorney fees, so Anderson could be credited with making a strictly moral decision.

"It was simply a matter of civil rights," said the lawyer. "I was committed to the fact that the First Amendment is a right guaranteed to everyone, even the Ku Klux Klan."

With the idea that he was defending the right of free speech, Anderson promptly filed for a temporary restraining order seeking to prohibit the school board from cancelling the contract with the Klan. Because the HEW telegram had been the reason the board denied the Klan use of the building,

HEW was included as a defendant. The matter was set for a hearing with Judge E. Gordon West of the Fourth Circuit Court of the United States' Middle District of Louisiana.

The following morning Duke and his counsel went to court in Baton Rouge to find out what the judge's decision would be regarding the restraining order. Anderson had prepared numerous studies of identical cases where groups were denied access to public buildings. Each time the courts had ruled in favor of the petitioners.

"Frankly," said Anderson, "I drafted a winner. The facts couldn't be disputed."

Attorneys for both the school board and HEW were present to defend their clients' actions. Judge West asked the parties to meet in his private chambers to discuss the matter. Unaware that Duke was not an attorney, West allowed the Klansman to join the legal combatants in the chambers.

Judge West sat down, glanced at the brief, tossed it aside, and announced, "I read the paper this morning and your motion is denied." The judge had decided to let an appeals court take the heat if the Ku Klux Klan were allowed to take over Belaire High School.

"I couldn't believe it," Duke said. "We had no justice, only judgment by newspaper!"

The judge's ruling did not come as a surprise to Anderson, who had already prepared a writ of mandamus. The writ was filed once again with Judge West. He hoped the judge would look at the merits of the case and force the school board to honor the contract. In an unusual Saturday meeting, all parties involved gathered again in the judge's chambers. This time Judge West took time to hear oral arguments from both sides, but once again denied Anderson's request.

"I knew at this time," Anderson said, "that this case was going to be protracted."

Never one to let an opportunity slip by, Duke called a Klan rally that evening at headquarters on Airline Highway. The gathering at Belaire High School had been cancelled, but word of the site change spread to the devoted quickly. Anyone who mistakenly showed up at the Belaire auditorium was greeted by three hooded Klansmen who directed them to the new location. Over three hundred people braved near-freezing weather to hear exhortations of "White power" from the back of a pickup truck.

Television reporters and newspapermen filled the parking lot as Duke began an attack on the federal government.

"Why are we standing in the cold?" he asked. And then he answered his own question: "Because this is where all white people have to stand."

Surrounded by hooded Klan members, Duke, dressed in a suit, strummed the crowd's emotions. "If you were black," he told them, "the federal government, the FBI, and HEW would have made sure you and your family were warm inside the Belaire gymnasium." The people in the parking lot cheered and shivered.

Duke ended his speech by saying, "I'm not for censorship, We're not against anybody, blacks or Jews. We are for the white race. We should have the same rights." As he spoke of equality for all people, the audience responded with shouts of "White power."

Anderson next filed for a preliminary injunction with the U.S. Fifth Circuit Court of Appeals in New Orleans. "I knew we were right about the case," he said. "If I could get the judges on the appellate level to give me a fair hearing, I felt certain we'd win."

What had begun as a request for a temporary restraining order had turned into a full-blown courtroom battle. The final decision would eventually set legal precedent in the area of First Amendment rights. Because of continuances, the case could not be heard by the Court of Appeals until April.

After Judge West had denied the Klan the restraining order, Anderson filed for damages against the school board and HEW in state court in the 19th Judicial District. He also filed for another temporary restraining order, but again was denied satisfaction on the state level. Every avenue was being taken to let Duke and his fellow racists have their say. Duke has persevered throughout the years by using the system he so very much wants to change.

In legal briefs before the appeals court, government attorneys argued that the Klan's presence at Belaire would represent a greater threat to the government and the interests of the school than any harm the Klan might suffer through denial of their First Amendment rights to free speech.

"The violent and illegal purposes and methods of the Ku Klux Klan," the brief read, "are well known throughout the country and, in particular, in the Louisiana Parish encompassing the East Baton Rouge public school system." The brief further stated that the Klan had no First Amendment right to use a school building "if the use of such facilities poses a clear and present threat."

The government's case was not strong, and Anderson knew he had a chance. "The facts were not disputed," he said. After looking at the request, the appeals court ruled in favor of the Klan and remanded the case to Judge West for a full hearing. The issue had not been settled, but at least Duke would be allowed his day in court.

Throughout the legal proceedings, life went on for Duke and the Klan. He was as busy as ever, speaking at colleges and at Klan rallies. He and Chloe had decided to move the Klan operation from Baton Rouge to New Orleans. "New Orleans is where I grew up," said Duke, "and it just seemed like the natural thing to do."

The Dukes first rented an apartment in Belle Chasse, a small town just south of the city. Chloe spent most of her time working for the Klan and taking care of Erika. Her husband was seldom around. Duke is devoted to one thing—the white race. He loved his wife and family, but "the struggle" has always come first. Duke's ideas and plans were expanding so fast that he could not spare the time to be a normal husband or father. The marriage was not yet on the rocks, but time — or the lack of it — would soon take its toll. The racist couple did their best to make a go of things, and Chloe became pregnant once again. She gave birth to their second daughter on June 24, 1977, and the parents christened her Kristin Chloe.

After he sold the Baton Rouge house on Swanee Drive, Duke purchased a home in Metairie for the modest price of $20,000. The house was in shambles, and Duke was forced to do most of the remodeling himself. Located at 3603 Cypress Street, the building served as home and office for the Dukes, the Klan, and Patriot Press.

The Belaire case finally had its day in court, but once again Judge West ruled in favor of the school board. Anderson appealed, and for the second time the appeals court ruled in the Klan's favor.

Before the case was concluded, Anderson and Duke had gone before the appeals court three times. The issue was finally settled by the U.S. Supreme Court. The highest court ruled that the Klan's rights of free speech had been violated. In a compromise worked out between Anderson and the school board, the Klan was allowed use of the Belaire auditorium and awarded a "nominal amount" of $2,500 for damages resulting from of the breach of contract.

Because he was acting on behalf of the ACLU, Anderson had not received any monetary compensation during the entire two-and-a-half-year legal battle. Relief was sought under the Civil Rights Attorneys Fees Award Act of 1976, and the government ruled in Anderson's favor. A bill of almost $37,000 was paid equally by the school board and HEW.

"It amounted to less than half the actual time I had spent on the case," Anderson said, "but it helped establish me as an expert in the field of First Amendment litigation."

Anderson was both surprised by and pleased with his racist client. "I was expecting a raging lunatic to come to my office for our first meeting," he said. "I found him to be very rational and easy to deal with. He was a good client." Duke had high regard for his attorney, whom he called "a man of principle."

A rally was finally held two years later and with the usual fanfare. A crowd of over four hundred Klan sympathizers jammed the Belaire auditorium to listen to Duke and other Klan leaders. Behind the podium was a huge Ku Klux Klan flag, flanked by robed Klansmen.

Klan member Karl Hand addressed the gathering and noted that a black man was in attendance. "According to law," he said, "this Negro has a right to be here. . . . Under no circumstances will we tolerate a disturbance of any kind." The crowd gave a chant of "White power." The observer was safe, however, because there were enough police patrolling the school to dissuade even the most fervent Klansman.

When Duke's time to speak finally arrived, the crowd was electric. "If we had been black and played our cards right," he shouted, "we not only would have gotten a public place for our meeting, we could've gotten a couple of federal grants to help hold our meeting!"

The crowd became subdued as Duke delivered a subtle but carefully crafted speech, concluding, "White people are no longer going to be slaves of fear. We're not stupid, evil people as portrayed in the media. We are white people protecting our culture."

Few grand wizards of the Klan would have thought to seek legal assistance from the American Civil Liberties Union, but Duke thought it quite natural. "All we were seeking was the same right guaranteed to everyone," he said. "Nothing more, and never anything less."

Building the Klan into a national organization with clout was a top priority for Duke. He knew that to be successful he first had to have a large corps of loyal supporters who believed in what he advocated.

One of Duke's most dedicated supporters was Don Black. Born and raised in Alabama, Black first met Duke at a White Youth Alliance meeting in 1970. Three years his junior, Black had an almost religious devotion to his racist idol.

"I could see David was totally dedicated to protecting the rights of white people," he said. An early "Dukie," Black soon moved up in the ranks of the Klan and in a short time became grand dragon for the state of Alabama. Like Duke, Black has sought public office, and he echoes his mentor's words almost verbatim.

Years later, in a strange turn of events, Black and nine fellow Klan members were arrested and charged with plotting to overthrow the tiny Caribbean island of Dominica. The island, inhabited mostly by blacks, was being ruled by a left-wing government that had recently deposed an anti-communist ruler. Black and his cohorts allegedly had hoped to reinstate the leader and rule the island. But things went awry, and the group was caught in an FBI undercover operation as they attempted to leave Louisiana by boat. All were charged with violating the federal Neutrality Act, which prohibits Americans from aiding any military operation against a nation with which America is not at war. Black was convicted and sentenced to three years in prison.

"We were acting as patriots," he explained. "We were trying to free the people from a communist government."

Duke was never connected with the invasion and has steadfastly denied any knowledge of the attempted coup. But he defended Black for "endeavoring to do the same thing Reagan later did in Grenada."

Another Klan leader was Tom Metzger of Fallbrook, California. A television repairman by trade, Metzger had long ties with right-wing extremists. The founder of such groups as the

White Brotherhood, he was regarded by some as the West Coast equivalent of David Duke.

The two first met in California following the death of a white U.S. marine who was murdered by eight black soldiers at Camp Pendleton. Racial tensions had been brewing between whites and blacks for some time, and a Klan chapter was organized on the base. Although the murdered marine was not a Klansman, Duke seized the opportunity to milk the event. Metzger had contacted the grand wizard, and the two racists met to plan strategy to deal with the incident. Duke was so impressed with his new associate that he made him grand dragon for the state of California.

The last thing the U.S. Marine Corps needed was for David Duke and the Klan to stir up an already complicated internal matter. Newspaper accounts of racial troubles at the base were amplified when Duke and Metzger arrived at Camp Pendleton demanding to meet with the base commander. The commandant refused their request, so Duke did what he does best. He met with the news media.

Surrounded by members of the Klan, the White Brotherhood, and the White Crusaders, Duke led a march in front of Camp Pendleton to bring attention to the plight of marine Klansmen. The group of white racists was met by members of the Marxist Progressive Labor Party, who were marching on behalf of black marines. The Klan members chanted "White power" while the Marxists shouted, "Kill the Klan."

Television cameramen and reporters lined up to record any possible action. As Duke walked over to speak with them, someone ran up behind him and hit him across the head with a large wooden board. He fell to the ground, bleeding from a wound on the side of his head. Metzger allegedly jumped on the assailant, touching off a brawl between the two protesting groups.

Only a few seconds elapsed before military police wielding billy clubs jumped into the fracas and ended the fight. Both sides were ordered to leave the base or face arrest. The incident at Camp Pendleton made national headlines and was the top news story on all major networks. Nothing conclusive was ever determined about the race issue at the marine base, but Duke was able to use it to further himself and his cause.

Metzger became one of Duke's favorite lieutenants, but later proved to be an embarrassment. The Californian was used to running his own organizations. He apparently was also much more radical than Duke and had no plans to become another "Dukie." Grand dragons were not supposed to speak their minds, but to echo Duke's philosophy.

"Metzger was very vocal," said Don Black. "He just couldn't work within the Klan."

Like Duke, Metzger ran for public office and was something of a media hound. The political marriage lasted only a few years.

The radical Californian later began his own Klan chapter before forming even more radical organizations. To Metzger, Duke was not a true white racist because he was "too soft" on racist issues. Duke generally limited his anti-Semitic attacks to Zionists, while Metzger is said to have focused on "the individual Jew."

In September 1976, the Klan participated in an international meeting in New Orleans dubbed the World Nationalist Congress. It was a racist version of a political convention. The five-day event drew over 1,000 delegates from "all over the world." There were meetings, seminars, banquets, and a parade through the French Quarter.

The Crusader described the convention as "filled with good comradeship of white people enjoying the company of other white people dedicated to the international struggle against Jewish-Communism." Right-wing extremist groups from Canada, England, Australia, Belgium, France, Germany, and Austria sent delegates to participate. Some were simply extreme conservatives, while some were, in fact, fascists.

"We allowed an open forum for anyone willing to discuss racialist issues facing all white people," Duke insists. "I don't have to agree with everything someone has to say. Including different viewpoints in discussion is the foundation of free speech."

At first, the convention went without a hitch. Wherever the Klan would go, regular and plainclothes police followed. "We were used to police harassment," said Don Black. Hundreds of hooded Klansmen marched down the main thoroughfare of New Orleans, giving the police department reason to worry.

A predominantly black city, New Orleans was the perfect place for a race riot to begin. However, citizens and the Klan did their utmost to avoid each other, and no trouble occurred during any of the marches. People lined Canal Street to gawk at the Klansmen dressed in white robes and pointed hats, waving Confederate flags, and chanting "White power."

Things were different in suburban Metairie where delegates were staying at the International American Hotel. After one day's meetings had ended, about twenty-five Klansmen returned to the parking area to find plainclothes police officers taking their photographs. "Dr." James Warner was summoned from a meeting in the hotel. He came outside and met with police, insisting that his members had "the right to meet without the chilling intimidation of police photographers."

Warner called upstairs for Duke to help resolve the matter. "It was absolutely police harassment," Duke said. "There was nothing going on illegally."

The sheriff's deputies informed Duke that the crowd would have to disperse or they would be arrested for inciting to riot. Duke argued the point with the authorities but they were not in a mood to listen to the grand wizard. Duke stood on the back of a pickup truck and, after three attempts, persuaded his fellow Klansmen to leave the parking lot.

Duke and Warner were contacted later that evening by Jefferson Parish deputies and told that they were under arrest for inciting to riot and failure to disperse. Warner was charged with battery against a police officer for grabbing a deputy's arm while speaking with him.

"It had been over ten hours since the incident in the parking lot," Duke said. "The whole episode was nothing but harassment by the police."

The two Klan leaders were taken to the East Jefferson Parish lockup, fingerprinted, and booked. It was not the first time behind bars for either of the racists. They were detained only briefly, however, because bail was easy to raise during the convention. Duke had learned long before to be prepared in case of run-ins with the law.

"We were arrested for our political beliefs," Duke complained. "The police and the FBI were doing everything they could to discredit the conference. They thought that by putting us in jail they could stop us from saying what was really going on in America. The Jewish-controlled press and influence just couldn't stand to watch us peacefully state our ideals."

Duke and Warner returned to the convention the next day to an enthusiastic welcome. The two immediately became martyrs in the eyes of the racists who had come to New Orleans. Duke spent the remainder of the convention lambasting the federal government for "denying good, honest, hardworking white people the same rights as a welfare recipient."

The Crusader would be the forum Duke and Warner would use to raise most of the money needed to pay their legal fees. The Klan paper would be filled with stories of unjust government treatment of the racist leaders. Articles asked the devout to donate to the "David Duke Defense Fund." The cost of defending the Klansmen exceeded $10,000 per man, so Duke and Warner had to raise money quickly. One Alabama Klan group headed by Don Black raised $5,000 through personal loans from members.

Duke has always been able to raise money in much the same fashion as a television evangelist. He never solicits funds for himself, but rather for "the struggle," or for "some legal defense fund." Whatever the cause, Duke has been successful in bringing in what was necessary to survive. This has enabled him to maintain his various organizations throughout the years, often with only a fraction of the paid members needed to cover expenses.

The Duke-Warner case was set for trial before Judge Thomas Wicker of the 24th Judicial District Court. After changing legal counsel, Duke settled on John Reed of New Orleans. Reed was not a Klan attorney, but as Duke put it, was a "very competent" trial lawyer. "I was never worried about being found guilty of inciting to riot," he said bluntly, "because there was no riot."

If the prosecution had tried the two Klan leaders on both counts, they could have demanded a trial by jury, which their lawyers felt would favor them. But the state dropped the charge of failing to disperse and let the sole misdemeanor charge of incitement to riot stand alone. This minor charge meant that Duke and Warner's fate would be decided by Judge Wicker without a jury trial. The legal defense team spent a great deal of time and energy in preparation, making sure their clients were properly represented. When the court date arrived, Duke and Warner were well prepared.

The legal proceeding was held at the Jefferson Parish Courthouse in Gretna. Duke took the stand for ninety minutes of cross-examination by Assistant District Attorney Shirley Wimberly. The grand wizard denied he saw Warner grab detective Melvin Cicero.

"We're only sitting in this courtroom now," an angered Duke declared, "spending our time and attorney fees because of our beliefs." He also denied making any aggressive actions or inflammatory statements in the hotel parking lot.

"On at least three occasions," he said, "I urged people to go back into the hotel . . . not because I did not think they had the right to be there, but because I was afraid of the police officers' conduct."

At the end of his testimony, Duke stressed he had never advocated violence in the Metairie parking lot or at any other Klan function.

Warner, a small man with a mustache and a high voice, then took the stand. Wimberly began reciting a list of incidents in which Warner was arrested during anti-integration demonstrations. She then asked the Klansman to explain them.

"I am a patriot," he replied, "just like the people who fought in the Revolutionary War. I am proud to have stuck my neck out for my country and my race."

It was very effective, but he was no David Duke.

Judge Wicker deliberated only a short time before rendering a verdict. In an unusual decision, the judge ruled that no damage had occurred and hence no riot had taken place, but still found both defendants guilty as charged. Since it was the first conviction for both parties and the charge was a misdemeanor, the fine was only $500.

"I knew the judge's mind had already been made up when the district attorney made a short summation," Duke said. "They wanted to find us guilty of something. It was purely politics. How can we be guilty of inciting to riot when there was no riot?"

The case itself was not major, but it further scarred Duke's already tarnished reputation.

"It's once again guilt by the press," Duke said. "When blacks are arrested for standing up for their rights, the media crusades it as a badge of honor. I am proud that I have stood up for my rights."

As long as Duke was grand wizard of the Ku Klux Klan, he continued to be a target for those who opposed him. He was now much wiser in the ways of promoting his ideas. Through trial and error, he learned how to use the system and still survive.

"I knew from an early age," he said, "that the struggle would be long and difficult. If we are to recapture the rights we have lost, it will take a lot of sacrifices from a few dedicated people."

David Duke (center) presides over a meeting of the Ku Klux Klan. (Photo by Michael P. Smith)

CHAPTER SEVENTEEN

Taking It to the Streets

WITH THE KLAN FIRMLY under his control, Duke set out to promote his racist philosophies worldwide. From television coverage on the "Today Show" in New York, to outfoxing Scotland Yard across England, to pursuing illegal aliens along the Mexican border, the grand wizard elevated racism and anti-Zionism to international headlines.

Duke enjoyed running the Klan. At no other time in his life was he so happy. It was easy to get publicity, easy to draw a crowd, and, frankly, easy to look good. As long as he did not appear for television interviews dressed in overalls and kept his teeth, he surpassed the stereotypical image of Klansmen. Observers joked that David Duke might very well be the only grand wizard to have had his name appear in the newspaper without being followed by the word defendant.

"It was a very exciting time," he recalled with a gleam in his eye. "We went from nowhere and made many people begin to listen. It was a very fulfilling period."

The demands on Duke's time increased with each new racist adventure. He found himself doing more television shows and radio interviews and attending fewer local Klan functions. The day-to-day Klan activities were left to trusted aides.

Appearing on the NBC "Today Show" with Barbara Walters was more pressing than speaking to twelve supporters at a truck stop in Wiggins, Mississippi. On television, he could reach millions with his message about the dangers of Jewish press domination or illegitimate black childbirths. Promoting the Klan was becoming less important than promoting his ideas of racial purity.

By using a political approach, Duke caused a rift in Klan leadership, especially among more radical members such as Karl Hand and Tom Metzger. Already distanced from Bill Wilkinson and Jerry Dutton, Duke had forged his own place in racist politics. But not all Klan members disagreed with Duke's leadership. Don Black was only one of many who felt Duke's approach was correct and followed the "Wiz of Racism" without question.

Spreading the "racialist" word throughout the world would not be an easy task. Not all countries value free speech in the same context as Americans. In the early spring of 1978, Bill Wilkinson got the idea to start a British version of his Invisible Empire. The thought of American agitators bringing their racist message to Great Britain did not please the government, and authorities turned Wilkinson back at the airport.

The Ku Klux Klan had long been banned in Great Britain as a subversive organization. This was not a good omen for Duke because he was scheduled to speak at universities in various parts of England just two weeks later. If he was going to enter the country, he would have to do so without being noticed by customs agents.

Because he was an American, Duke did not need a visa to enter Great Britain. He would have certain rights, and it would be much more difficult for the government to deport the grand wizard, but he first had to get through customs. Duke certainly did not want to give the British authorities any notice of his arrival. If he booked his flight through a major airline, government agents could simply look at the list of reserved passengers and wait for the Klansman's arrival.

Laker Airlines was a low-budget way to cross the Atlantic at the time. It provided a cheap, no-frills trip and, most importantly for David Duke, required no reserved seating. All anyone had to do was show up at the airport and stand in line for a ticket, which was issued on a first-come-first-served basis. To help hide his identity, Duke did not shave for two weeks. Bearded, wearing sunglasses, and dressed in a tropical shirt and blue jeans, Duke did not resemble anyone customs agents were expecting.

When the jet arrived at Gatwick Airport in London, Duke was ready for his attempt to get through customs without being noticed.

"I looked at the checkers," he said, laughing, "and noticed that some were traditional-looking British customs inspectors, but a couple were West Indies blacks. I walked over to one black checker and gave a big 'hey mon' in my best West Indies accent. It worked like a charm."

His passport was stamped and he was legally in England. It would take court action to deport him. He had learned a thing or two from past scrapes with the law, and now he was using it for his own purposes.

Duke had been invited to England to lecture at universities and to meet with the extreme right-wing National Front. Much like the John Birch Society in the United States, the National Front liked Duke's stands on immigration and other racist issues.

It had been arranged for the Klan leader to speak at leading institutions such as Oxford, Cambridge, and Brighton. In addition, he had hoped to hold Klan-style rallies, complete with cross burnings. This would be easier said than done once the British government understood the problem they had on their hands.

At first, things went smoothly for Duke. He was interviewed on radio shows and even appeared on "BBC Tonight," the most popular program in England. The show gave Duke over twenty minutes of national exposure, and he made the most of it.

"Why is it," he wondered, "that the government allows great numbers of non-British into the country who spit on the flag and will never assimilate into society? It is too bad that Europeans adopt the worst aspects of America — like fast food and integration."

The program made Duke an instant celebrity across Great Britain. "The response was overwhelming," said Duke. "Wherever I would go, people would wave and wish me the best."

Duke drews large crowds at cross-burning ceremonies to initiate new members into the British Ku Klux Klan. He also began to publicly attack the government's lax immigration laws, which were very unpopular with the British.

In addition to assaulting government policy, the grand wizard had organized an "alien watch." This outraged many in the government, and Duke was finally made an issue in Parliament. Home Secretary Merlyn Rees asserted Duke was "a big to-do about nothing." In a speech in Parliament Rees said, "I have no plans to use my powers to crack an unimportant nut."

But the more Duke continued to steal headlines, the more the pressure mounted for Rees to do something. The conservative newspaper *Daily Express* printed front-page articles about Duke, including one with the headline, "Get Him Out Of Here!" There was a picture of Duke dressed in full Klan regalia, standing at the River Thames with Parliament as a backdrop. It was all Rees could stand. He ordered the Klansman deported "forthwith." The grand wizard immediately took steps to elude Scotland Yard.

America's most famous racist quickly became Great Britain's newest media star. A game of cat and mouse ensued that left

Scotland Yard looking like Keystone Kops. Duke's right of free speech was supported not only by racist sympathizers but also by liberal factions who wanted to hear what the "Racist Pimpernel" had to say.

One daily newspaper displayed a front-page picture of Duke in a Klan robe standing outside the Tower of London posed next to a colorfully dressed Beefeater. The Tower guard grabbed the racist by the arm and smiled for the photographer. This display prompted the pro-Labor *Daily Mirror* to caustically ask the home secretary, "Where are your nutcrackers now, Mr. Rees?"

Questioned on a radio show as to why he was posing for pictures in his Klan robe, Duke responded, "I did it to annoy the home secretary. He's trying to make a fool of me, so I figured it was his turn."

Hopping from television stations to radio stations, Duke was able to keep one step ahead of the police with the help of the English people. A newspaperman was interviewing Duke in the lobby of a hotel when someone tipped off the grand wizard that bobbies were on the way to arrest him. Duke ran out of the lobby and was riding down the escalator as the bewildered bobbies rode up another, unable to grab the racist, who waved to them merrily.

Fleet Street was so impressed with the Klan leader that reporters began hiding him for hours in their press offices just to get a story. The BBC wanted a live television interview with Duke but Scotland Yard was keeping a vigilant watch on the station. It was decided that the broadcast would be shot live entirely in the back seat of a moving automobile. So there was David Duke, flaunting the British police and attacking the government's immigration policies as he rode through Trafalgar Square.

"Later," Duke said, "I did an interview with Peter Jennings, who was then the European bureau chief, for an hour and a half while I was on the run from authorities."

Scotland Yard had announced that all operatives were to memorize Duke's mustached face, but to their embarrassment Duke frequently walked freely throughout London. Law enforcement officials were so demoralized that James Jardine, the chairman of the Police Federation, protested that his members were not to blame.

On his tenth day in England Duke attended a dinner given in his honor in Warwickershire by a farmer sympathetic to his views. A Klan rally was scheduled, so Scotland Yard was ready to nab the elusive grand wizard, but Duke pulled a no-show. Thinking they had dissuaded Duke from any further performances, the police let down their guard. The Klansman held the rally the following evening, complete with a cross burning.

Mr. Robin Beauclair, whose Red Ascot Farm is located near Southham, was so impressed by the young racist that he was quoted in the *London Times* as saying, "I would be proud to have Mr. Duke for a son." His farm was the site of a small Klan rally, which was followed by a cross burning. The British press was there and filmed the entire episode for the BBC. Scotland Yard apparently learned about it after the fact on television.

Pressure was so great on the home secretary that he forbade the press from interviewing the Klan leader. Duke did not take the ban seriously and met with Robert McGowen, a reporter from the *Daily Express*. Not wishing to upset Rees, McGowen had told Scotland Yard the place and time of their meeting.

The two met at the Fox and Geese Pub in Ickenham in the northwest section of London. The reporter, who also sported a moustache, was enjoying a pint of ale with Duke when agents of Scotland Yard burst into the pub. With great pride the inspector promptly announced, "Mr. Duke, you've led me on a merry chase, but now I will serve this order on you! You are not to be detained. You have fourteen days to appeal."

Everything would have worked smoothly, except the officer handed the papers to McGowen by mistake. To make the deportation order official, Duke would have to be physically served. The Klansman rushed out the back door and a chase ensued.

True to form, however, Scotland Yard got its man. As he was being led back to the pub, Duke yelled, "God Bless Britain" and "God save the Queen." The embarrassed police officer promptly served the racist with the notice of deportation.

Down but not out, Duke did what he always does in this type of situation. He hired a lawyer. Duke chose Anthony Reed-Herbert as his solicitor and directed him to file an appeal. The action allowed Duke more free press and headlines for another week. When the newspapers tired of the Klansman's adventures, Duke voluntarily headed home to the United States. He had accomplished what he had set out to do by grabbing the attention not only of the European press but of the news media back in the States.

Duke was not so lucky with all his international endeavors, however. He thought Australia would be a fertile land to sow his seeds of racism. There were already Klan chapters Down Under, led by Darwin police officer David Jennings. But Duke wanted to lead the crusade himself. He made plans to appear at Klan rallies in Melbourne and Sydney, but authorities got wind of his trip.

Unlike in England, in Australia it was necessary for Duke to obtain a visa before entering the country. Officials had only to deny him a visa to keep the unwanted racist from entering.

"I was set to go," Duke said, "but the government cancelled my entry visa the day before I was to leave."

What does a racist do after he is thrown out of England and refused entry into Australia? Go north, young man, to Canada! A country with a long history of Klan activity, Canada has always been receptive to Duke. From television shows in

Toronto to rallies in Vancouver, Duke has been well received. "The western provinces were the best," he boasts.

Wherever he spoke in Canada, he blasted the government's immigration policies. "Some of the streets of Toronto, Vancouver, and Montreal bear more resemblance to the hovels of Calcutta, Hong Kong, or Timbuktu . . . than the gentle hamlets of Europe that Canada used to echo," Duke declared.

On April 1, 1979, Duke was participating in a three-hour call-in show on CJOR radio. After the program, the American grand wizard was greeted by three immigration officials, who questioned him. They promptly took him into custody for violating immigration statutes. Because of his conviction for inciting to riot the previous year in Metairie, Duke was considered an undesirable by the government. He had failed to list his conviction when he entered the country and was forced to face the charge before an immigration court.

Duke hired as legal counsel John Taylor, an immigration expert. The Klansman appeared at a press conference the next day dressed in ski clothes. "I've given up white power for white powder," he proclaimed with a smile. The story made national headlines both in Canada and the U.S.

At the hearing, Duke was formally charged with misrepresenting himself at the border and being in a class of inadmissable persons.

"Here I was," Duke said, "not breaking any laws, but once again charged with a crime for speaking my beliefs."

The government was seeking a permanent deportation order, which would have forbade Duke from ever entering Canada again. After a brief hearing, the court decided that Duke had not intentionally hidden his past. But under a technical rule, the grand wizard was banned from re-entry for a five-year period.

With globetrotting behind him for a while, Duke returned to New Orleans to find his family life in shambles. Chloe had been alone too long and decided to end their marriage. She had spent her time working at the Klan office and raising Erika and Kristin while her husband was gallivanting about the world.

"Working with the Klan put too much pressure on her," Duke said. "If I ever marry again, I would never allow my wife to work like that."

Duke was so wrapped up with "the struggle" that he rarely spent time with his family. "By the time I realized the problems it was causing my marriage," admitted Duke, "it was too late."

Chloe and the girls packed up their belongings and headed for Florida to live with Chloe's parents. Although they lived separately for several years, the Dukes were not legally divorced until 1986. Duke showed little outward emotion regarding the breakup.

"There was just so much to do," he said. "I really didn't have time to dwell on the past and feel sorry for myself."

As soon as Duke became a born-again bachelor, he was accused of womanizing. The grand wizard did encounter many women who were attracted by his celebrity status, and rumors abounded about Duke's alleged affairs with women throughout the country. "That's just one more unsubstantiated attack on my character by the media," said Duke.

Duke was not satisfied with bashing only blacks and Jews and turned his attention south to Mexican aliens. Working with radicals such as Tom Metzger, the Klan planned a Mexican Border Watch. The idea was to create a "civilian patrol" along the U.S. — Mexican border to help stem the flow of illegal immigrants.

The Border Watch extended from Brownsville, Texas, to the Pacific Ocean. Klansmen would drive the route in caravans from dusk to dawn. Six Klan "spotters" would work together, with about one-quarter-mile between vehicles. Klan members were instructed to report immediately to immigration officials any suspicious-looking people they might find.

Duke explained the Klan's position thusly:

David Duke leads the search for illegal aliens along the Mexican border. (Photo courtesy of AP/Wide World Photos)

"America was undergoing a tremendous demographic change. Until the 1960s, American immigration policy was pro-U.S. It was designed to allow white European immigrants who could assimilate into our society to enter the country. Things shifted to a liberal posture in the sixties, and the government encouraged South Americans, Africans, and Asians, who are all non-white and not easily assimilable, to have preference in immigrating.

"We were also trying to draw attention to the fact that illegal aliens were taking jobs away from hardworking Americans. We had to find some way to slow the loss of our natural heritage. Unless we change policies, America will have serious trouble in the future. Within a generation, whites will be the minority, and we will live under the whims of a cruel majority."

As could be expected, the news media turned out en masse. Television cameramen lighted up the roads as they followed the Klan looking for a story. Local law enforcement officials were not too happy to have the racist group patrolling the border. Because there were so many people involved in the Border Watch, it was impossible for any aliens to cross. With the Ku Klux Klan, an army of reporters, local sheriffs' deputies, and immigration officials all chasing each other, the Border Watch looked more Hollywood movie than a Klan stunt.

"We had proved our point," bragged Duke.

To make matters worse, local officials of the U.S. Immigration and Naturalization Service said they would welcome help from anyone, including the Klan. This upset San Diego Mayor Pete Wilson so much that he called on U.S. Attorney General Griffin Bell do something to stop the Border Watch. Wilson, who has since moved on to the U.S. Senate, said in a telegram to Bell, "I profoundly disagree with the attitude implied by your local officials, which seems to condone the assistance of the notoriously racist KKK."

Hand card distributed by the Klan. (Photo by Margaret Hawkins)

Duke made headlines from California to Texas, standing in an open jeep leading the Border Watch. The Klan had such a feared reputation that Mexican newspapers daily featured pictures of white-hooded members on their front pages. Mexicans who normally would not have feared being arrested by immigration officials were under the impression the Klansmen were out to hang them.

"It worked," reported Duke confidently. "We proved that if the government was truly serious about protecting American jobs from illegal aliens, then a solution could be found." The Border Watch continued off and on for the next year.

The fall of 1979 was once again election time in Louisiana. As had happened four years earlier, Duke set his aim on the state Senate. This time he was living in Metairie, in the district of incumbent Sen. Joseph Tieman. The Senator was extremely popular with constituents and would be very difficult for the young racist to unseat. Like Duke's first political opponent, Ken Osterberger, Tieman had a voting record that could withstand any Duke attack.

Qualifying day found not only Tieman and Duke in the race, but also Robert Namer and Robert N. Clarke. Namer was well known in Jefferson Parish and posed a possible threat to the incumbent Senator. Tieman was tied to the powerful Jefferson Parish courthouse establishment, and Duke would need much more than door-to-door campaigning and racist ideas to win this election.

"I was still learning about politics," admitted Duke. "I still felt I could win by running on my ideals. I didn't know the importance of election mechanics."

Duke spent the campaign crisscrossing the district in search of votes. Ku Klux Klansmen from across the nation descended upon Metairie as they had done four years earlier in Baton Rouge. Duke supporters stood at intersections waving signs bearing the grand wizard's face and the slogan, "Courage to Be Different." Tieman kept the race publicly low key and made certain Duke was never offered the opportunity to debate. Without plenty of news coverage, Duke's election was doomed.

Working day and night, Duke still found it impossible to unseat the popular senator. Election night results showed:

Tieman	21,329	57%
Duke	9,897	26%
Namer	4,635	12%
Clarke	1,824	5%

Losing the election was a bitter pill for Duke to swallow. He came in second, which was not a bad showing, considering his racist affiliations. But he was nevertheless disheartened by the defeat.

"After the second Senate race," he said, "I thought I would never run for public office again."

Although he was attracting attention from far and wide as the leader of the Klan, Duke felt stifled. He was tired of being a freak in a sideshow. Being grand wizard of the Ku Klux Klan had opened doors for Duke's career. He could get coverage in virtually any newspaper in the world just by speaking. So why was David Duke dissatisfied?

As had happened with the Citizens Council, the White Youth Alliance, and the National party, Duke had become bored with the Ku Klux Klan. He had come to the realization that he could never make a silk purse out of a sow's ear.

"I knew," he said, "that for me to be able to promote the ideals that I felt were crucial to the survival of the white race, I would have to find a new avenue [by] which to get my message across to those people I couldn't reach through the Klan."

It was difficult for Duke to communicate his racist ideas because they were always overshadowed by the fact that he was the grand wizard of the hated Ku Klux Klan. Duke constantly had to defend the violent reputation the Klan had earned over the years.

"I was tired of fighting the negative image the Klan had," said Duke. "It was impossible to discuss the issues that were so critical to the present when you spent all your time defending the past."

Competing with the Invisible Empire, United Klans of America, and various splinter groups all identifying themselves as the Ku Klux Klan was more than Duke could manage.

"I wanted an organization that was more politically motivated," Duke said. "Some members were more interested in the trappings and the ceremonies and the tradition of the Klan than in making real social change for the white race. It was simply a case of taking a new approach versus the traditional avenue of the Klan."

It was at this juncture that Duke met with Don Black, Jim McArthur, and others to plan the formation of the National Association for the Advancement of White People.

"We had discussed it for a long time," said Black, "and David felt the time was right."

But a problem now was what to do with the Knights of the Ku Klux Klan. Duke could not just walk away from the organization and leave it to an unknown. He would have to find the right person to take control of "his Klan." Black wanted to follow Duke in the NAAWP, so he was not a viable candidate. Those Klansmen close to Duke also wanted to follow him, so a search ensued to find an appropriate replacement for the departing grand wizard. After a while they decided it was hopeless, so the next best thing would be done. Duke would try to merge the Knights of the Ku Klux Klan with another Klan group.

A meeting was planned in Cullman, Alabama, with Duke, Black, and their old nemesis Bill Wilkinson to discuss the possibility of a merger between the Invisible Empire and the Knights of the Ku Klux Klan. Although they were enemies, Duke felt that turning the reins of the group over to Wilkinson "would be the best thing for the Klan."

The Klansmen met in an out-of-the-way farmhouse in a meeting that was supposed to be secret. Unknown to Duke and Black, Wilkinson had invited members of the press, who had hidden in bushes to videotape the meeting.

In what has become a long-standing dispute, Wilkinson claimed Duke had offered to sell him names and addresses of the members of the Knights of the Ku Klux Klan for $35,000. The grand wizard of the Invisible Empire was not impressed with his racist counterpart and allegedly declined the offer.

"He had already lost most of his members anyway," said Wilkinson.

Black remembers the night differently. "David wanted to let the Knights and the Invisible Empire join forces to make the Klan better. He wasn't sellin' out. It was a good plan for both organizations."

The version Duke tells is also quite different from Wilkinson's. Duke's idea was to give Klan members the opportunity either to remain with the organization or join the NAAWP. The Invisible Empire and the Knights of the Ku Klux Klan would jointly mail out letters to their memberships informing them of the new racist organization. Members could stay in the Ku Klux Klan under Wilkinson's leadership or switch to the NAAWP with Duke.

"We carried a copy of the mail-out to show Wilkinson," claims Duke. "At no time did I ever offer to sell the Klan membership list. It was a great opportunity for both groups. Bill Wilkinson was more interested in his own personal goals than in the struggle."

Since there could be no amicable way to merge the two Klan groups, Duke turned the Knights of the Ku Klux Klan over to his friend, Don Black. Duke had been a member of the Ku Klux Klan since his senior year in high school more than eleven years earlier. It was through the Klan that he had met Jim Lindsay, who, with the exception of Colonel Duke, was the most influential person in his life. The fraternal brotherhood of the racist organization had given Duke the feeling of belonging.

The fact that Duke had been the grand wizard of the Ku Klux Klan was the reason he had become a worldwide figure. David Duke had dedicated his life to the loathsome group and had extracted all he could from it. And now he moved on, once again alone, to begin the National Association for the Advancement of White People.

David Duke announces his candidacy for president on the steps of the
Georgia capitol, 1988. (Photo courtesy of AP/Wide World Photos)

CHAPTER EIGHTEEN

Finding Himself

DAVID DUKE WAS NO LONGER a member of the Ku Klux Klan. He now had to find a new way to keep his name and racist message before the public. In the past, he could depend on hooded Klansmen to pique the curiosity of the news media, guaranteeing a crowd of the faithful and the fearful. But now, even some of his most loyal supporters were following the lead of Bill Wilkinson by remaining true to the Klan. They looked upon Duke as a traitor and a fallen leader who had turned his back on the traditions of the Klan in order to further his own agenda.

But Duke viewed himself in a different light, explaining, "Whenever people were able to hear me, they almost always agreed . . . with what I had to say. I thought the NAAWP was the way to go. I was in the Klan because I wanted to advance certain principles. All groups have real meaning only as a means to an end. I was for any vehicle that could preserve the white race and Western Christian civilization."

Working out of his home on Cypress Street, Duke was virtually alone. He had an organization, but no members, and no money to pay for his first mailing. Don Black had stayed to run the Knights of the Ku Klux Klan, but the organization lost much of its clout once Duke bolted.

With the "media wizard" on his own, the Ku Klux Klan became just another bigoted group. No one really had much interest in the Klan. What made the Klan under Duke newsworthy was the radical philosophies wrapped in a normal-looking package. Somehow, the former grand wizard would have to find a new way to entice people to donate money to save the white race.

Even before he had left the Klan, Duke formed the National Association for the Advancement of White People. Incorporated as a federally recognized non-profit organization, the tax-free group was formed along the lines of the National Association for the Advancement of Colored People.

"That's the reason the name NAAWP was chosen," Duke admitted. "Our name and clear purpose make it impossible for minority racists to condemn us without exposing their hypocrisy."

Like every other group Duke has either founded or joined, the new organization would be spearheaded by a newspaper. Simply titled *NAAWP News,* the newspaper even looked like *The Crusader.* The difference, of course, was that it carried no mention of the Klan. It also was significantly less obsessed with "Zionist issues." David Duke had become, to borrow a phrase from George Bush, a kinder, gentler racist.

To help make ends meet, Duke continued his own mail-order bookstore. Fashioned after Patriot Press, Americana Books sold the same racist propaganda previously available through *The Crusader.* A long list of titles advertised in the *NAAWP News* was headed "Suppressed Books." Like *The Crusader,* the *NAAWP News* claimed to offer all sides of the issues to readers. A disclaimer contended, "It should be understood that this listing does not mean that this publication endorses or agrees with every book listed."

Many of the books dealt with racist issues such as integration, busing, and affirmative action, although Duke still continued to offer such anti-Semitic "literature" as *The Holy Book of Adolf Hitler, The Six Million Reconsidered,* and *White Power.*

The first issue of *NAAWP News* was a simple eight-page edition attacking Alex Haley's novel *Roots,* integration, and affirmative action. It also contained an article entitled "Genocide by School Busing" by former U.S. Cong. John R. Rarick of Louisiana. The four-term congressman had been voted out of office in 1974 and replaced by a Republican.

In an attempt to justify the NAAWP, Duke devoted a monthly column to "NAAWP vs. NAACP." This comparison also attempted to justify reading and subscribing to the *NAAWP News.*

One article began by asking, "Does the NAAWP believe in equality?" The answer was no. The negative response to equality was surprising to some, but should not have been unexpected. The credo that best exemplifies the NAAWP reads, "We believe that no two individuals or races are exactly equal in their inborn talents and potentialities. But, we believe that the best way to determine talent and reward it is through equal opportunity and equal rights."

There was also a page devoted to "Why the NAAWP is Necessary," "What the NAAWP is Doing," and "NAAWP Principles." The tenets espoused by the group, *i.e.,* Duke, included "Equal Rights for Whites" and "Preservation of the White Race and Its Heritage." It was classic David Duke. By claiming to be a champion of equal rights for all, the NAAWP could hide behind its true purpose — to promote the same philosophies Duke had advanced with the Ku Klux Klan.

There were advertisements urging readers to join the NAAWP for only twenty-five dollars a year. If a reader so desired, he could become a NAAWP organizer for an additional ten dollars. An organizer would receive ten copies of the *NAAWP News* and an organizer's starter kit. The kit included personalized calling cards, along with instructions on recruiting new members into the organization. It was a bit crude, but Duke was desperate to get his newest racist club off the ground.

Finally, there was the ever-present merchandise page. Duke knew he could make money by offering NAAWP tee shirts, calling cards, and Confederate and American flags, as well as various patches. Not to overlook the Jews, Duke sold his NAAWP booklet, *"Who Runs the Media?"* It was a technique straight out of *The Crusader.*

If the reader had not yet succumbed to Duke's pitch for money, an up-front request was made in an advertisement reading "Contributions Needed." No stone was left unturned, no possibility for fund-raising was left to chance. Duke even had a twenty-four-hour message service in case someone decided to phone in a contribution at three o'clock in the morning.

It was not much, but with the aid of the mailing list from the Knights of the Ku Klux Klan Duke was able to sign up three hundred NAAWP members for his first issue. It was nothing like the heyday of the Klan, but it proved more than enough to keep David Duke in the racist limelight.

Public attention would be needed quickly just to survive. Until this point, speaking engagements had been Duke's primary source of income. Audiences were much less likely to pay for a lecture from a former grand wizard. But after a while, Duke was finally able to book a few paid college dates through the Yardley Speakers and Entertainment Agency.

The first speaking date was at California State University at Northridge. Duke was invited by the Student Productions and Campus Entertainment Committee to represent the cause of white rights at a four-day human rights symposium. Duke had prepared to debate racist issues and was not ready for the protest awaiting him.

He was accustomed to pickets and hecklers, but students on the liberal California campus were so angered by Duke's racist past that the debate was delayed for more than an hour so security could be arranged to protect the speakers. Not only was it necessary for campus security to be called in, but twenty Los Angeles police were also needed to help calm the crowd.

Signs reading "Nuke the Duke" and "Death to KKK" surrounded the building where the symposium was being held. Duke had hoped his past affiliation with the Klan would be forgotten, but it was soon evident that was not going to be the case. Every time Duke began to speak, the crowd booed and screamed so loudly that he found it impossible to continue.

After an hour and a half, the event was cancelled.

"I feel sorry for the white students on this campus," Duke said. "If you think I've been badly treated today, wait and see how you'll be treated when you become a minority in this country." It was a rough start for the self-proclaimed president of the NAAWP but he nevertheless received a fee of $1,300.

Things were quite different when Duke appeared at the University of Montana in Missoula. There was a contingent of protesters, but it was much smaller and less vocal than at California State. He was greeted by what Duke refers to as "minority and Marxist elements." But this time the student body was almost totally white and gave the former Klansman a much friendlier reception.

His speech was almost the same one he had delivered as a Klansman, but was more toned down in racist rhetoric.

"It was not that I had changed my fundamental positions," Duke said. "It is just that I had matured from my role as Klan leader." He devoted the speech to blasting affirmative action and other liberal government programs. Although he mentioned the dangers of "the media masters," the fiery attack directed at Jews was no longer there.

Local newspapers gave front-page coverage to Duke's speech and the two-hour press conference that followed. All in all, it was a much better showing than the visit to California. He now realized he could not simply wave his magic wand to make his past Klan activities disappear. His critics were going to remain relentless in their attempts to expose him as a Klansman in a business suit.

Back in New Orleans, Duke spent most of his time in relative seclusion. A loner by nature, he became more of a writer than a political activist.

"I guess I needed time for reflection," he said. "The past ten years had been challenging, so I decided to set new goals and try and reach them." He even submitted himself to est training, a self-awareness program popular at the time.

"It was a chance to experience something new in life that might broaden my horizons," he said.

Working with ex-Klan member James McArthur, Duke devoted much of his time to promoting the NAAWP through the *NAAWP News.* McArthur was a former government employee turned "Dukie." A graduate of Temple University with a master's degree in library science, McArthur soon became the backbone of the NAAWP newspaper. Within two years of its inception, the organization could boast more than 4,000 paid members. It would not be long before the NAAWP surpassed the Knights of the Ku Klux Klan in actual dues-paying membership.

Duke soon discovered that the difference between leading an unknown organization such as the NAAWP and heading the Klan was accessibility to the media. He found it much more difficult to be taken seriously as president of the NAAWP. The name "grand wizard" could be reason enough for a press conference. But Duke had decided to take a course different from that of the Klan, a decision he insists he has not regretted.

"It is natural for people to resist change," he explained, "but I was willing to work to make that change occur."

To David Duke, creating social reform meant drawing attention to specific challenges to the rights of white people. At first, most NAAWP demonstrations were limited to the New

Orleans area for financial reasons. When the city attempted to tear down a statue regarded by some as commemorating white supremacy, Duke filed suit to stop the removal. During a rally in front of the obelisk, which marked a battle in 1874 between citizens and carpetbag police, Duke made a standard speech against government intrusion into the lives of "hardworking, white, middle-class taxpayers." It was a far cry from the flamboyant David Duke of Ku Klux Klan days.

Duke was frustrated in his attempts to find issues that could generate enough publicity to put him back in the national spotlight. He tried to create a new public forum called political theater, which was a cross between Free Speech Alley and a stage play. The object was for Duke to write a prepared text dealing with relevant issues, then read questions aloud to an audience. The audience would then respond to Duke in a structured form of public debate. With his new assistant Tom Wilson, a twenty-two-year-old graduate of Murray State University, Duke was trying to rekindle the enthusiasm of his Klan rallies.

Wilson and Duke decided to hold one of the political theaters in front of the Cabildo, in the French Quarter. The event was billed as the "White Survival Demonstration" to gain support against the Simpson/Mazzoli bill in the U.S. Senate. The legislation, which later became law, permitted certain illegal aliens living in the United States to become citizens automatically. Duke's idea of an intellectual racist discussion was not received well by the remaining "Dukies" who were used to his fiery Klan days, and the turnout was disappointing.

For the first time since Free Speech Alley, the NAAWP president had lost the ability to draw attention just by being himself. By publicly mellowing his racist and anti-Semitic positions, Duke had lost the very thing that had brought him fame, which was being more politically obnoxious than anyone else.

But Duke could not remain dormant forever. In 1986, racial unrest came to life in the New York City suburb of Howard

Beach. A black youth was killed by a group of white youths, causing national outrage. Black leaders from across America denounced the killing as a recurrence of pre-civil rights violence. Both whites and blacks were equally incensed by the tragedy. Duke knew a restless situation when he saw one and made his way to Howard Beach to see first hand what was going on.

"Nothing could more dramatically reveal the anti-white racism of the media and the government than the Howard Beach incident," he thundered.

Convinced that the slain black youth was responsible for the racial troubles, Duke retraced his steps of twelve years earlier in Boston. Many of the residents of the mostly white community thought the murder was a result of black outside agitators.

Duke walked the streets, talking with people he met. "The response was terrific," he boasted. "They really appreciated what I had to say." New York Mayor Edward Koch disagreed with the NAAWP president, declaring, "You would expect this type of thing in the Deep South, but not in New York."

Duke appeared on the "Bob Grant Show," on WABC radio, one of the highest-rated programs in New York City. Duke spent an hour and a half defending the "white victims of Howard Beach." He also used the platform to attack the federal government's positions on affirmative action and forced busing. It was vintage David Duke. His racist batteries had been recharged. Response from the "Bob Grant Show" was so positive that the NAAWP's membership increased by more than six hundred new members.

"It was like the 'Tomorrow' show all over again," gloated Duke.

Although Duke acknowledges there were atrocities committed against Jews in Europe during World War II, his true views surfaced in an article in the *NAAWP News* entitled

"Thoughts on the Holocaust." He claimed the Holocaust has been used as a political tool by Zionists, explaining:

"The Holocaust is the rock upon which Israel rests. Chronic Holocaust propaganda was the main justification used in the expropriation of Palestinian land to make way for the Jewish state. It has also been a crowbar used to pry billions in reparations from Germany and billions in aid from the United States. Finally, it is the specter used to silence any serious criticism of Israel.

"So exactly what is the 'fact of Dachau'? No doubters of the Holocaust question the fact that, at the end of the war, there was very little food and fuel in the camps and that there were accompanying epidemics. The victorious Allied armies bragged in the winter of 1944-45 that they completely smashed the major transportation systems of the Third Reich. There were severe food shortages all over Germany during this period. Finding a large number of emaciated, diseased bodies no more proves any deliberate extermination policy than the fact that there were many victims of the Chicago fire proves that the city administration deliberately set the blaze.

"There are probably a thousand different articles on the horror of the Holocaust in America's print media every month. In such an avalanche of emotionally-charged material, it is certainly difficult for anyone to calmly and deliberately analyze and evaluate the content of what is being said. One thing is certain. Every word written about the horrors of the Holocaust speeds money to Israel and muffles any criticism of a foreign policy that often flies in the face of our own national interest. It stifles much of the legitimate criticism of the men who dominate America's media, men who also happen to be of the same people as those of the Holocaust, and blunts any sympathies for the Palestinian victims of ethnic persecution."

The "Duke of Racism" was back, and this time he was roaring.

In an article entitled "National Disgrace" in the *NAAWP News*, Duke blasted Congress for passing legislation declaring Dr. Martin Luther King's birthday a national holiday. In a front-page editorial, an incensed Duke wrote:

"Nothing could more bitterly toll the passing of a great nation than the recent travesty committed by the Congress of the United States in passage of a national holiday in honor of Martin Luther King.

"Just who was Martin Luther King? He was a communist sympathizer, a person revered by only a small percentage of Americans, a man who was elected to no political office and whose policies were opposed by the vast majority of Americans, a man whose personal integrity was in the gutter, a man whose record is so damning that the government agreed to hold it in secret for 50 years. Congress has now chosen to give this man the highest honor ever accorded an American.

"Even George Washington does not now have a holiday exclusively in his honor. He shares his birthday as 'President's Day.' In one fell swoop, the Congress of the United States minimized giants such as Thomas Jefferson and Abraham Lincoln to honor the black revolutionary M. L. King.

"In fact, in the last day's voting, the Senate rejected a proposal of Sen. Gordon Humphrey [of New Hampshire] to substitute Lincoln's birthday for King's. The proposal was soundly defeated, clearly demonstrating the Senate's view of the obviously inferior status of Lincoln to that of MLK. By any stretch of the imagination, can even mattoid liberals really believe that King deserves a national holiday in his name more than Lincoln?

"The inescapable fact is that the majority of the congressmen and senators of this nation are simply political prostitutes who have sold their souls and those of their countrymen for the approval of a handful of ugly aliens in the national media and the black votes that they savor more than honor.

"I know that these are harsh words, but words any less strident would be less than truthful.

"Have these men acted to prevent the destruction of our educational system by massive busing and integration? Have they acted to protect our nation from the millions of non-whites pouring over our borders each year, taking American jobs, soaking up welfare, committing unnumerable [*sic*] criminal acts, and fundamentally changing the racial and cultural makeup of America? Have they raised a finger to stop the massive racial discrimination going on against the descendants of those who created America? Have they moved to stop the racist, anti-white bias of our alien media? Have they lived an example of real honor for our youth to emulate and aspire to? No, they have been the supreme examples of dishonor who have not dared to raise even their voice in opposition to the remaking of America into a black and brown country!

"We of the NAAWP issue a call to every true American who loves his nation, and his sacred heritage. The time for vacillation and equivocation is long over. We either fight now, openly and honestly for our heritage and our rights, or lose both. No running or hiding can obliterate that fact. No pleasurable diversions can expel it from the minds that know. No cowardice can change it. No avarice can lessen it. You and I must rise above this madness engulfing our country. Whether we win or lose, honor demands nothing less."

DAVID DUKE

So bitter was Duke about the King holiday that he devoted the entire issue of the *NAAWP News* to lambasting the slain civil rights leader. The paper contained pictures of King surrounded by members of a "communist training school." It was a great platform for Duke to use in attacking blacks and big government. He was now ready to return to his leadership role as America's number one racist.

The *NAAWP News* quickly became a campaign tool to further Duke's latest ambition, running for president of the United States. If he were going to regain his national stature, he would have to find a way to draw media coverage. The campaign would be a great way to increase not only his personal visibility but also that of the NAAWP.

In January 1987, Forsyth County, Georgia, came under the national spotlight. Although in the Deep South, it was totally white. The county, located north of Atlanta, was targeted by black groups as an example of "held-over racism." Black leaders from across the nation converged on the rural county in an attempt to integrate it. A plan was being devised to build in the county large, low-income housing projects to be occupied by displaced Atlanta blacks.

In no time, the matter became a national story, and Duke could not wait to enter the fray. Don Black and the Knights of the Ku Klux Klan had already been trying to organize white opposition to the black marches, but with little success. A group calling itself the Committee to Keep Forsyth White was formed by Frank Shirley and Mark Watts. They were familiar with the NAAWP and requested Duke's assistance in organizing the county residents to oppose the blacks. The former Klan leader accepted.

Duke met with members of the committee as soon as he arrived in Atlanta. "They were simply looking to keep their basic rights to live as they choose," Duke argued. "If they get massive numbers of blacks from Atlanta into Forsyth County, they know that their children are more likely to be hurt or robbed or raped or killed."

Accepting the role as spokesman, Duke immediately met with the media. He appeared on every local television station, as well as the ABC, NBC, and CBS evening news programs. Local radio talk shows once again were jammed by callers talking to and about David Duke.

In interview after interview, Duke asked the same question: "How much white blood will have to be spilled to satisfy race mixing?" Duke continued to flame the fires of racism. "I'm not opposed to helping these people with job training and education, but don't take away the rights of the majority, and for heaven's sake, don't put our people in danger. It's the worst form of tyranny when the government forces a program that results in harming innocent people."

A rally was planned by black leaders for Saturday, January 23. As he had often done since his college days at LSU, Duke planned a counterdemonstration.

"We wanted to show that the hardworking white majority of people in Forsyth County wanted to remain free to chose how they lived," he contended. "The press had an obligation to show both sides of the story."

Although Duke was there as president of the NAAWP, former Ku Klux Klan leaders such as Don Black made it impossible for the event not to take on the look of a Klan march. Over 5,000 whites from across the U.S. joined Forsyth County residents in following Duke to the courthouse. In subfreezing weather, the normally sleepy Georgia town of Cumming was transformed into a snow-covered battle ground.

The intent of the black demonstrators was to march from one end of Cumming and finish with speeches on the courthouse steps. Later, Duke and his white brigade would enter the town from the opposite direction and would also be given the opportunity to speak at the county square.

"We met just outside of town," Duke said, "and got everyone in place. It was really terrific! You could see 5,000 non-violent white marchers fifteen to twenty abreast and stretching from hilltop-to-valley-to-hilltop, almost a half-mile in length."

Both groups were led by officers from the Georgia Bureau of Investigation to make certain nothing got out of hand. So tense was the situation that thousands of Georgia national guardsmen were called into service for possible riot duty.

Flanked by television cameras and newspaper reporters, Duke led his group through Cumming. Marchers armed with American and Confederate flags waited for the much-larger black demonstration to end.

Sporting a "Keep Forsyth White" button and speaking through a bullhorn, Duke harangued the crowd:

> "This is one of the first battles in a long struggle to regain our rights in America. Today, we declare that we have the right to associate with whom we desire, the right to preserve our culture and heritage, the right of our children to a good education, and the right of all people, young and old, men and women, to live in communities without the black plague of crime, murder, and terror of our citizens.

> "White people in Forsyth County are demonstrating, in spite of the media's attempt to paint them otherwise, not out of hatred of blacks and other minorities. We are motivated by an absolute determination to have a society that represents the highest attributes of civilization and not the violence, incompetence, corruption, and decay of black-run cities or counties. We are fully aware of the deplorable state of every non-white nation in the world.

> "In our minds and hearts we have visions of white communities, strong, clean, and healthy; excellent schools where our children learn of the greatness of their forefathers and are inspired to play an important role in the continued evolution and the advancement of our people.

> "Media will reflect the high values and culture of our people and serve to inspire and kindle a common vision of greatness. Violent crime and illegal drugs will not be tolerated, with swift and sure punishment for those who prey on the innocent. Government will be the servant, not the master, of the people.

> "Such a vision seems far away. Yes, there can be no doubt that the journey will be long and hard, but there is also no doubt that it will be made. Millions of our folk united in a common purpose and a steel will cannot be

denied. The awakening has been long coming, but the sleepy white giant, the founder and the backbone of America, is finally stirring.

"You and I are going to make it all possible. We will be blessed to live in the most threatening and also the most exciting time in the long history of our people. Let us make good use of the life God has given us!"

The marchers, standing in snow, responded with wild enthusiasm. They had traveled to Georgia from all parts of the nation to see Duke in person, and the "Gandhi of Racism" did not let them down. His articulation of white fears brought joy to the masses that heard his racist message.

So pleased were the marchers that they became restless waiting for the black protesters to arrive. Numerous times Duke shouted through the bullhorn for the crowd to remain nonviolent. "The worst thing we can do for the cause," he told them, "is to break the law!"

The plea for nonviolence fell on deaf ears as many in the all-white crowd began chanting, "No niggers in Forsyth!" Duke once again beseeched the marchers not to give law enforcement officials any reason to make arrests. But the whites who braved the cold Georgia winter weather to make their point were too angry to listen to Duke's counsel of peace.

Authorities of the Georgia Bureau of Investigation had heard about as much as they could stand and decided to put an end to the demonstration. Duke, Don Black, and Frank Shirley were called over to the police command post and abruptly arrested. They were charged with parading without a permit, handcuffed, and imprisoned in a barbed-wired stockade surrounded by combat-uniformed national guardsmen.

Duke was astounded that he was charged with failure to obtain a parade permit because he had been advised by the sheriff's office the day before that Forsyth County did not require permission to march publically.

"Someone from the GBI asked us to meet with them to discuss the demonstration," said Duke, "and then suddenly arrested us. It was the most gross violation of civil rights I had ever witnessed."

Along with a handful of other marchers, the three racist leaders stood for eight hours in ankle-deep snow and slush without being given water or permission to call a lawyer. Five hours later, the count of parading without a permit was changed to reckless conduct and obstruction of a highway, a charge normally reserved for drunks or vagrants.

"They wanted to muffle what we had to say," Duke fumed. "We were all held until after the march was over and the blacks had had their say. What they did was to cancel our civil rights march."

Finally, Duke was allowed to use a telephone and called one of the local organizers, who arranged bail for him and Black. "I was determined to fight it with every means possible," Duke said. He paid a $2,000 bond and was ordered to return to Georgia for a court appearance on February 23.

As he had done in the past, the NAAWP president hired a lawyer and prepared to defend himself. The problem was that the charge was so minor that it would not have behooved Duke to fight the case, especially with his presidential campaigning about to begin.

Ten days before the trial the state of Georgia added the charge of inciting to riot. Then, sensing a weak case, prosecutors offered to drop the charges in return for a guilty plea to jaywalking. On the advice of counsel, a deal was cut and Duke pleaded guilty to walking on a highway. He paid a fine of fifty dollars and was glad to have the issue behind him.

Back in New Orleans, Duke began putting together a campaign for the White House. A lifelong Democrat, Duke entered the Democratic primaries in hopes of going head-to-head with Jesse Jackson.

The April 1987 issue of the *NAAWP News* sported the head-line, "Duke May Run for President—David Duke vs. Jesse Jackson." Referring to Duke as "the charismatic National President of the NAAWP," the article claimed the former Klan leader had tentatively lined up organizations with 500,000 supporters to back his candidacy and read as follows:

"The truth is that neither the Democratic leadership nor the Republican leadership has acted to preserve our heritage and rights. Under both the Republicans and the Democrats the founding white majority of America is heading for oblivion. There is a tremendous dissatisfaction among the rank-and-file working people in the Democratic Party. A sizeable segment is angry about the organized minorities, feminists, and ultra-liberal domination of the party, yet it is still the party of the white working person. Many have deserted the Democratic Party in the general election and voted for the Republican candidate. However, in their hearts they know that the Republican Party doesn't really speak for them either, and that it is just as controlled by the international banks and money interests as are the Democrats.

"Gary Hart's dropping out from [sic] the race has put Jesse Jackson in the position of front-runner. Jesse Jackson's presence in the race will clarify the issues at stake in 1988. Just as this black racist symbolizes the mono-racialation [sic] of America, so David Duke will symbolize the hopes and aspirations of millions of white, middle class Americans.

"When millions of votes come rolling in from New Hampshire to Florida, from North Carolina to California, American politics will never be the same again. Candidates from all over America will begin to realize that they are not alone, and that they no longer fear the alien power that dominates us.

"We are the backbone of America, we are the great minds and strong arms of this country. It was our fore-fathers who tore this nation from the wilderness and from

Foreign domination. The election of '88 will give White Americans who truly care about the future of this country the chance of a lifetime."

Duke was now clearly running for president of the United States. A formal announcement had not been made so that the campaign would not be subject to any federal election restrictions. Because the NAAWP was a non-profit organization, it could not participate directly in campaigns. Duke needed all the support and publicity he could muster, so the *NAAWP News* would be his launching pad. Even a long-shot campaign such as Duke's would be expensive, and the newspaper, as always, would be a good way to raise money. The article ended by noting that "the knowledge that he [Duke] is the President of the NAAWP will inevitably result in thousands of new members and supporters for our organization."

Even though he had no real chance to win the Democratic nomination, Duke thought he could surprise some people. "If the party played by the rules, I knew I could win at least as many delegates as Jesse Jackson," he said.

With only a few thousand dollars in his bank account, Duke decided formally to proclaim himself a candidate for president in Atlanta, the site of the Democratic National Convention. He originally had rented a conference room at the Stouffer Waverly Hotel, but his reservation had been cancelled a week before the announcement was to occur. The hotel claimed that Duke was a risk to the security of its patrons and staff, but the *NAAWP News* insisted the denial was prompted by "the Jewish-Black Coalition."

Another reservation was made at the Ritz-Carlton, but once again the hotel cancelled as soon as it was understood who David Duke was. Finally, Duke was able to book a conference room at the Atlanta Marriott Hotel, but not without loud protests from the management. They insisted Duke would have to obtain a million-dollar insurance bond to guarantee the hotel's security. The cost: $600 for the day. The racist leader balked, arguing, "How can it be we live in a free country, and it is impossible for a presidential candidate to announce his candidacy?"

The day before he was to announce for president, Duke had scheduled interviews on various Atlanta radio and television stations. To his chagrin, the hosts were belligerent and gave him little time to discuss his platform. One host even suggested that blacks should "beat him with whips and chains."

On Tuesday, June 9, David Duke made his formal announcement for the nation's highest office on the steps of the Georgia state capitol in front of the statue of racist Sen. Thomas E. Watson. The ex-wizard was joined by about 150 supporters, who were enthusiastic at the idea of their idol's entering the fray. Duke laid out plans for his presidency by railing against affirmative action, illegitimate welfare childbirths, government set asides, income taxes, the Supreme Court, and "Zionist control over the media."

In his opening address he declared, "I expect a tremendous fight over the next few months. I can't dismiss the danger. We all know what happened to George Wallace. A lot of people are afraid of David Duke. The Democrats will be Tweedle-Dee and Tweedle-Dum. I can beat them because I'm not afraid to offend Jesse Jackson. I'll be the only one articulating the issues that are important to the Democratic Party."

Borrowing from Jesse Jackson's Rainbow Coalition, Duke dubbed his campaign the Sunshine Coalition.

"I don't know if I can win," he acknowledged, "but I know in this state I can beat Jesse Jackson. With the same type of constituency George Wallace had in 1972, I think I can do well."

The setting of Duke's announcement was very uncomfortable and not appreciated by the local news organizations, which were priming themselves for the "real Democrats" in August. But all was not lost on the news media on announcement day. After his speech, Duke headed to Washington to

appear on CNN's interview show, "Crossfire," which was televised nationwide.

As could be expected, the Democratic party bosses were
not happy about having the former Ku Klux Klansman rain
on their parade. It might be a bit distracting to have a debate
involving Jesse Jackson, Michael Dukakis, and David Duke.
The Democrats were concerned with focusing on the Republicans in the fall, not on Duke all year long.

While in Washington, the racist presidential aspirant attempted to meet with Democratic National Committee Chairman Paul Kirk to discuss the possibility of participating in
the scheduled debates, only to be informed that he would not
be allowed in the DNC headquarters.

The DNC was so strongly opposed to the idea of Duke's
participation in the primaries that Kirk wrote to all Democratic state chairmen urging them to do everything legally
possible to distance themselves from the NAAWP president's
campaign. Calling Duke's campaign "a fraud and a sham on
the political process," the DNC chairman made it clear that
he wanted no part of the former Klan leader's politics.

"I have as much right [as anyone] to run for any office
within the Democratic party, having been a lifelong Democrat," roared Duke.

Kirk finally changed his tone regarding Duke and issued a
letter saying that the racist candidate had the legal right to
participate in the Democratic primaries. But Kirk added that
the DNC was opposed to everything Duke stood for and would
never endorse his candidacy.

Duke hoped to be on the primary ballot in thirty-three states
and thus qualify for federal matching funds. The problem
Duke faced was viability within his party. Because he was considered a pariah by the Democrats, he was denied the opportunity to appear in DNC-sanctioned debates, thus making
Duke a virtual non-candidate.

The former grand wizard learned that a nationally televised debate was going to be held at Tulane University in New Orleans. This would be the perfect opportunity for him to gather his local supporters and give a great show of support. The trouble was that all the candidates were invited except Duke, who lambasted everyone in sight:

"The Democratic Leadership Conference, a committee of the party bosses, would neither invite me, nor would they accept my appearance there. And the Democratic National Committee and the organizations holding the debate did not offer my name as a potential candidate or a potential debater. I don't think they want a young person who is standing up for the rights of the American majority to be in a situation where he can call on other candidates for their records and really debate the issues in a sincere fashion."

Whenever Duke feels his civil rights are being threatened, he files suit, and it would be no different this time. When asked if he planned to protest his treatment by the DNC, Duke answered, "We will file suit in federal court in New Orleans in an effort to win a place on the debate platform at Tulane University. We have an excellent campaign coordinator, Mr. Ralph Forbes, who did a masterful job of research and legal writing and who initiated this suit."

The suit, however, was filed too late and the debate proceeded without Duke and his racist platform. "What we really were [asking] in this suit," he explained, "was [whether] the basic right of freedom of speech and the right of Americans to participate in the political process had to be open to all."

Trying to avoid a shutout, Duke showed up outside Tulane's McAllister Hall, where the debate was being held, to stage his own one-man debate. It was Free Speech Alley revisited. Duke stood on a bench and gave the waiting press and curious students a lecture on racist politics. Without a microphone, Duke held the attention of the crowd with his views on affirmative action, immigration, the Ku Klux Klan, and black teenage illegitimate births. The students seized the opportunity to question the former Klan leader and the event lasted over an hour. "Real democracy," he told the crowd, "is not inside that closed hall, but out here with the people."

The New Hampshire primary was scheduled for January 1988, and Duke hoped to make some inroads in the almost all-white state. If he could get even a small percentage of votes in the important first primary, the national coverage would be a boost to his long-shot campaign.

He worked around the state trying to draw as much attention as he could. But he soon found it more difficult than he imagined because the the New Englanders were not receptive to his brand of politics. Also, he had to compete for media attention with Massachusetts Gov. Michael Dukakis, not to mention Republican Sen. Robert Dole and Vice-President George Bush.

The results of the Democratic presidential primary were not surprising. Dukakis led the field with 44,112 votes, with Cong. Richard Gephardt of Missouri and Sen. Paul Simon of Illinois trailing badly. Duke managed to win a paltry 264 votes, which gave the Democratic party good reason not to let him participate in sponsored debates.

Things took a bizarre turn in New Hampshire. The Granite State has an unusual law which allows candidates to run for vice-president. "We knew we were being blacked-out by the Democratic party bosses," said Duke, "so we decided to also put my name on the vice-presidential ballot." The results there were much better for the former Klansman, who received 10,531 votes, or almost 60 percent of the total. "It proved that people would vote for my ideals if given the opportunity," he asserted.

Running in an uncrowded field of unknowns for vice-president would not be the same as going up against the big boys in the real races. But Duke's fortunes would be no better in the other thirty states he competed in as a Democrat. Before the primary process had ended, the Democrats had chosen Governor Dukakis to head their ticket, completely shutting Duke out of the race. "If we [had been] given the opportunities that Jesse Jackson was given," reasoned Duke, "we would have gone to the convention with at least as many delegates."

Democratic leaders disagree with Duke and insist he was awarded the same opportunities as any other minor candidate. As one party official said, "If we let all the nuts who wanted to run for president participate in every debate, we'd have to hold them in football stadiums."

Although he had no chance to participate in Democratic politics, Duke was far from finished in the presidential race. During the Democratic primaries, he had attracted many extreme right-wing supporters. Among them was Ralph Forbes, who has long been associated with neo-Nazi causes and who lent a very unsavory aroma to Duke's campaign.

Don Black was on the board of directors of the Populist party, and felt the party's nomination could be Duke's for the asking. After some persuasion by Black and Forbes, Duke agreed to attend the convention in Chicago to try to lead the Populist party ticket.

The convention was attended by only a few hundred party loyalists, who ranged from the extreme to the very extreme. Former Nazi party members, ex-Klansmen, and Skin Heads were only some of the radicals who came to choose a man to lead their cause in the November presidential election. People such as Don Black and Ralph Forbes were not the only decision-makers in the Populist party. At first, the nomination seemed locked up for Duke, but there were others who wanted be the party's standardbearer. One was Cong. John Trafficant, a Democrat from Ohio, who was Duke's strongest opposition for the post. A maverick within the Democratic party as well as in Congress, Trafficant is considered to be a libertarian in philosophy and practice.

The nomination process was preceded by short speeches on behalf of potential candidates, and Duke won on the first ballot without much fanfare. It would be a far cry from the original nomination he had sought, but at least "the struggle" could continue.

During the election, Duke did anything but distance himself from the Populist party and its ideology. He had long espoused his brand of "racist populism," which fit right into the scheme of the party he was representing. His vice-presidential running mate was a man named Bo Gritz of Nevada, a decorated Vietnam veteran and the man on whom the motion-picture character Rambo allegedly is based.

Although the Populist party is out of the mainstream of American politics, it still managed to raise a substantial amount of money for the campaign. Well over a half-million dollars was spent trying to elect David Duke to the highest office in the land. It was much more money than he could ever have dreamed of raising through the NAAWP. Populists, libertarians, and other neo-groups, however, all exist because they know how to trigger a delicate mechanism within certain people to extract support, and most importantly, money, to keep their crusades going.

Campaigning by Duke for the fall election was restricted primarily to radio talk shows and some television coverage. "We really were running on a shoestring," said Duke.

Duke's campaign advisors decided to produce a thirty-minute television program, which was aired on October 25, just days before the election. Duke sat across from an attractive young woman who asked prepared questions. It was the old David Duke:

> Questioner: "How do you feel about being classified
> as a racist?"

Duke: "I don't see any racist here. Jesse Jackson is not here in the studio. I think it's interesting [that] if a person is white and they believe in equal rights for everybody in this country . . . they are called racists. George Bush and Michael Dukakis . . . both of them are now embracing so-called affirmative action, which is nothing more than blatant racial discrimination against better-qualified white people in hiring and promotions, scholarships, college admittance, union admittance, and rewarding of contracts [at the] municipal, state . . . and . . . federal level. So what we've got going on now is massive racism being emphasized against white people in America, and I'm being called a racist because I believe in equal rights for everyone. . . . I think that's quite hypocritical."

The rest of the program was a David Duke retread. He lashed out at the leading presidential contenders.

"Zionist PACs have long ago bought Bush and Dukakis," he said.

Calling for "an America First policy," Duke said his administration would revamp the welfare system, end all forced busing to achieve racial balance in schools, and dramatically limit immigration. He also proposed strong protectionist tariffs on competing nations that threaten America's work force. No longer under a Duke administration would foreigners be able to purchase land or businesses. Another plank in his platform was the abolition of the Internal Revenue Service. Income tax under Duke would be a flat 10 percent of earnings.

In a disguised attack on Jews, Duke suggested that a new banking system of his creation would "be committed only to the people of the United States and their welfare."

Duke has long claimed that the largest and most important banks are controlled by Jews and therefore monetary policy of the U.S. supports Zionism. He argued that "foreign aid and military assistance must be based solely on the direct interests of the majority of the American people. We should review our Mideast policy and make it more evenhanded so that our economic and strategic interests are served, rather than [those] of the tiny minority that has such excessive influence in the media and in government."

Finally, he called for the lifting of sanctions against the minority white government of South Africa, which he referred to as "our kindred people."

The show ended with a direct appeal for votes. "Voting for the lesser of two evils," he cautioned, "is still voting for an evil. The only vote you truly waste is a vote that you cast for a principle or person you don't believe in. The Populist party of the people is America's fastest-growing movement. We need a party that puts America first, that puts the American workingman, the American majority, first in American politics."

The program was seen by millions of households across the country. It gave Duke the exposure he had wanted when he first decided to run in the Democratic primaries.

Duke returned home to Metairie to wait for the will of the people. When election night came and the ballots were finally tallied, Duke had received only 150,000 votes. "We could have done much better," he claimed, "if we [had been] allowed to run the campaign with the same rules as Bush and Dukakis. We were denied federal matching funds. Why? Because those in power don't want the truth to reach millions of households that television money could buy. A perfect case in point is what happened in the New Orleans area. There is only one daily newspaper in New Orleans, the *Times-Picayune*. It is owned by the largest newspaper chain in America, the Newhouse group. The family is one of Zionism's biggest benefactors, and all of their papers have taken a slavishly pro-Zionist position and at the same time a liberal/minority bias that would shame perhaps even the Sulzbergers of the *New York Times*."

With any presidential aspirations temporarily behind him, Duke planned to return to running the NAAWP and take some time off. He had been on the road for almost two years, and he wanted to relax and regroup. But only days after the election Duke was paid a visit by his friend Howie Farrell, who pointedly reminded him that the local House of Representatives seat would soon be up for grabs.

"I was exhausted," remembers Duke, "but I knew this could be a great step for the struggle. There wasn't any time to relax."

He was now known across the country as the "Rolls Royce of Racism." By hard work, David Duke had finally found himself.

Louisiana state Rep. David Duke. (Photo by Nancy Moss)

CHAPTER NINETEEN

Today and Tomorrow

THERE WOULD BE NO TIME for Duke to adjust to his new role as a member of the Louisiana legislature. After all, he was still reeling from the shock of actually being elected to office. It is sometimes easier to lose than to win, and Duke finally faced the prospect of having to do something about the issues he had so long championed.

Political observers were burning with curiosity as to how Duke would behave once he began introducing legislation. No one was sure what to expect from the first grand wizard of the Ku Klux Klan ever to hold a legitimate public office in the United States. Rumors abounded throughout Baton Rouge about Duke's proposed legislation dealing with welfare recipients. Was he going to demand that welfare mothers be neutered in order to receive benefits? Not even a conservative Southern state such as Louisiana had ever seen the likes of David Duke.

Less than ten days after being elected, Duke was submitting bills he hoped would become law in a special session of the legislature. He was administered the oath of office on Monday, pre-filed his first piece of legislation on Tuesday, and appeared nationwide on the "Larry King Live" television show Thursday night—not bad for a guy in office only four days. Duke has always been the consummate manipulator of the press simply because the material he works with is so reportable. No other state legislator, including Julian Bond of Georgia or Tom Hayden of California, has ever produced the type of emotionalism that David Duke generates.

True to his word, the first piece of legislation proposed by Duke was House Bill 77, which "prohibits state and local entities from using public funds by participating in certain discriminatory practices in the letting of contracts." Since his early days with the Ku Klux Klan, David Duke has trumpeted what he saw as the evils of affirmative action and set-aside laws. He made their removal from state government his top priority.

Both affirmative action and set-aside laws were unpopular with Louisiana voters and even with most lawmakers. But Duke's bill was still construed by many as racist legislation aimed at countering gains made by blacks since the civil rights movement began in earnest in the 1950s.

"David Duke has never been the friend of black citizens," said the Reverend Avery Alexander, civil rights leader, dean of the legislative Black Caucus, and Democrat from New Orleans. "The NAAWP and all that other stuff is no more than George Wallace all over again."

Alexander was not the only black legislator who felt animosity toward the former Ku Klux Klan leader. Rep. Diana Bajoie, also a Democrat from New Orleans, went to the microphone and announced before the entire House of Representatives, "Blacks will be watching you very close, Mr. Duke."

Unmoved by the Black Caucus, Duke proceeded as scheduled. "I think it's hypocritical," he said, "that Reverend Alexander and the rest of the blacks can belong to the NAACP and still call me a racist for belonging to the NAAWP."

At the beginning of the first special session, Duke was shunned by most of his colleagues as though he were Libya's Moammar Khadafy at the White House. Wherever the racist went, he was followed by a battalion of photographers looking for a photo opportunity. Anyone caught speaking with him was fair game for front-page news. An amiable person, Duke had a habit of walking through the House chamber, smiling and shaking hands with members as he passed.

One day early in the session, he leaned over and shook hands with Rep. James St. Raymond, and cameras began clicking. The next morning, the *Times-Picayune* carried a front-page, color picture of Duke and St. Raymond, hand in hand. St. Raymond represents an affluent area of uptown New Orleans that includes the largest Jewish community in Louisiana. Understandably, his telephone rang off the wall with calls from outraged constituents wanting to know what their representative was doing posing with their worst nightmare.

St. Raymond sent a letter to all local newspapers notifying them in no uncertain terms of the differences between him and Duke. "I wanted to distance myself as far as I could," St. Raymond explained. "If Duke wanted to join the other Republicans in the legislature, that was fine. But when I saw he had his own agenda, I got as far away as I could."

Duke saw St. Raymond's predicament in a different light: "He bent to the pressure of the *Times-Picayune.* It's remarkable what happens when Jews apply pressure."

St. Raymond's rebuke did not really matter, because Duke was caught up in the euphoria of the moment. He filed HB 893 that would increase the sentence of anyone convicted of violating the controlled-substance law in a public housing project.

"If we are really serious about cleaning up projects," he challenged, "then let's make it a more serious crime to sell drugs there."

The bill was almost identical to one proposed by Sen. Cleo Fields, a Democrat from Baton Rouge. The difference was that Fields is black, and his motives were not perceived by the news media or other members as racist. The outcome was that SB 9 became law and Duke's bill died a quiet death.

Quickly, the former grand wizard learned that his past would make the present very difficult, indeed.

HB 1569, which Duke also filed, proposed "that an adult who is convicted of a violation of the Uniform Controlled Dangerous Substances Law while participating as a recipient in a public assistance program, in addition to the criminal sanctions, becomes ineligible to receive further benefits thereunder."

Even a bill that punished convicted drug pushers was hard for Duke to get passed through both the House and the Senate. "David said the same things a lot of us had been sayin'," admitted one North Louisiana legislator, "but it was just impossible for anyone to stand up and vote with him in the beginning."

The special session was a failure for Duke as far as legislation was concerned, but he was not discouraged. "The civil rights movement for blacks was not won in a week," he reminded anyone who would listen. "But keep in mind, the legislature debated ideas that would never have been talked about before. I think it was a great step forward. I may have been the personal focus of some attacks on my legislation, but very few people disagreed with what I was saying. Liberals cannot intelligently argue the point that affirmative action is discriminatory against whites."

In an attempt to save money while in Baton Rouge, Duke stayed in a friend's empty one-bedroom apartment. Unlike the rest of the House members, Duke was not invited to dine each night by the throngs of lobbyists who fight for legislators' attention. The atmosphere was tense in the special session, and everyone walked a very fine line with Duke.

If a lobbyist was regarded as being too close to Duke, he faced the possibility of being linked with the former Ku Klux Klan leader in the press and thus would lose any influence he may have had with the Black Caucus. But David Duke was not in the legislature to eat dinner with a lobbyist from the Chemical Association. Most people would be offended by someone who acted friendly toward him in private, then became distant in the crowded House chamber. But not Duke. After a lifetime of extremist politics, he has accepted life as an outsider.

But all not was gloom and doom in Baton Rouge. Republican legislators such as Charles Lancaster, Jr., of Metairie, Emile ("Peppi") Bruneau, Jr., of New Orleans, and Roy Brun of Shreveport treated Duke as an equal.

"You can't judge a man on what happened ten years ago," Lancaster said. "As long as David behaves himself in a dignified manner, then I can work with him. If he wants to neuter people, then that'll be different."

Before he was elected, Duke had made a commitment to attend the Populist party's convention in Chicago. It was not a smart political move to go, but Duke is far from being a smart politician.

"I had made a commitment long before I was in the legislature," Duke explained. "A man has to keep his word."

Duke was followed to the convention by Republican activist Beth Rickey, who had notified the local press that the former presidential candidate would be in attendance.

"It was incredible," she said. "There were the absolute worst kinds of people in the room. I mean Skin Heads, the whole bit . . . and David did not make one effort to distance himself from them."

After the meeting, Duke was being interviewed by a Chicago television station when Art Jones, who has been identified as a former Nazi party-member, walked up and shook Duke's hand. Cameras began rolling as a bewildered Duke stood in shock. To make matters worse, Jones staged a confrontation with newsmen, screaming and calling them names. An embarrassed Duke stood by as photographers videotaped the entire episode.

"I had never met this guy before," Duke later said of Jones. "I heard he's some Nazi kook."

Back in Baton Rouge, Duke asked the Speaker of the House for special privilege to address the body. A subdued Duke addressed his new colleagues and apologized for any embarrassment the incident may have brought to the legislature.

Whatever the issue might be, Duke continued to be the focus of media attention. Many longtime legislators were jealous of his ability to get seemingly unlimited coverage. When Gov. Buddy Roemer's fiscal reform tax package was being debated, Duke was constantly on television as though he were an expert on state taxes. One member of the Senate Finance Committee was not shy about his appraisal of the state's newest legislator.

"This guy's been in office a week," he complained, "and he's been in the papers more than Huey and Earl Long put together."

By a very narrow margin, Governor Roemer's tax package had passed both the House and the Senate and faced a tough fight for voter approval. The governor and many business and civic leaders took a high profile in support of the tax revision. With the power of the governor's office and the help of big business, they were successful in raising over a million dollars to help advertise the benefits of changing Louisiana's backward tax code.

Because he was on a roll from his recent victory, Duke became the leading opponent of the governor and fiscal reform.

"It is no more than a seven-hundred-million-dollar tax increase," Duke liked to say. "Read my lips, Gov. Buddy Roemer. No new taxes!"

Duke was basking in the limelight, and Roemer finally lost his composure. When asked what he thought about Duke's vocal opposition, the governor responded tersely, "I don't care about David Duke and the American Nazi party!"

Once again, Duke made great copy. Newspapers and television stations covered the political battle daily. What had begun as a simple tax reform election had turned into a referendum on the governor himself.

Roemer is one of the brightest politicians in America and has had his eye on the White House all his life. If he were able to get the tax reform package passed, then he was practically guaranteed re-election. After re-election, he planned to launch a campaign as a Southern moderate for the Democratic nomination in 1996. But first he had to convince a skeptical Louisiana electorate that shifting the tax burden from big business to homeowners would spur new investment and create more jobs in a devastated economy.

The election was scheduled for April, and it immediately took on the air of a major campaign. Bumper stickers reading "Support the Movement for Fiscal Reform" sprouted all over Louisiana. Households were inundated with television commercials and direct mail touting the tax package. Roemer traveled the state from one end to the other in pursuit of votes. Legislators met daily with local civic clubs in an attempt to sway voters to turn out on election day and support the tax package.

Foes of fiscal reform were led by Duke and Baton Rouge Rep. Woody Jenkins, a staunch conservative. Considered almost a libertarian in political philosophy, Jenkins has long been one of the most vocal anti-tax legislators in Louisiana. He has one of the sharpest minds in the House and often takes positions contrary to the governor. Although he has run twice for the U.S. Senate and is well known, Jenkins was still overshadowed by Duke's skill in attracting coverage from the news media.

All campaigning by the anti-tax reform forces had to be done on a shoestring as they had virtually no money. What they did have was the best free publicity machine anyone could hope for, David Duke. Wherever the former Klansman went, people and the press would show up to get a look at the man they had heard and read so much about. It was just after Duke's victory over John Treen, and he was still a public curiosity.

One night before the election, Duke and Roemer were in Shreveport campaigning in different parts of town. The governor met with a number of Chamber of Commerce members, area legislators, and civic leaders to promote his plan. Duke, on the other hand, held a simple rally which drew a throng of white middle-class citizens wanting to see the former grand wizard in person.

The next morning, the Shreveport *Journal* carried a headline reading, "Duke Outdraws Roemer." An elated Duke responded, "It proves that the people are listening to what I've been saying!"

Newspapers throughout the state printed polls indicating that the fiscal reform package would pass with over 55 percent of the vote. Buoyed by the polls, Roemer confidently crisscrossed the state for a final campaign swing. The election proved to be as exciting as political forecasters had predicted. The entire state had become locked in debate not only on tax reform, but on the governor and Duke personally.

The Wednesday before the balloting Duke was invited to speak in opposition to the tax package by fellow Rep. John ("Juba") Diez. Diez's district encompasses a middle-class union constituency, which is the core of Duke's support.

Although a Democrat, Diez, like Duke, was opposed to the governor's tax proposals and hoped to draw support from Duke's popularity among blue-collar voters. A public meeting was held at seven o'clock at the VFW hall outside of the city of Gonzales, about fifteen miles south of Baton Rouge. An overflow crowd of more than six hundred people spilled out into the parking area to hear what Duke had to say. They politely greeted Diez, who promptly turned the podium over to Duke.

The former grand wizard was given a standing ovation, which he received with a broad smile. "What we are here about tonight," he said in a preacher-like tone, "is whether we are going to stand by and let Gov. Buddy Roemer raise our taxes by seven hundred million dollars! What do you say?" The hall answered with a thunderous no!

Knowing he had the crowd eating out of his hand, Duke began railing against affirmative action and set asides. In an attempt to mollify opposition from black lawmakers, Roemer had included a portion of the tax package for minority contractors through a set-aside program. This gave Duke one more reason to fight the referendum, and he made the most of it.

"If it is wrong to discriminate against a person because he is black," Duke said, "then it is equally as reprehensible to discriminate against a person because he is white."

That drew Duke's second standing ovation of the evening.

Throughout the speech, Diez sat beside Duke looking somewhat amazed at the reaction of the voters of his district. After all, these were French Catholics who stood fanatically applauding a former Ku Klux Klan grand wizard. "I've known every one of these people my whole life," Diez quipped. "These are not David's old Ku Klux Klan gang."

But the night resembled a Duke rally from his past days with the Klan. The parking lot was filled with pickup trucks, and most in attendance were lower- to middle-class whites. Most importantly to Duke, they all agreed with him.

After lambasting Roemer, Duke reminded those faithful in the gathering, "All we are asking for is equal rights for everyone. Even white people!"

That is precisely what the audience had come to hear, and they all jumped to their feet in a wild frenzy. Loud chants of "Duke! Duke! Duke!" drowned out Diez's attempt to thank his friends for coming out. Duke stood up and motioned Diez over to him. The crowd became quiet in order not to miss anything Duke might say.

"I want you to know," he told the crowd, "that Juba Diez is working for the interests of working people, and you can be proud of him."

The blessing by Duke awarded Diez his only standing ovation of the night. Clearly, he would be indebted to his new racist colleague.

The election was only three days away, and forces in support of fiscal reform had done everything possible to inform voters of what passage of the referendum would do for the state. The amendment was endorsed by every leading newspaper in Louisiana, in addition to gaining almost universal political support. Mayors, sheriffs, and local constables had all come aboard the governor's band wagon. As the polls closed, Roemer and key aides huddled in the Governor's Mansion in Baton Rouge to await the outcome.

Down in Metairie, more than three hundred Duke supporters gathered at the Electrical Workers Hall to be with their hero. These were the same workers that just months before had stood beside the guru of racism in his winning legislative campaign. There were no bands, and only one keg of beer and homemade sandwiches. This was in direct contrast to parties hosted by supporters of the referendum. They were confident of winning, and large victory celebrations were scheduled throughout the state.

Results of the election began coming in about 8:30 P.M., and it was clear from the outset that Roemer and fiscal tax reform would be overwhelmingly rejected by voters across the state. Rep. Robert Adley of Bossier City, one of Roemer's closest allies, met with the press outside the Governor's Mansion about 9:30 P.M. to concede that the referendum had indeed failed. Everyone around the governor tried to downplay the effects on the state's chief executive, but it was obvious by the size of the defeat that his clout had been greatly diminished.

It was a totally different picture at the Electrical Workers Hall, where a jubilant Duke was once again basking in the effulgence of an upset victory over what seemed to be unsurmountable odds. Reporters from Louisiana and across the nation wanted to hear what Duke had to say about the election result.

"The people have spoken," Duke declared in an excited voice, "and they said, 'Gov. Buddy Roemer, no new taxes!'"

The packed hall began shouting "Duke! Duke! Duke!" When asked by a reporter why he thought the tax package had failed, Duke responded, "The voters spoke loudly and clearly. They reject any new taxes, and they reject the anti-white racism called set asides."

Thus, a man who had built his career on racism had suddenly become the leading opponent of new taxes. Although Duke would continue to be no more than a gadfly to the governor in the legislature, he had proved to be very effective with direct appeals to the voters. The members of the Louisiana legislature are some of the most astute politicians in America, and they quickly saw that their constituents were not in the mood for either taxes or set asides.

When the legislature reconvened the following Monday, Duke found legislators more inclined to mix with him on a political level. Many still tried to avoid being associated with Duke in the press, but most members of the House were willing at least to listen to what the former Ku Klux Klan leader had to say. The Republican Caucus and the powerful Jefferson Parish Caucus have welcomed Duke with open arms and taken him in as "one of the boys."

Although Duke enjoys being a Republican member of the legislature, he is still shunned by many within the GOP. Twice the state Republican Central Committee has attempted to censure the former Klan leader, in response to heavy pressure from Democrats. Duke escaped official rebuke both times, but only after long and acrimonious debate.

Many from the Treen camp still harbor ill feeling toward the man who defeated their candidate only months before.

Some party leaders believe that since censure would have no legal effect on Duke's ability to hold office or to campaign under the Republican banner, the resulting publicity would only benefit him in the end.

At one committee meeting, state Sen. Ben Bagert of New Orleans, who later would win the party's endorsement over Duke in the 1990 race for the U.S. Senate, urged members not to "make this maggot into a martyr." After all, both President Bush and RNC Chairman Lee Atwater have stated emphatically that Duke will never be welcomed by the Republican party.

Representatives in the House sit beside one other member. Because he had just been elected and was so controversial, Duke was assigned a single desk at the very rear of the House chamber. But Duke has long been used to going it alone and politely went about his business. Anyway, he was never going to be just one member out of 105 who blended quietly into the background.

Duke spent much of his days at the special session on the telephone, either with his office back in New Orleans or doing radio talk-show interviews. Unlike other representatives, Duke was an international figure and was in demand among reporters on a daily basis. Almost hyperactive, he rocks back and forth, drumming his fingers across his desk as he reads legislation and talks on the phone. He has never forgotten what his father taught him about idle time and makes the most of his day.

Appearing during the session on the "Donahue Show," Duke managed to reach his largest audience to date. The program was filmed in Denver and, as usual, Duke surprised the television audience with his placid demeanor. Dressed in a conservative blue suit and with his moustache newly removed, he was now state Rep. David Duke, rather than the grand wizard or NAAWP president.

Although he still headed the white-rights organization, he was on the "Donahue Show" because of his recent election victory. At the end of the program, Duke asked viewers to write him at the state capitol if they wanted to hear more about him or the NAAWP. For weeks following the show, Duke's House desk was covered with mail from viewers from every state curious about what he was saying. Envelopes were filled with handwritten words of encouragement from people who agreed with Duke's racist philosophies. Most of the letters contained checks for two, three, or five dollars.

"It was the damnedest thing I've ever seen," exclaimed one rural House member. "I've been in office for sixteen years, and the only letters I get are complaints from voters back home. This guy gets money from people he don't even know."

Not only had Duke's fortunes improved in Baton Rouge but things back in New Orleans also were booming. All the coverage he had been receiving from the media during his House election and the fiscal reform referendum had helped the NAAWP grow beyond even David Duke's wildest dreams. Thousands of people became first-time members of the organization that previously had been known only by right-wing extremists. NAAWP headquarters was now operated by full-time employees, with help from a staff of volunteers. Whenever a letter was received, the name and address was immediately fed into one of Duke's many computers so they could be used in future fund-raising efforts.

Duke has become a celebrity without equal in Louisiana politics. No longer forced to live as an outsider, the racist representative works within the system. He has been welcomed into the homes of some of New Orleans' most elite families and is often seen hobnobbing with people who just months before would have shunned him.

But contrary to the general perception, Duke has not spent all of his past without some social acceptance. One of New Orleans' wealthiest and most flamboyant socialites, with very

strong political connections, has been a closet "Dukie" for
years, even though public knowledge of their relationship
would be devastating to her socially.

Many prominent businessmen, as well as one of the leading
writers for the *Times-Picayune,* have also secretly shared long-
term friendships with the champion of the racist right. A New
Orleans-bred entertainer with international credentials continues to keep company with him, despite the knowledge that
it could jeopardize television or recording contracts.

"I didn't just happen along," Duke insists. "I've had long
relationships with many people who I'm certain would rather
not have their names linked with mine."

The private David Duke is far removed from the driven
racist portrayed in the press. Time spent away from politics
or the NAAWP is normally spent alone. In his cramped, one-
bedroom apartment, Duke is most at ease reading or playing
the piano with his cat, Minnie, on his lap.

A health enthusiast, Duke works out almost daily at a local
health club and makes an effort to watch his weight. Ever
since his mother taught him golf, it has been one of the few
luxuries he has allowed himself. One day while at the driving
range in New Orleans' City Park, Duke complained about the
three-dollar-charge for the rental of golf balls.

"It would only cost half this much," he calculated, "if the
city didn't have to subsidize welfare recipients."

A doting father, Duke spends a great deal of time with his
daughters Erika and Kristin, who live in Florida with Chloe
and Don Black. During the regular session of the legislature,
the children stayed with Duke and could daily be seen following
their famous dad throughout the House chamber.

Because of the controversy surrounding Duke, security for
him and his daughters was tight. While their father was busy
trying to end affirmative action, someone would watch the
girls or take them to the cafeteria for ice cream.

One day the fire alarm was set off and the capitol had to be quickly evacuated. Duke panicked when he realized Erika and Kristin were nowhere to be found. He ran out of the chamber and down the stairs and found them in the basement.

Slight and pretty, the two girls have their father in the palm of their hands and enjoy the playful attention he showers on them. They are extremely defensive about what people say about Duke and cannot seem to understand why their father is so maligned.

Being a bachelor, Duke enjoys the role as America's most eligible racist. He can be seen buzzing about town in his sports car, which he bought used for $5,000. He has always devoted his financial efforts to "the struggle," and lives an extremely spartan lifestyle.

His apartment furniture consists of a metal kitchen table, four chairs, a king-sized bed, a bed for the girls, a chest of drawers, a television set, and some stereo equipment. Other than a piano, Duke owns very little else. When he is accused of profiting from the NAAWP, he throws a tantrum.

"What do they think?" he demands. "Do they think I like driving used cars or buying clothes at discount stores? I'd like my daughters to have nice things other children have. Look at the way I have to live!"

During the regular legislative session, things looked as if they would only get better until one day Beth Rickey, an activist for Duke's own Republican party, notified the press that she had some damaging information about Duke. News regarding the racist leader is almost always guaranteed to get attention, but something that might be disparaging will probably make the front page of every Louisiana newspaper.

Rickey met with the news media in the capitol rotunda and displayed Nazi literature she said she had recently purchased at Duke's bookstore. An embarrassed Duke responded that he had discontinued the books and was only selling the remaining stock on the shelf. The revelation linking Duke with the Nazi literature was one more setback in his attempt to distance himself from his checkered past. Duke has more political baggage to carry than most politicians and makes a tempting target for a hungry reporter looking for a big story.

No matter what Duke does, he still manages to make headlines. Hardly a day goes by that he does not appear on a radio talk show somewhere in the country. Local newspapers carry articles weekly on some aspect of his life. If there were such a thing as a teflon racist it would be David Duke. It is amazing that he has survived the barrage of accusations about past ties to the Klan and to Nazis, but after each attack he seems to rebound.

"Sure," he readily admits, "I was strident in my youth. But I was taught as a boy that if you stood up for what you believed in, it wouldn't be held against you for the rest of your life. People have said horrible things about the early lives of many revered Americans. They said at one time Ronald Reagan was a member of left-wing socialist groups, and that John Kennedy was a womanizer. They accused Goldwater of [planning to] drop . . . the bomb if he was elected. I can take the heat."

Knowing he must ride the wave of public recognition or fade into the background, Duke now stands at an important point in his career. He understands that he can never really get his agenda into law as long as he remains in the Louisiana legislature.

"Even if I managed to get a bill to outlaw affirmative action through both houses," he said, "the governor would just veto it. The issues I am most interested in can best be addressed on a national level."

In early 1990, a restless David Duke announced he would run for the U.S. Senate against J. Bennett Johnston, who has held the seat for eighteen years. Although he lost the Republican party endorsement to state Senator Bagert, Duke continued to campaign against heavy odds, as he did in his successful 1989 House race.

With Democrat Johnston and Republicans Bagert and Duke running in the same open primary, and many Louisiana voters still angered by Johnston's 1987 fight to defeat Reagan's nomination of Robert Bork to the U.S. Supreme Court, pollsters began to voice the unthinkable: David Duke had a chance.

At first, Johnston denied being concerned about the Duke challenge. The Johnston campaign, however, began running television commercials statewide in March, seven months before the October 6 election. Duke supporters interpreted this early campaign kickoff as a sign of panic in the Johnston camp, while the Senator's supporters viewed it as merely prudent.

Political consultant Nancy Todd of Baton Rouge, a veteran of scores of national Democratic races, says that although the early Johnston advertising campaign is not unprecedented for an incumbent, it is "a common strategy for a candidate in trouble."

The election of Duke certainly would send political tremors throughout the nation. It also would deliver to the U.S. Senate a controversy-packed sideshow not seen since the heyday of the Louisiana Kingfish, Sen. Huey P. Long, more than fifty years ago.

The idea of becoming president of the United States is a goal that Duke thinks is attainable. He will not turn fifty until the year 2000, so he has a long time to convince voters that racist politics are good for America. "If the ideals that I stand for are addressed, then I will only be a footnote in history," Duke says. "But if the deterioration of the white middle class continues, then I will be president."

Duke's position remains steadfast: "I've got to stand up for what I believe to be right."

Duke feels the time is right for his brand of racist politics.

"Things are worse now in America than they have ever been before. The liberal experiment has failed. That's why I'm getting more support than ever. The liberal multi-racial dream has helped lower educational standards and created an underclass of poverty that is dragging the country down. The rapidly changing racial demographics will change forever the way we and our children live.

"We need to preserve the white race to preserve America. Everyone, including minorities, would be better off. If we lose the heritage of America's founding race and the multi-racial society doesn't work, there will be no turning back from the United States' becoming just another third-world country. America is facing a dangerous crossroad."

As he looks toward tomorrow, David Duke stands as a man still firmly committed to "the struggle." He is someone whose fundamental ideology has remained unchanged for more than a quarter of a century. From radical days at LSU, to the Klan, to the NAAWP, to his election to the Louisiana legislature, Duke clings to the same principles he has always held.

No matter how well he succeeds in his quest to ensure what he calls racial survival, Duke will never see the world he envisions. It will never come to pass. But nothing will ever deter him from seeking his dream of a Norman Rockwell America, led by white Christians with strict ethics. Even when it looks as though he is finished politically, there is a little boy inside the man that pushes him on.

He has been threatened, insulted, punched, spat upon, clubbed, jailed, shunned, deported, and ceaselessly ridiculed, but still he maintains his convictions.

As long as there is one "Dukie" left in the world, David Duke will continue fighting for what he believes.

As one elderly woman said on a recent radio talk show, "The rich people, they got the Republicans, and the blacks, they got the Democrats. But us working people, we got David Duke!"

Index

299